Systems Engineering
with SysML/UML

Morgan Kaufmann OMG Press

Morgan Kaufmann Publishers and the Object Management Group™ (OMG) have joined forces to publish a line of books addressing business and technical topics related to OMG's large suite of software standards.

OMG is an international, open membership, not-for-profit computer industry consortium that was founded in 1989. The OMG creates standards for software used in government and corporate environments to enable interoperability and to forge common development environments that encourage the adoption and evolution of new technology. OMG members and its board of directors consist of representatives from a majority of the organizations that shape enterprise and Internet computing today.

OMG's modeling standards, including the Unified Modeling Language™ (UML®) and Model Driven Architecture® (MDA), enable powerful visual design, execution and maintenance of software, and other processes—for example, IT Systems Modeling and Business Process Management. The middleware standards and profiles of the Object Management Group are based on the Common Object Request Broker Architecture® (CORBA) and support a wide variety of industries. More information about OMG can be found at *http://www.omg.org/*.

Related Morgan Kaufmann OMG Press Titles

UML 2 Certification Guide: Fundamental and Intermediate Exams
Tim Weilkiens and Bernd Oestereich

Real-Life MDA: Solving Business Problems with Model Driven Architecture
Michael Guttman and John Parodi

Architecture Driven Modernization: A Series of Industry Case Studies
Bill Ulrich

Systems Engineering with SysML/UML
Modeling, Analysis, Design

Tim Weilkiens

AMSTERDAM • BOSTON • HEIDELBERG • LONDON
NEW YORK • OXFORD • PARIS • SAN DIEGO
SAN FRANCISCO • SINGAPORE • SYDNEY • TOKYO

Morgan Kaufmann Publishers is an imprint of Elsevier

Acquisitions Editor: Tiffany Gasbarrini
Publisher: Denise E. M. Penrose
Publishing Services Manager: George Morrison
Project Manager: Mónica González de Mendoza
Assistant Editor: Matt Cater
Production Assistant: Lianne Hong
Cover Design: Dennis Schaefer
Cover Image: © Masterfile (Royalty-Free Division)

Morgan Kaufmann Publishers is an imprint of Eslsevier.
30 Corporate Drive, Suite 400, Burlington, MA 01803, USA

This book is printed on acid-free paper.

Copyright © 2006 by dpunkt. verlag GmbH, Heidelberg, Germany.
Title of the German original: Systems Engineering mit SysML/UML (ISBN: 978-3-89864-409-9)
Translation © 2007 Morgan Kaufmann Publishers, an imprint of Elsevier, Inc. All rights reserved.

Library of Congress Cataloging-in-Publication Data
Weilkiens, Tim.
  [Systems Engineering mit SysML/UML. English]
  Systems engineering with SysML/UML: modeling, analysis, design/Tim Weilkiens.
    p. cm. — (The OMG Press)
  Includes bibliographical references and index.
  ISBN 978-0-12-374274-2 (pbk. : alk. paper) 1. Systems engineering. 2. SysML (Computer science).
3. UML (Computer science). I. Title.

  TA168.W434 2008
  620.001'171—dc22

                    2007047004

ISBN: 978-0-12-374274-2

For information on all Morgan Kaufmann publications, visit our
Web site at www.mkp.com or www.books.elsevier.com

Printed and bound by CPI Group (UK) Ltd, Croydon, CR0 4YY

Transferred to Digital Print 2011

Contents

Foreword by Richard M. Soley

According to the Boeing Commercial Aircraft Company, a Boeing 747-400 aircraft has a maximum gross take-off weight (including a typical 416 passengers, 171 cubic meters of freight in the cargo hold, and over 200,000 kg of fuel) of nearly 400,000 kg. Four behemoth engines push the bird at up to 88 percent of the speed of sound for unbelievable distances, up to 13,500 km, without refueling. The length of the aircraft alone (45 m) is longer than the Wright brothers' entire first flight.

But these amazing statistics, after 30 years finally to be eclipsed by even larger passenger aircraft, are nothing compared to the complexity of the system of systems which makes up the Boeing 747-400. The aircraft's electrical systems comprise some 274 km of wiring alone; high-strength aluminum and titanium parts are designed to work both standing still and heated by rapidly passing air. Backup systems keep navigation and life-sustaining systems running if primary systems fail; and even the in-flight entertainment system is one of the more complex systems on earth. In fact, the Boeing 747-400 comprises some 6 million parts, about half of which are simply fasteners like screws and bolts. It's no wonder that a Boeing spokesman once quipped, "We view a 777 as a collection of parts flying in close proximity." As a frequent flyer, I constantly and fervently hope that that proximity goal is respected!

All of these facts reflect a fact that all engineers understand: complexity is difficult to manage, and most interesting systems are complex. Worse, the compounding of systems into systems of systems—e.g., back to our airplane, the electrical, hydraulic, propulsion, lift surface, life support, navigation, and other systems of aircrafts—tends to introduce new complexities in the form of unexpected overlaps of parts and unexpected behavior of previously well-behaved systems.

The net result of the rising complexity of systems is the crying need for ways to express component systems in ways that those designs can be easily shared between design teams. A shared language is a crucial component of the design methodology of any system or process, be it electrical, software, mechanical, or chemical. And if that shared language is based on a pre-existing language, the team which must share design will be up to speed more quickly and more able to complete the design task—and the more-demanding long-term maintenance and integration task—better, faster, and cheaper.

This line of thinking was the thought process behind the Systems Modeling Language (SysML), an open standard developed and managed by the Object

Management Group (OMG) and its hundreds of worldwide member companies. OMG's SysML has quite a lot of positive aspects:

- It is based on (an extension of a subset of) the OMG's own Unified Modeling Language, or UML. Thus software developers comfortable with UML can move to SysML easily and tool developers with UML tools can easily support SysML as well.
- It is graphical. I have always been struck by the way software developers will share design with other developers using graphics (boxes and lines), but then write (for example) "C++ code" when communicating that design to a computer. Likewise product engineers will work out the details of a family of products using graphs, boxes, and lines but then outline those choice points using a textual approach, e.g. PDES/STEP. Graphical languages are a natural choice for design and have been used for thousands of years (witness building and ship blueprints, electrical circuit diagrams, etc.).
- It has many implementations. International standards simply aren't worth the paper they are printed on (or the hard disk space they occupy) if they are not implemented. Even before the SysML final specification became available in early 2006, several companies announced implementation of the standard.

It is important to understand that SysML is not just another software development modeling language. While software is an important component of nearly all complex systems today, it is almost never the only component—planes, trains, and automobiles all have software, and so do building controllers and chemical plants, but they also have plumbing, hydraulics, electrical, and other systems that must be harmonized and co-designed. Likewise the human and automated processes to use complex systems need to be mapped out as well in order to get good use from them (as well as maintain and integrate those systems for future requirements and into future systems). And all of these co-design issues need to take into account the fact that all complex systems are available in multiple configurations, based on facilities requirements, personnel hiring issues, and myriad other variables.

This is the focus of the SysML language, a language to model all of these different factors in the course of engineering complex systems and systems of systems. The purpose is not to mask the complexity of those systems, but rather to expose and control it in the face of constantly changing business requirements and constantly changing infrastructure.

SysML is likely not the last language for engineering complex systems; the fast-paced change in most engineering fields (and in fact introduction of completely new engineering fields, like bioengineering) will likely cause change in the specification language itself. This shouldn't be a surprise to any engineer; other long-lasting xispecification languages have changed over time. One simple example: building blueprints are several hundred years old, but those made before about 1880 didn't feature the international symbol for electrical outlets, since that feature didn't exist yet. Languages change to suit changing requirements in engineering, and fortunately SysML itself is designed to change, by being based on a metamodeling infrastructure also standardized by the OMG, the Meta Object Facility (MOF). This same technology can be used to transform and integrate existing designs in older engineering modeling languages, including IDEF (a language heavily used in many fields, including aviation).

This brings us full circle, back to that collection of 6 million parts flying in close formation. There is no hope of developing such a large collection of parts—and people, facilities, hardware, software, hydraulics, navigation, and HVAC—without a shared design language which takes into account the constant change of component systems. SysML was specifically designed to address that need, and is already doing so in parts from tiny embedded robotics controllers to huge industrial components.

So enjoy learning the language. While not simple—complex problems often require complex solutions—it's logical and based on good engineering design practice. And keep those parts flying in close proximity!

Richard Mark Soley, Ph.D.
Chairman and Chief Executive Officer
Object Management Group, Inc.
Lexington, Massachusetts, USA

Author Biography

Tim Weilkiens works as a consultant and trainer for German consulting company oose Innovative Informatik GmbH. He is a member of the OMG working groups about SysML and UML and has written sections of the SysML specification. His son Ben helped energetic writing the book. You can reach both at twe@system-modeling.com

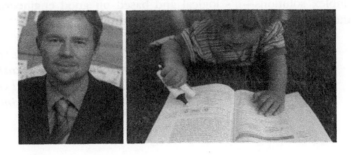

Introduction

Technology evolves from the primitive over the complicated to the simple.

(Antoine de Saint-Exupéry)

When you have read this chapter you can answer the following questions:[1]

- Why is this book around?
- What is systems engineering?
- What relation is there between SysML and UML?
- How does the content of this book relate to topics like CMMI, V model, or AUTOSAR?

1.1 Preliminaries

"Things had been much simpler in the past. You had been able to put something up and get it running with just a handful of people. Today the number of people you need quickly runs up to a hundred to develop a decent system. And even then they don't normally get things right … With all those experts from all kinds of disciplines…"

I hear such and similar talk increasingly often. As a trainer and consultant, I meet a lot of people from most different industries. But the tone is always the same. What's the reason? Very simple: progress.

We have reached a point where what's needed are complex and distributed systems, but where conventional development methods are not yet ready to make such systems available fast enough and at acceptable cost.

We cannot expect to develop increasingly progressive, larger, and better systems while continue using the same tools. Our approach, the modeling languages we use, and the development environments have to be part of this progress and evolve in line with it.

---

[1] If you can't please write to me and ask me: *twe@system-modeling.com*.

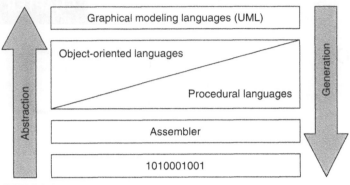

FIGURE 1.1

Increasing abstraction of programming languages.

In software development, e.g., this evolution can be seen quite clearly. Development tools have known increasingly larger components (from 0/1 to classes/objects) from the times we used punch cards, and then Assembler, and then procedural programming languages, and eventually object-oriented languages, thus facilitating the description of complex systems. The evolution to the next generation has already begun: The graphical *Unified Modeling Language (UML)* has become increasingly popular for developing software systems, and it is being used to solve more and more tasks that had been previously done with conventional programming languages (Figure 1.1).

In systems engineering (system development) the boundaries between the different disciplines continue to blur. Especially software is used in more and more fields. These hybrid systems represent a particular challenge to the development.

We can use proven methods to efficiently develop individual components of a complete system. However, the complete system is more than the sum of its components. The interplay between all the elements can be extremely complex and hard to control.

The need for a holistic line of thinking is particularly strong in the software development field. Embedding a piece of software in a system is a critical complexity factor. The consequence is that both approach models and notations are required to be able to develop these systems effectively. Otherwise the development cost will rise out of proportion compared with an acceptable price in the near future.

Systems engineering has been dealing with this problem for quite some time. The development of large systems in which many different disciplines participate requires holistic lines of thinking. This means that the requirements and structures of a system are looked at totally detached from the knowledge of specific details. The entire lifecycle from the idea to the disposal is planned to develop a system that fulfills the wishes of all participants.

Software development can learn a lot from systems engineering. But there is no taking without giving. Systems engineering can also learn from software development, where highly developed modeling tools and methods are available.

The *Unified Modeling Language (UML™)* is a modeling language from this field. It has established itself as a worldwide standard. What systems engineering has been lacking is a standardized modeling language. This situation will change with the new *Systems Modeling Language (OMG SysML™)*. SysML is based on UML and is supported by leading organizations from the systems engineering industry, including the *International Council on Systems Engineering (INCOSE)*.

1.1.1 Is This Book for Me?

This book will be interesting and helpful to you if you

- want to familiarize yourself with the new SysML modeling language.
- write, specify, and develop systems, i.e., if you are active in system analysis and design.
- work with complex systems.
- want to use SysML or UML in systems engineering.
- develop systems with mixed disciplines, e.g., software and hardware.
- want to create a holistic model in which analysis and design elements relate in a reproducible way.
- want to familiarize yourself with a universal way that leads you from the system idea to the system design.
- are active in software development and have a holistic view.
- cannot identify yourself with any of the above points. In cases of doubt ask me: *twe@system-modeling.com*.

This book will introduce you to a toolbox you can use to take a uniform road all the way from the idea of a system to its design. We keep the results in detailed and expressive models. The modeling language is SysML or UML. You will learn both languages as well as their common features and their differences. The tools described here work both with SysML and UML. To give the child a name I call the toolbox *SYSMOD*—derived from "system modeling."

1.1.2 What Will I Get from This Book?

You find the following in this book:

- A toolbox for system development from the system idea to the design (SYSMOD).
- Summaries about each of the tools so that you will be able to easily put them together to an individual approach. In fact, the book outlines a standard path for you.
- A description of the *SysML*.
- A description of the *UML*.
- An introduction to systems engineering.
- Marginal notes, e.g., on variant management, simulation, testing, and modeling patterns.

1.1.3 What Motivated This Book? And Thanks!

The first time I thought about writing this book was approximately at the year 2003. At that time I had held many seminars on using UML for system analysis and design. Most of the participants/attendants came from software development—from programmers to project managers. However, I found in one particular seminar that an unusual group of people had gathered: engineers, including telecommunication engineers, but not a single software developer. They planned a large project that was to include software, but also construction work, hardware, and other disciplines. As the training course went on I reduced the software aspect and explained the analysis and design techniques in more general terms. What the attendants gained from this was an excellent approach for their project.

This particular constellation of attendants has not been an exceptional case from then on. It was followed by more seminars, workshops, and coaching contracts that were not attended by software developers, but by engineers from other disciplines who wanted to familiarize themselves with system analysis and design using UML for their work. I found myself thinking more and more about issues, ideas, and further considerations: How much software does UML actually contain? How can I describe requirements in UML for non-software fields? How do I handle hybrid systems? I gradually became aware of the fact that the UML language and the approaches it supports can be used in many fields independently of software.

A glance over the fence helped me arrive at the systems engineering discipline. I found this a discipline where my line of thinking fitted well. It was by pure chance that, as I had been working on UML 2 within my work in the *Object Management Group* (*OMG*), I was asked whether I could support the development of the *SysML*. That was a perfect match with the ideas I had back then and I accepted immediately. Since then, I have been actively participating in the development of SysML, and I am a coauthor of the SysML specification.

The general approach was to analysis and design, the field of systems engineering, and the SysML modeling language—the mosaic was complete. I want to show you the picture that results from this perfect match in this book.

I was able to find the matching pieces for the mosaic only because my ideas found a fruitful soil in many discussions with my customers to fully mature. My sincere thanks! I'd like to mention first and foremost Reiner Dittel, Marc Enzmann, and Ulrich Lenk.

The creative disputes in the SysML work group with very competent modelers and system engineers have taken me huge steps forward. I'm particularly grateful to Conrad Bock, Sanford Friedenthal, Bran Selic, Alan Moore, and Roger Burkhart.

Extremely important for my professional and personal development are the environment and freedom of movement I enjoy from oose Innovative Informatik GmbH, the company I work for. My special thanks to my colleagues and particularly to Bernd Oestereich for their support. Several pictures in this book are by courtesy of oose Innovative Informatik GmbH.

Praise and thanks to my publisher, first and foremost to Christa Preisendanz!

It's always a pleasure to communicate with Richard M. Soley. Thanks for your great foreword.

No book can achieve sufficient quality if it weren't for domain-specific review. Looking things from outside is important. I'm particularly grateful to Wolfgang Krenzer of IBM Automotive Industry, and Andreas Korff of ARTiSAN Software Tools GmbH.

I'd like to thank Pavel Hruby for his excellent UML Visio template (*http://www. phruby.com*). By the way, it is also used for the official UML and SysML specifications.

My sincere thanks to you, of course, for having bought this book and for being interested in the subject. I'm interested in your feedback. Please write to me: *twe@ system-modeling.com*.

1.1.4 How Do I Read This Book?

This book consists of two parts: Chapters 1 and 2 are intended for consecutive reading, while the second part from Chapter 3 on is the reference part suitable for looking things up.

You are currently reading Chapter 1. This chapter informs you about the book itself, e.g., how to read this book in this section, and introductory basics about systems engineering, SysML, and UML.

Chapter 2 describes the SYSMOD approach used to collect and model the requirements to a system, and to derive a design that meets these requirements. The type of system—whether hardware or software—doesn't play an important role. The results from the approach are modeled using SysML. However, you don't have to fully rely on SysML tools; you can also use UML and its stereotypes.

At the end of Chapter 2 I'll briefly mention various other issues that are important for this approach, such as variant management, simulation, and others.

In Chapters 3 and 4 I will explain the SysML and UML modeling languages. Since SysML builds on UML, the SysML chapter describes only the extending elements. Accordingly the UML chapter discusses only those language elements that are also used in SysML. So these two chapters together represent the entire SysML language. The demarcation shows you clearly what UML can do and what SysML adds to it.

Chapter 5 describes the language extensions (stereotypes) needed in the approach discussed in Chapter 2. They do not belong to the SysML and UML language standards.

1.1.5 What Next?

This is not the end. It is not even the beginning of the end. But it is, perhaps, the end of the beginning.

(Winston Churchill)

Together with SysML, UML proliferated further. Starting as a pure modeling language for software development, UML extended its use to business process modeling (BPM) [33], and more recently became a modeling language for systems engineering. What next?

It seems that UML is fit and ready to become the *lingua franca* for modeling. It has the potential. UML is extendable, which means that it can be adapted to specific needs. It is used, proven, and accepted all over the world. And behind it is the *OMG*—a globally active consortium with members being leading IT corporations—as well as SysML and the *INCOSE*.

Although I am a strong advocate of UML, considering it to be unrivaled in its role, I don't think it will become the *lingua franca* for modeling. I think (and hope) that no language will achieve this. A certain diversity is necessary. But UML is sowing the seed for future modeling languages, which will lead to a situation where these languages will have a similar core and be compatible to a certain extent.

The future will bring about a great demand for modeling languages. The systems we develop will become increasingly complex. It is therefore a good idea to first thoroughly design them on the drawing board and perhaps simulate them before using them in practice.

The modeling language allows me to move on different abstraction levels. The more abstract I get the simpler the system appears to be. This is the art of being concrete on an abstract level.

> *In a collection of parts called A300*
> *flying in close proximity somewhere*
> *high above Germany in May 2007.*
> (Tim Weilkiens)

For further clarifications, please refer to:

- The homepage to this book:
  http://www.system-modeling.com
- Direct contact:
  Twe@system-modeling.com
- Consulting, seminars, project work:
  http://www.oose.de
- OMG™:
  http://www.omg.org—main page
  http://www.omgsysml.org—OMG SysML™
  http://www.uml.org—UML™
- INCOSE:
  http://www.incose.org

1.2 Systems Engineering

Every discipline and every industry have their own methods. Be it software development, hardware development, mechanics, construction, psychology, and so on. These demarcations work fine as long as you stay within one discipline with your project. Things get harder, however, if your project extends over several disciplines. It means that interfaces have to be created and coordinated between the methods of these disciplines. Product management has to introduce its requirements to the system development process, marketing is involved, and so on. Then project management is confronted with the challenge of having to consider the particularities of all disciplines.

The large number of jokes about the peculiarities of physicians, engineers, IT people, mathematicians and other engineers underline the fact that different worlds collide in interdisciplinary projects.[2] Misunderstandings and conflicts are preprogrammed.

For example, a team of software developers think about a new high-performing architecture. They find that it requires more memory resources. Unfortunately, they find this only much later when they start integrating it on the target hardware. The hardware developers see a way to expand the hardware to sufficient memory. The problem seems to have been solved. The bad thing is that they find out much later that the expanded hardware will no longer fit in the enclosure since nobody told the enclosure designers that there had been a couple changes. The new hardware develops more heat, exceeding the required upper limits. In the end product management finds that such a high-performing software architecture wasn't actually necessary. Each of the disciplines involved had contributed the best possible solution from its area and its view. Unfortunately, the sum of all these good individual solutions is not the best solution for the overall system.

So 1 + 1 makes 3. The development of single subsystems is well under control. The "+" increases the complexity and leads to a wide range of different problems. It is found all too often that projects lack a role responsible for forming sums, i.e., the holistic view across the entire system. That's a real pity because there are proven methods and strategies for this role. Systems engineering is a discipline that has been dealing with this issue for more than 50 years.

"Wow, that's pretty complex!" You've certainly heard this at least once. What do people mean by that? What does "complex" mean? There is a similar word: complicated. Do they mean the same? No! Something complex doesn't have to be complicated. The following definition stems from [28].

Complexity refers to the number and type of relationships between elements in a system.

Intricacy refers to the number of different elements.

Based on this definition, many systems are complex, while hybrid systems are additionally complicated, or intricated. That's the core challenge in systems engineering.

1.2.1 What Is Systems Engineering?

You've surely heard of a discipline called systems engineering. But even if you haven't, the term will probably ring a bell. Both *systems* and *engineering* are well-known general terms. Hearing them combined, everybody has a certain idea of what this discipline is all about. The trouble is that these ideas are often very different.

---

[2] An engineer, a chemist, and an IT guy are in a car driving across the desert. All of a sudden the car stops, and the three of them start quarreling about what might have been the cause of failure. Says the chemist: "Got to be an unexpected entropy increase in the engine compartment!" The engineer: "Crap! Either the V-belt is broken or the ignition distributor is gone. Simple as that!" ... and so on till the IT guy lost his patience: "Who cares. Let's just get off, then back in the car, and you'll see it'll run again."

What do you mean by a system? An airplane? A car? An inventory management system? A navigation system? A word processor? Your laptop? A company? All examples are correct.

A system is an artifact created by humans that consists of components or blocks that pursue a common goal that cannot be achieved by each of the single elements. A block can consist of software, hardware, persons, or any other units [45].

This definition of a system is intentionally very general. You can also think of very large systems in the sense of systems engineering, e.g., a country's aviation system, consisting of airports and air traffic routes.

When looking at the size of a system you have to clearly distinguish between the size of the real system and the size of the system model. A country's aviation system is clearly larger than a car in real life. However, when you look at the underlying system models it could be just the opposite. It all depends on the detailing depth of the model. For example, we could model a car to include even the tiniest little screw. In the system model for an aviation system, however, we have airplanes and airports as our smallest units.

You have just learned what the first part of the term *systems engineering* means. The second part, *engineering*, generally stands for a discipline that uses methods and tools in a structured way to develop a product.

Putting the two words together, the term *systems engineering* describes methods used to successfully develop systems.

Systems engineering concentrates on the definition and documentation of system requirements in the early development phase, the preparation of a system design, and the verification of the system as to compliance with the requirements, taking the overall problem into account: operation, time, test, creation, cost and planning, training and support, and disposal [45].

Systems engineering integrates all disciplines and describes a structured development process, from the concept to the production to the operation phase and finally to putting the system out of operation. It looks at both technical and economic aspects to develop a system that meets the users' needs.

As such, systems engineering stands above specific disciplines, such as software development, for example. As a so-called meta-discipline, systems engineering deals with the entire approach, from the idea to create a system (trigger) to the development, realization, and use to the disposal of the system. This holistic line of thinking can also include solutions to problems that emerge only as a new system is introduced.

Figure 1.2 shows a bundle of systems engineering tasks in the form of a SysML package diagram. The individual areas are considered on the system level, rather than diving into the details of one single discipline.

Here, you find the concepts of systems engineering in the specific disciplines again. The way how problems are formulated and solutions are developed here shows many parallels that are generally described in systems engineering. For example, contents include the description of lifephase models and problem-solving cycles.

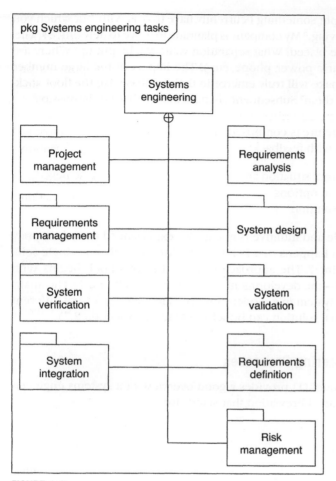

FIGURE 1.2

Group of tasks in systems engineering.

A lifephase model describes several time sections: development, realization, use, and disposal. The problems in the development of systems arise from the fact that consequences of the decisions that have to be made during the development phase will only become effective in later phases. In the later lifephases, however, there is normally no way to influence the system properties to a larger extent. This situation poses important questions that we have to answer in the development phase:

- What problems does the system solve?
- What problems does the system create?
- In which environment will the system be used?
- How long should the system be used?
- How will the system be replaced by a successor?

Here is a simple example, something I currently have to deal with, but which you surely know very well: moving.[3] My company is planning to move to new office space. Where will which desk be placed? What separation walls will be put up? Where are which connections (electric power, phone, etc.)? The impact of the large number of decisions we have to make will truly emerge in the use phase. Are the floor sockets really where we need them? Subsequent changes may be hard or impossible.

A problem-solving cycle describes the way from when a problem emerges to its solution. Its rough structure is composed of three steps that are to be traversed not only linearly, but also with feedback:

1. Describing the current situation and formulating the goal to be achieved.
2. Working out solution options.
3. Selecting the best solution.

What sounds so simple and intuitive is not always experienced as such in practice. For example, it often happens that Point 1 is omitted, or only one single solution is considered in Point 2. The approach discussed in this book begins with the formulation of a goal—the development of a system—(Section 2.1). The analysis and the design of the system in a model support us in viewing several different variants so that the optimal solution can be selected (see also Section 2.7).

1.2.2 Systems Engineering Processes

The *SIMILAR* process model [1] provides a good overview of a systems engineering process. The name is an abbreviation that stands for

- **State the problem**
- **Investigate alternatives**
- **Model system**
- **Integrate**
- **Launch the system**
- **Assess performance**
- **Re-evaluate**

The following subsections briefly describe these tasks.

State the problem

At the beginning of a system development project there is a description of the tasks involved. A good solution can be found only provided that the task is well formulated. Errors in this phase can become very costly, in terms of both money and image. A task should define what the system is to perform, or which requirements it is to meet. A systems engineer deals with requirements on the system level.

The requirement model does not describe the solution. If it did it would hinder us from evaluating alternative solutions.

---

[3] Development of the system "new office."

Investigate alternatives

One of the important tasks of a systems engineer is to investigate and weigh alternative concepts. Unfortunately, this task is often neglected. The human urge to concentrate on one single solution to a problem blurs the sight on the fact that an alternative solution may be better suited.

This means that, based on the requirement model, a systems engineer does not only develop a system design, but normally additional alternative designs. This allows the systems engineer to weigh several solutions against one another. It will hardly ever happen that all benefits are united in one single solution. This means that different criteria and priorities have to be considered. Typical aspects include, e.g., cost, size, weight, development time, time-to-market, and risks. Simulation parameters are derived from the system models to make the required aspects directly visible, comparable, and measurable in the model. SysML supports this work, e.g., by the parametric diagram (Section 4.6).

Model system

Design models are created as early as when we weigh alternative solutions. This step is the detailing of the selected solution's model. From the system engineer's perspective the model also serves for managing the entire lifecycle of the system, in addition to being used to specify the system design.

Modeling with SysML offers a good traceability of aspects, e.g., the realization of a requirement in the design (see *satisfy* in Section 4.3.4).

Integrate

A system will not exist in solitude and serve an end in its own. It is embedded in an environment, and it will interact with this environment. This step integrates the system. It includes, e.g., the definition of system interfaces.

Launch the system

A system is created on the basis of a specified design model and taken into operation. The models from the previous steps specify implementation requirements for software, hardware, mechanics, etc.

Assess performance

Once the system is ready for operation it is tested and measured. The values resulting from tests and measurements have to comply with the requirements. In SysML the connection between test model and requirement model is made by use of the *verify* relationship (Section 4.3.6).

Re-evaluate

This task ranks above all other activities. Results from the process are critically verified and evaluated. As a consequence, the findings gained are fed back to the process.

Risk management

Another important issue in systems engineering is risk management, or—positively formulated—provisions management, which is not part of the SIMILAR abbreviation.

A general basic understanding among all participants is necessary to ensure good risk management in a project. There is no absolute perfection in any work, including the work of a project team, and project managers cannot work wonders. Things just tend to go wrong. That's the normal situation.

Risk management is responsible for identifying potential risks and defining measures to minimize risk, or solve the problem when a risk event has occurred. Risk management is part of the decision processes in a project, and it needs to be regularly observed to be able to discover the occurrence of a forecasted risk event in time and react accordingly.

1.2.3 The Systems Engineer

A system engineer is the connecting link between the disciplines in a project, which are sometimes very different. System engineers think along the line of the entire system, independent of software, hardware, or other specific views.

From the organizational perspective, the systems engineering discipline ranks like a staff unit. It reports directly to the corporate management on the entire project which, in turn, communicates directly with the other development departments. Systems engineers should not be mediators between the project management and the development departments. They are the architects[4] on system level. They have to be capable of dealing with different development departments about domain issues rather than just playing the role of observers and go-between for messages. In particular, a system engineer has decision authority. According to INCOSE, 20 to 30 percent of the entire project budget should be allocated to systems engineering [45].

Many projects lack the organizational unit *systems engineering* shown in Figure 1.3.[5] Its tasks are handled by the overall project management and the individual

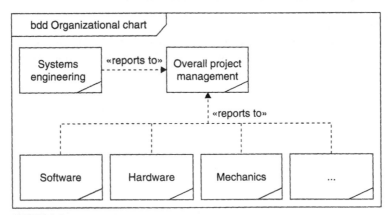

FIGURE 1.3

Positioning systems engineering in an organizational chart.

---

[4] Though the term *architect* is quite overstressed.
[5] The figure shows an organizational chart in the SysML/UML notation. You find more information on BPM with UML in [33]. The chart is a block definition diagram (*bdd*). These diagrams are described in Section 4.5.

development departments. Although the overall project management would be capable of assuming systems engineering tasks as far as the contents are concerned, it usually does not have the time available other than for its management tasks. The development departments communicate only with their direct neighboring disciplines, to which there are interfaces. Though this widens their view to a certain extent, it doesn't give them a holistic system view. This leads to the problems often observed in practice that the overview of complex systems is easily lost.

A frequent scenario is that the discipline that normally dominates (for historical reasons) in the company assumes the systems engineering tasks. This constellation leads to potential conflicts and misunderstandings at the latest as soon as other disciplines become more important. For example, an engineer with an increasingly dominating software discipline.

The development departments of a project solve partial problems of the overall problem. Each partial solution is a choice taken from a set of several solution variants. Without a system engineer role the selection criteria are characterized by the respective disciplines. The interplay between the solution variants of the individual development departments remains unnoticed. The applied divide-and-conquer principle works only provided that someone focuses on the overall problem and ensures that the sum of the best partial solutions results in the best of all possible overall solutions. So this means first conquer, then divide. And that's one of the tasks of systems engineering.

Trying to integrating systems engineering in the project structure shows that it cannot be introduced without the support of all departments—particularly the management. In addition to the organizational change, it also means a change to the project culture. Clear rules and transparent task descriptions for all stakeholders are important tools when introducing a development process. It will only work if it is driven both from the top (management) and from the bottom (development), meeting in the middle, or getting very close.

1.2.4 Systems Engineering History

Humanity developed systems already 5000 years ago. Back then, the Egyptians built their impressive pyramids. At that time nobody talked about systems engineering. Even if this is partially seen as the beginning of this discipline, we will make a huge time leap forward to the beginning of the 20th century and set the birth of systems engineering there. The industrial revolution produced many systems that can be better connected with systems engineering: cars, airplanes, machines. However, engineers still hadn't known systems engineering. A head engineer was capable to see the entire system, and the partial disciplines were able to develop more or less autonomously, since the interfaces were simple.

Systems engineering as we know it today emerged toward the end of the 1950s. At that time humanity started tackling systems, the complexity and project implementation of which surmounted everything known then. The race of the world powers in space, or the military race, has brought about projects that had to develop extremely complex systems on the one hand and, on the other hand, were forced to be available as soon as possible and successful. This enormous pressure led to a situation where methods of systems engineering had been developed.

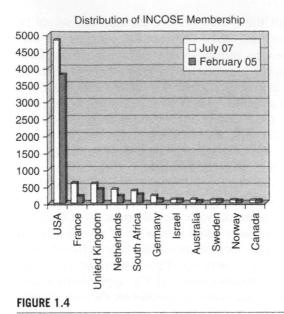

FIGURE 1.4

Distribution of the INCOSE membership (July 2007).

In commercial fields, too, systems had become more complex, and the need for holistic methods grew. For example, an early publication, "Methodology for Systems Engineering" by Arthur Hall [21] came from the telecommunication industry in 1962.

The significance of systems engineering has grown slowly but surely. The techniques of this discipline are used not only for huge projects in aviation and space, but also in "common" projects. In 2002, the process framework ISO/IEC 15288 [24] that describes processes along the lifecycle of a system had been introduced. This turned systems engineering formally into an accepted discipline in the development of systems.

1.2.5 **International Council on Systems Engineering**

An organization by the name of *National Council on Systems Engineering* (*NCOSE*) was founded in the United States in 1990. Its goals had been the development and promotion of systems engineering in the United States. It took only 5 years to extend these goals to the international level, when NCOSE became *INCOSE*.

The largest part of the INCOSE members of over 5000 comes from the United States (>3300 members) and the United Kingdom (>400 members). Germany has about 100 members (Figure 1.4). The US members include employees of NASA, Boeing, and General Motors. German representatives include Siemens, BMW, and oose Innovative Informatik GmbH. INCOSE is organized in geographic regions with local chapters.

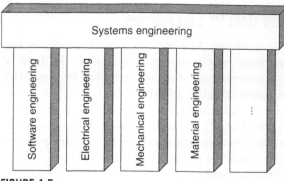

FIGURE 1.5

Systems engineering disciplines.

1.2.6 Systems Engineering versus Software Engineering

I often hear the question: "What has systems engineering got to do with software engineering?" especially from software developers. The answer can actually be found in the previous sections. Nevertheless I want to repeat it here explicitly again. Software engineering, hardware engineering, process engineering, automation technique, and so on are all disciplines that develop certain components of a system. Systems engineering takes a holistic view on the system: the overall architecture, the correct interplay of the components, the requirements as well as their implementation and verification, and all the other lifephases of a system, such as operation and disposal, in addition to the development.

Figure 1.5 shows the superior cross-section functionality of systems engineering. In particular it shows that systems engineering does not replace software engineering. It will interfere with the matters of software engineering only to the extent as requirements are given to bring about the best possible integration in the overall system.

1.2.7 Marginal Notes

General systems theory was founded by the biologist Ludwig von Bertalanffy. He carved out common features from different fields of knowledge and described them in his book [58]. In the sense of general systems theory, technical systems are only one of many possible fields of application. Others would be, e.g., economics, sociology, and psychology. Human social systems could be seen as a system just as well as the world economy, or an automobile. We will only look at systems made by humans in this book.

This means that general systems theory is on a very abstract level. Transferring it to a concrete field of knowledge, we can derive many important and specific tools and methods. Systematic thinking allows us to interact with systems without knowing the details of the individual components they are composed of.

1.3 The OMG SysML™ and UML™ Languages

The central topic of this book is modeling. And models require modeling languages. The *UML* has established itself as a modeling language in the field of software development. UML is an international standard specified by the *OMG*. UML is also accepted as an ISO standard (ISO/IEC 19501).

Despite a number of initiatives to standardize the processes of systems engineering (e.g., Process ISO/IEC 15288, EIA-632), no uniform modeling language had resulted. This had led to considerable friction losses in interdisciplinary projects. Information in the form of models is hard to communicate leading to misunderstandings and an immediate need for different tools.

In 2001 the *INCOSE* decided to make UML a standard language for systems engineering. UML essentially meets the requirements, it is widely used, it can be adapted to specific needs, and there are a large number of modeling tools as well as consulting and seminar vendors. Thanks to the extension mechanism (stereotypes) new modeling vocabulary can be defined, so that UML can be adapted to specific domains and disciplines. Together with UML Version 2.0[6] the range of applications has further increased versus UML 1 (see, e.g., [33]).

The adaptation of UML for systems engineering has the name OMG Systems Modeling Language (OMG SysML™), and its Version 1.0 is based on UML 2.1.1. The most important extensions are:

- UML classes are called *blocks* in SysML, and the class diagram is called *block definition diagram*. The UML composite structure diagram is called *internal block diagram* in SysML.
- Item flows in the internal block diagram. For both diagrams several extensions were defined.
- Support of *Enhanced Functional Flow Block Diagrams* (*EFFBD*) and continuous functions by action and object nodes in the activity diagram.
- Two new diagram types: requirement diagram and parametric diagram.
- Support of the neutral ISO AP-233 data format for exchanging data between different tools.
- Explicit omission of UML elements that are not needed in systems engineering, e.g., software-specific components.

The question whether these extensions were necessary at all is justified, or in other words: "Why yet another modeling language?" The answer is that, though UML is quite a mighty language, it has some shortcomings with regard to systems engineering, such as a lack of requirement modeling. Another reason for the need of SysML is the fact that UML is rather software-specific and strongly characterized by object orientation, while modeling in systems engineering is interdisciplinary. The use of UML can easily lead to acceptance problems and misunderstandings when in interdisciplinary communication.

---

[6] I use "UML 1" and "UML 2" for UML Versions 1.*x* and 2.*x* in the further course of this book. If I mean a specific version, I will write it fully, e.g., "UML 2.0."

OMG SysML™ Version 1.0 was accepted by OMG as a standard in April 2006. Several manufacturers already support the language, including ARTiSAN Software Tools, EmbeddedPlus Engineering, Telelogic, NoMagic, and Sparx Systems.

The *Finalization Task Force* has worked on the fine tuning of Version 1.0 for a full year. In April 2007, OMG SysML™ 1.0 was finalized as the official standard of OMG and published in September 2007.

The approach described in Chapter 2 uses SysML. Chapters 3 and 4 describe the SysML and UML languages separately and independently of one another. This way you will learn which elements are from UML and which extensions were introduced by SysML. This knowledge helps you to use only UML in systems engineering and to apply the approach discussed in this book without the SysML extension. Chapter 5 introduces more elements in the form of a profile, which are used in the approach described in this book.

1.4 Book Context

This section briefly introduces the immediate environment of this book so that you can classify it better and draw a line against similar topics. Figure 1.6 shows a book context diagram[7] that follows the system context diagram described in Section 2.3.

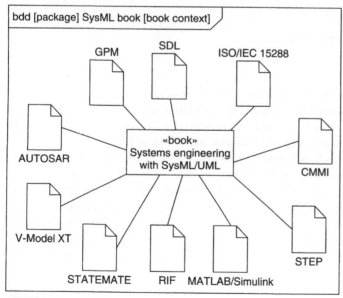

FIGURE 1.6

Book context.

---

[7] Of course, the stereotype *«book»* is not part of the SYSMOD profile (Chapter 5). But it could easily be added.

1.4.1 Autosar

AUTOSAR stands for *Automotive Open System Architecture*. Behind this idea is an international organization aimed at specifying an open standard for electronics architectures in cars. Most of the organization's members are car manufacturers and suppliers. One basis of AUTOSAR is the *EAST-EEA* project.

The goal of AUTOSAR is to find better ways of exchanging automobile electronics components between suppliers and manufacturers as well as between various product lines. The standardization required to achieve this goal maintains competition. It considers a wide range of fields, including body electronics, drive, chassis, security, multimedia systems, telematics, and man–machine interface.

The acronym *EAST-EEA* stands for *Electronics Architecture and Software Technologies—Embedded Electronic Architecture* [13]. It is a project of the European *ITEA* (*Information Technology for European Advancement*) program. The results of this project form the basis for AUTOSAR.

The participants in EAST-EEA include car manufacturers and suppliers. The *EAST-ADL* (*Architecture Description Language*) was born within the scope of this architecture. ADL is a profile of UML2 for modeling of electronic systems in the automotive field. It focuses on requirement modeling, consistency across several abstraction levels as well as validation and verification. EAST-ADL is organized in six areas:

1. Structure
2. Behavior
3. Requirements
4. Validation and verification
5. Support
6. Variants

Language constructs are available for each of these areas.

This results in considerable overlapping with the capabilities and goals of the SysML language. Some initiatives have been started to bring the two languages closer together. For example, the requirement modeling of EAST-ADL is an extension of the SysML approach, but based on SysML Version 0.3. Since SysML is more general, i.e., independent of the car industry, the language will certainly achieve a higher degree of proliferation. I expect and hope that the two languages will not compete in the future, but complement each other, and be used together.

SysML and AUTOSAR cannot be directly compared. AUTOSAR is an architecture with standardized interface descriptions, components, and so on. SysML is "only" a modeling language. It can be used to describe a system according to the AUTOSAR architecture.

1.4.2 Capability Maturity Model Integration

It has (had?) long been accepted as normalcy that software development projects fail. The successful completion had been the exception, i.e., functionality as required and development time and cost as planned. To improve this situation, the US Department of Defense encouraged the development of the *Capability Maturity Model (CMM)* to be able to better evaluate their principals/contractors. CMM was developed by the *Software Engineering Institute (SEI)* of Carnegie Mellon University at Pittsburgh in the mid-1980s.

CMM defines five steps that characterize the quality of an organization and its processes. For example, it looks at project planning, risk management, and requirement management.

The *Capability Maturity Model Integration (CMMI)* is the successor of CMM; it was published in 2000. It integrates experiences gained from working with CMM. In addition to software development, CMMI also examines systems engineering.

The SysML language cannot be directly compared with CMMI, since they are two different things. Good SysML models and the processes that create them help to meet the quality criteria of CMMI. For example, it demands the traceability of requirements, which can be easily mapped in SysML.

1.4.3 BPM

Systems engineering does not only deal with flows within a (technical) system. The processes in the environment of the system are equally important. Which work flows are to be considered in development, in production, in operation, and when the system is disposed of?

Modeling these flows is a field of *BPM*.[8] Rather than at technical systems, BPM models, develops, and optimizes business systems, i.e., companies. Between the two disciplines there are not only tangencies, but also many parallels. The modeling tools and approaches are similar in many areas [33].

1.4.4 ISO/IEC 15288

The ISO/IEC standard 15288 had been developed to provide a framework for processes to develop technical systems that ranks software and hardware on an equal scale. There had not been such a type of hybrid process framework when work at the standard began in the 1990s. This standard is based on ISO/IEC standard 12207, which refers to software only.

The framework is equally suitable for small and large corporations. Moreover, it is independent of a specific domain. Accordingly, the standard is general to ensure that it can be easily adapted for a specific project.

The V-Model®XT [54] allows you to map conventions for ISO/IEC standard 15288. This means that it puts terms and concepts from both standards in relation. For example, the process *stakeholder requirements* definition from ISO/IEC 15288 is mapped to the activity group *requirements and analyses* from the V-Model XT.

The standard describes five process areas:

1. Acquisition processes.
2. Corporate processes, e.g., quality assurance, resources management.

---

[8] SPICE is an evaluation method for standard ISO/IEC 12207.

3. Project processes, e.g., project planning, risk management, controlling.
4. Technical processes, e.g., requirements analysis, architecture, implementation, operation, disposal.
5. Other processes, e.g., tailoring.

SysML is a possible language to describe results from activities in processes.

1.4.5 MATLAB/Simulink

MATLAB (Matrix Laboratory) is a proprietary development environment and programming language of *The Mathworks* designed to visualize, compute, and program mathematical expressions.

Simulink is an extension of MATLAB designed to model, simulate, and analyze dynamic systems using block diagrams. *Stateflow* is an extension that allows you to model and simulate finite state machines.

MATLAB/Simulink is a widely used tool. Despite its impressive capabilities, its major drawback is that it is a proprietary system rather than being a standard like SysML, for example. A SysML modeling tool is not directly competing with MATLAB. Although there is some overlapping, e.g., with regard to state modeling, the two environments can complement each other. SysML is more powerful with regard to requirements modeling and the overall system design, while MATLAB/Simulink has its strengths in the simulation area. If you use both environments you need a chain of tools to ensure that you won't lose continuality of your models.

1.4.6 The Requirement Interchange Format

The *Requirement Interchange Format (RIF)* is the product of an initiative of the automotive industry.[9] It was designed to exchange requirements between car manufacturers and suppliers. Despite this background, RIF is independent of the automotive industry and can be used in other domains.

The principal/contractor constellation is a typical scenario in which requirements have to be exchanged. Between the two roles there is normally the corporation boundary, and access to a common requirements database is hardly ever possible. The friction losses, and thus errors, costs, time delays, and discords can easily exceed the limits to pain. And when something hurts, it's time to change it.[10]

RIF closes the gap, allowing you to exchange requirements beyond tool limits and company boundaries. It describes a generic format for filing requirements. In addition to the requirements themselves, you can also describe groups, hierarchies, relationships, access privileges, and more.

The RIF model is described in UML and implemented in XML. This means that it can be imported to and exported from a SysML model. The hard part that remains in all variants is the traceability of requirements beyond model boundaries.

---

[9] The initiator was the *Herstellerinitiative Software (HIS)*, a group of car manufacturers including Audi, BMW, Daimler-Chrysler, Porsche, and Volkswagen. Adam Opel AG also participates in the RIF specification.
[10] Kent Beck would probably have called it the limits of smell (*If it stinks, change it.*) [2].

Though SysML integrates several arrangements to improve this situation, the successful realization depends on the modeling tools.

1.4.7 Statemate

STATEMATE is a graphical modeling tool of I-Logix designed for the development of integrated systems. It is popular in the automotive and aviation domains. The central model in STATEMATE are state machines. It is based on the seminal work by David Harel, cofounder of I-Logix [22].

STATEMATE had been developed before UML emerged. I-Logix used UML to publish the *Rhapsody* modeling tool that features a large number of STATEMATE functions. Rhapsody is also a SysML modeling tool. I-Logix was taken over by Telelogic in 2006.

1.4.8 Step

STEP describes a series of ISO 10303 standards and stands for *Standard for the Exchange of Product model data*. It is a sort of building kit, consisting of several documents, including:

- the EXPRESS language for describing object-oriented data models.
- implementation methods for realizing data models, e.g., a text format (ISO 10303-21), an XML format (ISO 10303-28), or an API (ISO 10303-22).
- basic models for data classes, e.g., product identification and product configuration (ISO 10303-41), visual representation (ISO 10303-46), or mathematical descriptions (ISO 10303-51).
- application models that extend the basic models, e.g., for finite elements and methods (ISO 10303-104), or kinematics (ISO 10303-105).
- application protocols for describing product data under a specific aspect, e.g., ISO AP-214 to describe product data in the automotive domain (ISO 10303-214).

The application protocol ISO AP-233 for systems engineering data is also developed within the scope of STEP. It includes elements to describe the following:

- Requirements
- Functional and structural data
- Physical structures
- Configuration data
- Project and data management data

Together with OMG and INCOSE the AP233 work group has established the requirements for SysML and participated in the development of SysML. SysML and ISO AP-233 had been tuned to ensure that SysML models can be exchanged between other systems engineering tools via ISO AP-233. For example, ISO AP-233 is also supported by *DOORS*, the requirements management tool of Telelogic. Models can be exchanged via *XMI* (*XML Metamodel Interchange*) or an API according to the STEP implementation methods.

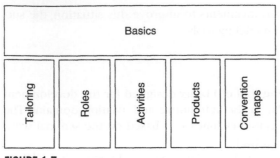

FIGURE 1.7

Overview of the V-Model XT.

1.4.9 Specification and Description Language

The *Specification and Description Language* (*SDL*) was developed in the tele-communication industry [36]. It is published as a standard by the *International Telecommunication Union* (*ITU*). Meanwhile SDL is used outside the telecommunication industry, e.g., to develop medical systems, or in the aviation and space domain.

The SDL is a language that has many common features with UML and thus SysML. For example, the sequence diagrams stem from the *Message Sequence Charts* (*MSC*) of SDL [37]. The large number of common features supports the mapping of SDL models to SysML/UML models [43].

1.4.10 V-Model XT

The V-Model is an approach model that was developed by commissioning of the State of Germany for planning and implementing system development projects. It considers the entire lifecycle of a system nicely fitting the line of thinking in systems engineering.

The current V-Model XT from 2004 is based on V-Model 97, its predecessor. The model's revision was motivated when, after 7 years, the old V-Model was found to no longer comply with the current state of the art in projects. It was no longer suited for supporting the most recent techniques and methods.

The V-Model XT is a toolbox consisting of defined roles, products, and activities (Figure 1.7). This means that the approach can be adapted to a specific project. The "XT" stands for *Extreme Tailoring*. Rules ensure that the composed approach is logical and consistent.

In contrast to several other standards, the V-Model is concrete and does not first have to be interpreted before it can be practically used.

Trying to directly compare the V-Model with SysML is similar to the famous comparison of apples and pears. SysML is a language and does not contain any instructions of the kind that can be used in projects. In contrast, the V-Model does contain the instructions. For the results that are thereby created, SysML can be used in many different domains. The SYSMOD approach described in this book covers parts of the V-Model.

The Pragmatic SYSMOD Approach

2

The wise man never takes a step too long for his leg.

(African saying)

In this chapter you will be introduced to the SYSMOD approach for modeling of complex systems based on a practical example used throughout this book. I selected a practical system that is easy to understand, and includes all necessary aspects. The approach scales very well and can be used both for much larger and much smaller systems than the one in our case study.

Using the same example throughout this chapter will make it easier for you to gain an overall insight, to better understand the approach discussed here, and to easily apply it to your practical environment. In fact, we don't jump from one island solution to the next in our practical projects either, but have to consistently apply our approach.

We will begin with the project context, looking at our system as a black box,[1] studying the environment, and will then successively delve into the details. This approach corresponds to a widely used pattern: identify an element, describe some context (external view), and then immerge (internal view). Since we will be starting in the green meadow, the approach covers all areas pertaining to a development process. Of course, the approach would also work if you were to start off from an existing system, the difference being that you would probably leave out a few steps or slightly modify some steps.

Look at the individual steps of the approach as if they were packed in a toolbox from which you simply take those you need in your project. This is not a rigid recipe that can be used only in the sequence described here. The path discussed here has proven in practice and belongs to the best practices of many approach models—in particular, special iteratively incremental processes. Of course, you can use SysML in other approach models too.

---

[1] The term *black box* means that the system is a black box we can't look into. This means that the internals of the system are not considered. All you see is what goes into the system and what comes out of it. The opposite is termed *white box*.

This chapter is described from the view onto a project that is intended to realize a technical system for a rental car firm. To be able to better understand the entire system and the principal's requirements, we will take a holistic look at the system, independently of its hardware- and software-specific aspects. There are plenty of discipline-specific books. We are more interested in the tasks involved in systems engineering and in the particularities of both the analysis and the design of complex systems.

The intricacy of the example we use in this book is intentionally small to ensure that you will be able to concentrate on the approach itself and the SysML/UML languages. Both the approach and the language scale very well and can be used for systems of any size.

Each section begins with a *reference card* that outlines the step within the approach discussed in that section. This abstract describes the step with incoming and outgoing information. Moreover, it includes a short description, helpful guiding questions, and a list of the most important SysML model elements required in the respective step. Finally, the summary lists elements from the SYSMOD profile.

The blocks can be put together to form the entire approach. Figures 2.1 (analysis) and Figure 2.2 (design) show you a possible way of how to proceed, but there are other ways. In particular, we will be doing without modeling results, because we either won't need them, or they are already at hand, so that we won't have to create them within our approach.

The figures that describe the approach and the sequence of sections in this book have a purely sequential character. However, this won't work in practice when you won't start a step before you have fully completed all previous steps. For example, you should start working on your domain modeling at the latest as soon as you have finished modeling your first use case (Figure 2.1).

2.1 Case Study

Assume we are a company called *System-Modeling.com*, specialized in project work in the field of systems engineering. Our principal is a rental car firm by the name of *SpeedyCar*.[2] They have decided to use innovative IT systems, allowing them minimum manpower to offer unbeatable prices in the market. Of course, they don't want to compromise on their quality of service. To the very opposite: Their service should be clearly better and visible versus their competition.

Our contract with SpeedyCar consists in developing an on-board computer for rental cars, with the primary task being to make it simpler for their customers to pick up and return cars without their staff's intervention.

In a first meeting with the principal, we learn the more specific ideas they had already worked out for the planned system. We prepared a meeting minutes (Table 2.1).

---

[2]Both *System-Modeling.com* and *SpeedyCar* are fictitious companies.

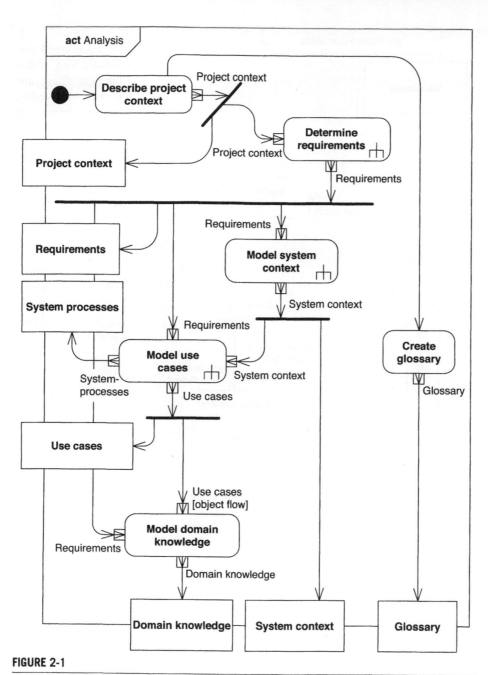

FIGURE 2-1

The approach model for analyses.

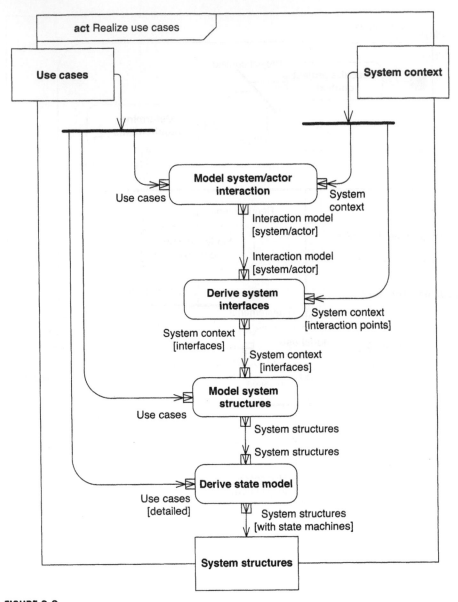

FIGURE 2-2

The approach model for designs.

PROJECT DIARY

Project Time 2160

Markus Witte, Project Manager, System-Modeling.com

I decided to write a project diary to be able later on to track the course of the project. As is customary with diaries, it is intended for my eyes only. I got the idea when I read the excellent book *The Deadline* by Tom DeMarco [9]. The novel's hero, Mr. Tomkin, writes a diary that was a good possibility for him (and thousands of readers) to reflect and learn. Of course, I won't publish my project diary.

Mr. Speedy's ideas of the on-board computer we are supposed to develop are too specific. Though using a competitor system as a guiding example provides a feasible solution, why shouldn't there be better alternatives?

Unfortunately, Mr. Speedy doesn't have much time. So we'll start our project with only superficial knowledge of the system. On the other hand, Mr. Speedy has promised us good communication with his domain experts.

Altogether I have a good feeling that there will be a good cooperation with SpeedyCar.

Table 2.1 Minutes of the first brainstorming meeting with SpeedyCar.

Title:	Brainstorming meeting with principal SpeedyCar.
Place, date:	SpeedyCar Headquarters Hamburg, November 28, 2005, 14:16.
Participants:	Mr. Tim Weilkiens (oose Innovative Informatik GmbH, Moderator); Mr. Hugh Speedy (SpeedyCar, Project Manager; CEO); Mr. Kevin Corsa (SpeedyCar, Manager Car Service); Mrs. Steffi Schoning (SpeedyCar, Marketing); Mr. Markus Witte (System-Modeling.com, Project Manager).

Mr. Speedy briefly introduces the planned system. He uses the system of a competitor as an example.

The on-board computer is to be built into the radio compartment in the car. Accordingly, it also has to assume the radio functionality, since it will replace the conventional car radio. Behind the windshield, a card reader is attached that can read from a customer card placed onto it from the outside, and transmit the information to the on-board computer. The on-board computer itself has to communicate with the booking center to be able to verify the validity of a customer's booking. Mr. Speedy thinks of realizing this communication via SMS. The cell phone functionality of the on-board computer thus required should also be made available to the customers so that they can make phone calls over the on-board computer.

The car key is placed in a special holder inside the glove compartment. The on-board computer registers when the key is removed and returned.

As a security mechanism—which is also required by the insurance company—the customer has to type a personal secret code (PIN). The electronic drive-away protection deactivates as soon as the customer entered their correct code.

(Continued)

Table 2.1 (Continued)

The returning of a car follows the procedure in reverse order.

In addition, Mr. Speedy presents a navigation system that the competitor system cannot offer. However, he's afraid that there might be a cost problem. Therefore, he first wants to have a feasibility study on this.

Mr. Speedy gave us a couple pictures of the competitor system (Figure 2.3).

FIGURE 2-3

Competitor system: card reader and on-board computer.

2.1.1 Describe Project Context

The project context is shown in Table 2.2.

At the beginning of the project we will first of all think about the goals that the system under development is to pursue: Why? What for? Where to? It is extremely important to recognize the goals and system ideas, and to document them and communicate about them with all project participants. Motivating common goals weld together a team and provide for direction.

> Alice: "Would you tell me, please, which way I ought to go from here?"
> The cat: "That depends a good deal on where you want to get to."
> Alice: "I don't much care where."
> The cat: "Then it doesn't much matter which way you go."
> Alice: "So long as I get somewhere."
> The cat: "Oh, you're sure to do that, if only you walk long enough."
> (Lewis Carroll, Alice in Wonderland [7])

Goals help make decisions. When there are controversial discussions, a decision will be made in favor of the idea that best supports the goal.

Contradictive goals can be detected early. For example, our principal would like to offer a highly comfortable usage with the system but, on the other hand, he wants the system to be secured against misuse. High security usually reduces the usage comfort, since the user will generally have to do additional steps.

We prepare the goals and ideas for the system in a workshop. We invite our principal and two of his staff. From our own team, the project manager and an analyst will participate.

Table 2.2 Summary: Describing the project context.

Reference card: Describe the project context.	
Describe project context ⋁ project context	*Incoming and outgoing data* **Project context:** Basic ideas and goals for the system; background situation; framework conditions and other information from the project environment.

Motivation/description

Why? The system ideas and goals as well as the project environment have to be known to all participating parties to ensure that the right decisions and measures are taken along the way toward the finished system.

What? Describe all relevant information from the project context, particularly ideas and goals for the system.

How? The information is prepared in workshops and described in text documents. System ideas and goals are worked out in the form of a product box.

Where? The project context forms the basic knowledge for all subsequent steps, particularly for determining the stakeholders.

Guiding questions
- What are the three most important system goals?
- Are all project participants informed about the goals?
- How does the background situation of the project look like?
- What goals does the project NOT pursue?

SysML elements
None.

Now, it won't make much sense to think of common sentences about the goals next to the flipchart and to discuss commas and other textual nuances. Things can be done in a much more productive and, at the same time, entertaining way: We develop a product box.

A product box shows the goals (Why should I buy this one of all products?), the system idea (What can I do with this product?), and perhaps some additional information, such as system requirements, price, content, and so on.

We take our unmarked little box and imagine that it is to become the box for our system. The box has to present the product attractively to arouse buying interest. This approach has clear benefits:

1. It's fun and, at the same time, an extremely creative and productive method.
2. The metaphor of a product box creates a uniform vision about the result among all workshop participants.

3. The space available on the box is limited. You can't accidentally drift off writing a user specification as you formulate the system idea. And you cannot get lost in details as you formulate the goals; rather you limit yourself to the most important goals that can then be focused on much easier.

4. With some luck you will find a good metaphor for your project.

Of course, we want to achieve a meaningful result with our product box. That doesn't necessarily mean that we'll have less fun. Don't hesitate to think about crazy things; play with your ideas, and think about a great name for the system, a logo, striking advertising slogans. You will see that the result is very good. A relaxed atmosphere normally encourages creativity among all participants. And if you need a document that is more formal than the product box, you can easily derive it from the product box.

A logo or a striking slogan can serve as a metaphor for the system. It will be much easier for the project staff to remember it than dryly formulated goals. In fact, it's "a story everybody—customer, developer, manager—can use to intuitively explain the functionality of the system" [2].

Pay attention not to lose your goals out of sight during the course of the project. It often happens that a project is successfully completed and celebrated from the technical perspective. However, as it often turns out, it is eventually a big failure when the primary goal was cost savings, and if the development, maintenance, operation, and/or disposal costs no longer complied with the planned budget.

Place the product box somewhere well visible in your office. This way you'll always have your goals in front of your eyes, and you can quickly show the system you are currently working on in case somebody was interested. Though there is usually a certain amount of blindness with regard to the permanent inventory in an office, it is rewarding to now and then throw a glance at the goals originally formulated weeks or even months after the project started. Does the system you are developing still fit into the box? Or are you smiling at the original goals? If the latter is the case, you need a more exact analysis. Have the goals changed? Or has the project moved in the wrong direction?

Of course, your system doesn't really have to fit into the box. This technique also works if the system you have to model is for a port logistics system [59] or a car.

In addition to the system ideas and goals, you have to document other information on the project context. This additional information includes, e.g., the following aspects:

- Has someone perhaps tried to create such a system, but the attempt was unsuccessful? Why?
- What framework conditions and restrictions are there? For example, the budget.
- What steps had been undertaken? For example, the board of directors encouraged the project, but the money had not been approved.
- Project organization, team structure.

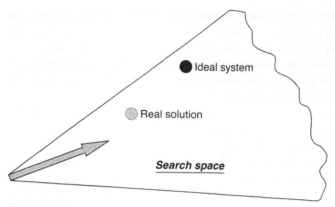

FIGURE 2-4

The solution search space.

The project context is written in text form. The structure of the document is optional. It should be simple enough to ensure that the document is easy to read and friendly.

We are at the very beginning of our project. Nevertheless, there are concrete visions about the solution. There will be a card reader in order for customers to identify themselves with their customer cards. The on-board computer and the booking center are to communicate via SMS. And so on. All these things are solution ideas our principal had seen in the on-board computer of one of his competitors. But perhaps there is another way. And it might even be a better one.

In the systems engineering discipline, we normally develop several solution approaches and then weigh one against the other before we go for one. So we question the solution ideas of our principal and think about alternatives. Unfortunately, it is often the case that our look into alternatives is foggy, since we already know one possible solution, or because the project doesn't have enough time to examine alternatives more closely.

This is the point where a thinking experiment comes in handy: searching for the ideal system. Of course, we always want to develop an ideal system. But what is THE ideal system? The ideal system meets all user requirements without existing itself. Wait a minute! Don't close the book just yet. This thinking process is really helpful.

Thinking about this obviously unreachable goal limits the search space and focuses on a successful direction (Figure 2.4). Let's look at a concrete example: Consider the locking system of a car. Start thinking of old times when you had to put a key into the lock and turn it to unlock the car door.[3] Is this what you'd want as a user? Think of all its nice side effects: the lock freezes in winter, or you scratch the paint as you try to find the key hole, or you have to dig deep in your pocket to find the key. As a user, you'd want to have a locked car. Nothing more!

---

[3]You know how old you are if you really remember.

Modern cars all have central locking systems that can be unlocked from the remote control at the key. Get your key, press the door unlock button, and off you go. The locking system itself is less evident for the user, but it offers the same functionality. However, there is still no ideal system, and there are new inconveniences. For example, you realize only when you already buckled up that the key is still in your pocket, but you need it to start the car.

A very recent technique comes pretty close to the ideal system. As soon as a hand approaches the door knob of the car, the locking system checks whether or not there is an encoded chip nearby and, if so, unlocks the door. A finger print scan at the gearshift can start the engine. The system is nearly inexistent for the user, but the desired functionality is there.

Look at the systems in your environment and think about how these systems have evolved over the years. They normally aspire to becoming ideal systems.

The idea of an ideal system was first expressed by Genrich Saulowich Altshuller, who founded the theory of inventive problem solving (TIPS) in 1956 (see box below). Searching for the ideal system is aspiring for simplicity. Or in the words of Goethe: "*All intelligent thoughts have already been thought; what is necessary is only to try to think them again.*"

Now, let's apply this technique to our system. We find that the user of our system is not keen on carrying around a customer card, or memorizing a secret code. One possible alternative would be a keyless access system, similar to the car locking system described above. The system could then do without card reader and without PIN. Another idea is to allow the user to access the system via their cell phones (the customer sends an SMS with the code to the on-board computer). We don't want to lose these ideas as we proceed; we want to consider them as feasible alternatives until sufficient information will be available to opt for one solution idea.

TRIZ/TIPS

TRIZ is an acronym that stands for "Teorija Rezhenija Jzobretatel'skich Zadach," which is Russian and means "Theory of Inventive Problem Solving (TIPS)." This theory is based on a systematic methodology for innovative processes. The father of TRIZ—Genrich Soulovich Altshuller (*15.10.1926–†24.09.1998)—was convinced that inventions are no coincidence.

Altshuller analyzed thousands of patents and found that the problems and their solutions repeat themselves—on an abstract level—in various disciplines. The patterns he found form the basis of TRIZ. One of Altshuller's particularly interesting findings was that real innovation happens only when several different disciplines cooperate.

Altshuller wrote a letter to Stalin about the deplorable state of affairs in the Soviet Union. He was sentenced to 25 years and continued his studies with his fellow inmates while at a labor camp. After Stalin died Altshuller was released from prison, and when the Soviet Union broke up, TRIZ was taught in the West too [29].

2.2 **Determining Requirements**

Probably the most important step in a system development process is collecting requirements. If this step is neglected you may still be able to develop a system, but it will probably be no big success, since you haven't considered what the system's environment—e.g., your principal or the system users—want and demand.

Figure 2.5 shows the details of our approach step *determine requirements* from Figure 2.1. The approach splits this step into two areas that will be described in the following sections. The results are the requirements to the system. On the

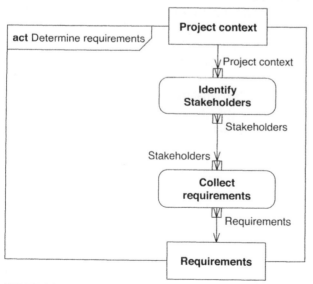

FIGURE 2-5

The "determine requirements" step within our approach model.

basis of these requirements, the subsequent steps will then develop an analysis model and eventually one or more design models.

2.2.1 Identify Stakeholders

Identifying stakeholders is shown in Table 2.3.

We barely know the functions that are desirable for the system and its goals. This amount of knowledge is not sufficient to develop the system. We have to deal with the issue of where all the information on system requirements will come from or, more exactly, from whom.

Table 2.3 Summary: Identifying stakeholders.

Reference card: Identify stakeholders.	
Project context → **Identify stakeholders** → Stakeholders	*Incoming and outgoing data* **Project context:** Basic ideas and goals for the system; background situation; framework conditions and other information from the project environment. **Stakeholder:** An individual or organization that has an interest in the system and may have requirements.

Motivation/description

Why? It is decisive for the success of the project that the needs of all stakeholders are sufficiently fulfilled.

What? Identify all individuals and organizations that may have requirements to or an interest in the system.

How? The list of stakeholders is initially elaborated in a workshop and continually reviewed during the project.

Where? Stakeholders are the sources of requirements. Their interest is described and analyzed in further steps within the approach.

Guiding questions
- Who has an interest in the system?
- What if we were not to consider this or that stakeholder and his interests?
- Who will use the system?
- Who would be concerned if the system failed?
- Who will be in charge for disposal of the system?

SysML elements
Perhaps use case diagram, SYSMOD: stakeholders.

All individuals and organizations that may have an interest in the project are equally important. They are the potential sources for requirements, and we call them *stakeholders*.[4]

We initially identify our stakeholders in a workshop. We invite a suitable group of individuals to ensure that we gain a broad domain knowledge about the system. We could also combine the workshop with the preparation of the system ideas and goals (product box), since this requires a similar group of participants. Moreover, depending on the project size, both issues can be worked out jointly.

For brainstorming, we gather all potential individuals and organizations that have an interest in the planned system. The following list briefly outlines where to look for stakeholders:

- System users
- Domain experts
- Principal, investors, board of directors, corporate management
- Laws and standards
- Customers
- Service staff, training staff
- System engineer, system maintenance
- Buyers of the system
- Marketing and sales
- System adversaries and advocates
- Stakeholders of supporting systems, e.g., production system, training system, or maintenance system
- Stakeholders of related systems, e.g., predecessor or competitor systems

Be creative! It is better to have one potential stakeholder too many on your list than missing one out. The forgotten stakeholder could show up shortly before or after the project ends and contribute important requirements, such as legal regulations that have to be observed, and which your system doesn't cover yet. That would cause a serious problem.

Even if the result will now be pretty extensive it is not complete yet. But completeness cannot be seen as the goal of a workshop. Its goal is to find as many stakeholders as possible to create a good working basis. We will discover more stakeholders as the project progresses, and we can add them to out stakeholders list as they emerge, and then take them into consideration.

To be able to work effectively with a long list, we have to assign priorities. Simply use a scale ranging from 1 = high to 4 = low and ask yourself the following question about each stakeholder: "How high is the risk of project failure if I don't consider this stakeholder and his interest?" A healthy gut feeling will help you handle this task quickly. If you are not sure, lengthy discussions won't help. Just select a higher priority for the stakeholder you are not sure about. This ensures that the stakeholder won't be left out, since we initially presume that all stakeholders have important requirements.

---

[4] The word presumably goes back to the gold digger era, when the *holders* of claims used *stakes* to mark their rights. These stakeholders had an enormous interest in their claims and put forward certain requirements (that were fiercely fought for in the gold digger times).

Table 2.4 Stakeholders (selection)

Stakeholder	Priority (1–4)	Comments/Interests
Customer	1	Wants easy and comfortable access to a car and low prices.
Reservation system	2	Requires interface to the on-board computer.
Car manufacturer	1	The on-board computer must control the central locking system and the drive-away protection, and collect mileage information.
Cellular communication vendor	1	The on-board computer and the reservation system will presumably communicate via SMS. Both speed and availability must be ensured.
Insurance company	1	Is break-in protection coverage for the on-board computer sufficient?
Car service	2	Installation, maintenance, and configuration of the on-board computer.
SpeedyCar call center	2	Handles customer enquiries with regard to the on-board computer's operation.
Navigation system manufacturer	4	SpeedyCar wants the on-board computer to have navigation system functionality.
Car radio manufacturer	2	The on-board computer should integrate car radio functionality since it will replace the regular radio.
Card reader manufacturer	1	The access device will be purchased from third party.
Legacy systems takeback law	3	What does the law say about the disposal of old devices? Who is responsible?
Lawmaker	1	What size/weight is permitted for the on-board computer? Other legal provisions have to be checked yet.

Table 2.4 shows a few stakeholders we found for our system.

To make sure we obtain requirements we have to ask our stakeholders. And to do that we need additional information about the stakeholders, including:

- Person to contact.

    If we have a stakeholder who cannot be addressed directly we need a person to contact. This is the case, e.g., with insurance companies, reservation systems, or customers.[5] In particular, persons to contact in lieu of important stakeholders (priority 1) should include vacation leave substitutes.

---

[5]It often happens in projects that the customer cannot be contacted directly. Potential persons to contact are members of the customer's marketing department, or market survey firms.

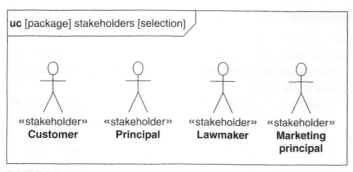

FIGURE 2-6

Using SysML to model stakeholders.

- Category:

  It is normally helpful to group stakeholders in categories, for example:
  - Domain experts;
  - a person in charge for requirements, i.e., somebody who is authorized to specify (and pay for!) requirements; and
  - system users.

    Notice that the categories overlap, i.e., one stakeholder can concurrently belong to more than one category.
- Open points and other remarks.

Note that we have used neither UML nor SysML in this approach step. Though there are methods to model the stakeholders with actors (using the *«stakeholder»* stereotype) (Figure 2.6), I think this is "over-modeling" and not useful in most projects. It's quick and easy to create stakeholders–actors and their relationships. The thing is that this model information has to be maintained and used, which could become very time-consuming. It is normally a better idea to manage your list of stakeholders in a wiki, a text processor, or spreadsheet. Many SysML/UML tools allow you to embed external sources at the appropriate places.

PROJECT DIARY

Project Time 5381

The cooperation with our principal has started off very well indeed. My suggestion to meet once in a week to check the project status was accepted right away. The regulars in these meetings are Mr. Speedy and myself. Other participants will be invited as needed. Since we put great weight on regularity, we want to conduct the meeting at least over the phone if we can't agree on a personal meeting date, even though this is a poorer form of communication. But it's clearly better than e-mails.

2.2.2 Collect Requirements

Collecting requirements is shown in Table 2.5.

The fact that we know who the stakeholders of the planned system are doesn't mean that we know their requirements. So, how do we get hold of the requirements? Well, we simply ask them.

This sounds more trivial than it is in practice. I remember a company where a department had developed a piece of software to support their staff in creating a help text system. The software turned out to be a failure. The future users of the help text software had never been asked about their requirements. In fact, they didn't even know about their "luck." And all this while they sat only a couple rooms away from the development department.

Turn to your stakeholders and ask them about their requirements. Run interviews and workshops. Collect documents, manuals of legacy systems, and the like. Also ask your stakeholders for further stakeholders.

Table 2.5 Summary: Collect requirements.

Reference card: Collect requirements.	
Stakeholders ⩒ **Collect requirements** ⩒ Requirements	*Incoming and outdoing data* **Stakeholders:** Individuals or organizations that have a direct interest in the system and may have requirements. **Requirements:** Requirements to the system.

Motivation/description

Why? Requirements form the elementary basis in system development. They determine what the system has to offer.

What? Requirements are obtained from stakeholders and documented and put in a structure.

How? Requirements are determined by survey techniques such as workshops and described in a SysML model.

Where? Requirements are a direct or indirect prerequisite for most steps involved in system development.

Guiding questions
- Do you ask the right people?
- Are the responses official?
- Do you ask the right questions?

SysML elements
Requirement diagram, requirement (SYSMOD): categories (e.g., functional requirement), containment, refine, trace.

Of course, there will always be stakeholders who cannot be addressed directly. For example, a lawmaker could be a stakeholder out of your reach. In this case, you have to find a suitable substitute, e.g., someone in the legal department, or you consult the relevant legal code book.

There may be other stakeholders who are extremely hard to reach. For example, you can't talk directly to a customer of SpeedyCar. What you could do though is think about a survey. In this case, you'd have to weigh the costs against the benefits. Again, there may be a suitable substitute, e.g., the marketing department of SpeedyCar; they should know their customers' wishes and expectations.

Requirements won't just fall into your lap as you conduct interviews or workshops, or browse documents for requirements. I will briefly introduce a few techniques you can use to check natural language for information.

Words like *easier*, *better*, *simpler*, *faster* should have a signaling effect on you. They can be examined more closely by asking the following questions:

- What does the comparative or superlative refer to? What is the point of reference?
- Which measuring method can be used to check the required feature?
- Which unit is meant, e.g., second, minute, or hour? What tolerances are permitted?

Ask yourself these questions. The answers are important for your requirements.

Pay attention to generalized terms like *never*, *always*, *ever*, *everybody*, *all*. You will find them in many sentences. These words generalize a fact. There are certainly exceptions. Ask them:

- Really always? Really everybody? Really never?

The general situation is often correctly mapped to a system. It is the exception that causes problems. In my car, e.g., the navigation system's display is linked to the car light. When I switch the headlights on the display switches automatically to night mode, which is better readable in the dark. Now, it is customary in my area to drive with the lights on during the day too. The display in night mode is then rather hard to read.

An acquaintance of mine has a habit of putting his briefcase on the passenger seat. Then, however, the car refuses to start driving. It expects the passenger to buckle up first.

I'm sure that you have made similar experiences with a system in exceptional cases.

You can recognize conditions in words like *if*, *then*, *unless*, *provided that*, *depends*. They describe variants. Ask for completeness:

- Are there other variants? What if not?

A condition is a junction that leads to something else. For example, a statement says where you'll most likely be getting to if you turn right. Be glad about the information and ask what if you chose to turn left.

The result from interviews, workshops, and studies are stakeholder requests. In the first go, you have no predefined granularity or structure. If you're informed by a stakeholder that he requires this or that system, then you have a stakeholder request. If you look at it more closely you may find that it is a functional requirement which is further refined by several use cases. Or it is a performance plus a physical requirement and something of a functional requirement.

We add the requirements identified to our model. SysML offers a suitable model element for this purpose (Figure 2.7). It describes in a very general way a requirement to the system, i.e., a contract between the customer or stakeholder and the systems engineer.

Each requirement gets a unique ID. SysML does not dictate a given format. You can choose any character string. Moreover, each requirement comes with a piece of text—also an arbitrary character string—that describes the requirement. It can optionally contain a reference to external sources, e.g., a requirements management tool. The requirement element is then only a reference in the SysML model to the external source.

Requirements are usually described in text form. Modeling with SysML means nothing else but storing the text in a standardized format and representing the text blocks in rectangles in the diagram to visualize their relationships. In turn, you can generate pure text documents from SysML requirements. They are a non-standardized view on the SysML requirement model.

Figure 2.7 shows another model element connected with the requirement by a dashed line. This is a *rationale*. You can use it to document the Why?, which can be very valuable information. If the reader cannot answer the Why?, then this can have a blocking and stifling effect on his further work [56].

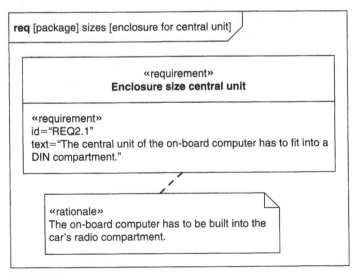

FIGURE 2-7

Requirement for enclosure size.

Requirements can be grouped into various categories. One example for categorizing requirements is the *FURPS* model developed by Robert Grady (Hewlett-Packard) [19]:

- *Functionality*—functional requirements.
- *Usability*—usability requirements, e.g., usage concepts, corporate identity.
- *Reliability*—reliability requirements, e.g., failure frequency.
- *Performance*—quantifiable requirements, e.g., response times, speed, bandwidth.
- *Supportability*—testability, configurability, installation, service.

There are other categorization catalogs, including the one by Robertson [38], which also describes categories like *policies*, *operation*, and *security*, among other things; or the quality characteristics defined in ISO/IEC standard 9126 [23].

Since there is no uniform standardized catalog here, SysML does not dictate categories. Use the extension mechanism of stereotypes to add your project-specific categories in the modeling language. Section 5.3 describes the categories of the SYSMOD profile.

Of course, the requirements are not isolated from one another. One requirement results from another or is part of another requirement. It is important to model these relationships to ensure that future changes to requirements, which always occur, can be integrated into the model in a reproducible way.

There are requirements on different hierarchical levels. Generally formulated requirements are broken down into several sub-requirements which, in turn, are broken down into several detail requirements, and so on. We use the *containment* relationship to model the requirements hierarchy (Figure 2.8).

Some requirements can be derived from existing requirements. For example, we have the size of the DIN[6] radio compartment where the central unit enclosure is to be built in. We can derive the size of the enclosure from this (Figure 2.9). These requirements already include technical aspects for a possible system design. You will read further below how we handle this. For now, let's first add this customer wish as it is.

Pay attention to the direction of the arrowheads. In SysML/UML arrows are often used in exactly the opposite way of what you would normally expect. As a rule of thumb, the arrows can be read in the direction they point. The size for the central unit is derived from the DIN radio compartment (Figure 2.9). Another helpful rule: arrows are also often dependencies. This means that the enclosure size depends on the DIN radio compartment, and not vice-versa, which would hardly make any sense.

There are other requirement relationships that produce a connection to the design and test models. They answer questions like "What does which requirement implement?" and "What checks whether or not a requirement is implemented correctly or at all?" These relationships will be explained in the course of our approach, or in the appropriate SysML chapter (Section 4.3).

---

[6]DIN = Deutsches Institut für Normung e.V. (German Institute for Standardization).

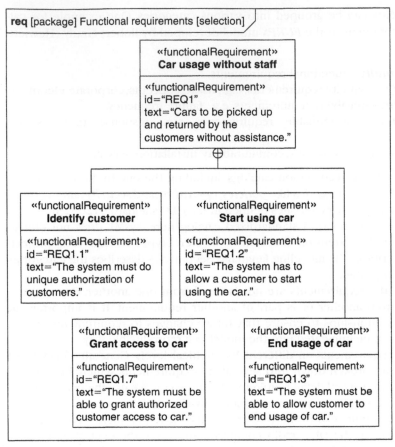

req [package] Functional requirements [selection]

«functionalRequirement»
Car usage without staff

«functionalRequirement»
id="REQ1"
text="Cars to be picked up
and returned by the
customers without assistance."

«functionalRequirement»
Identify customer

«functionalRequirement»
id="REQ1.1"
text="The system must do
unique authorization of
customers."

«functionalRequirement»
Start using car

«functionalRequirement»
id="REQ1.2"
text="The system has to
allow a customer to start
using the car."

«functionalRequirement»
Grant access to car

«functionalRequirement»
id="REQ1.7"
text="The system must be
able to grant authorized
customer access to car."

«functionalRequirement»
End usage of car

«functionalRequirement»
id="REQ1.3"
text="The system must be
able to allow customer to
end usage of car."

FIGURE 2-8

Requirements hierarchy.

We have added the customer's requirements more or less directly. These requirements often include solution approaches, e.g., the requirement to the enclosure size for the central unit. Technical solution approaches also have an influence on the list of stakeholders we identified (Section 2.2.1). For example, it includes the *cell phone manufacturer* stakeholder. However, this is not desirable, because solution approaches don't really belong to the requirements analysis. You probably have a hunch telling you that we can't simply omit them. Unless there is a solution idea, it is very difficult to find good and correct requirements. So allow for solutions and derive solution-free requirements from them, provided you need the higher abstraction level at all.

We give our requirements model some structure to separate technical system requirements from pure domain requirements. If product families or several solution variants are to be evaluated, then we need an additional way of differentiation. We will deal with this issue in Section 2.8.1.

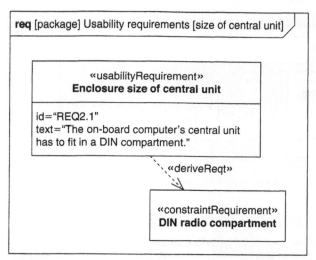

FIGURE 2-9

Requirement to the size of the on-board computer.

We define the two different types of requirements as follows:

An **essential requirement** describes the purely domain-specific intention and is independent of the technical implementation (solution). Accordingly, we speak of a **technical requirement** if it is based on a solution approach.

We take the technical requirements and ask ourselves the question about the Why. Why should the enclosure size for the central unit be such that it fits into the DIN radio compartment of a car (Figure 2.9)? What's the purpose? The car driver should be able to operate the on-board computer and read information from it as they drive. There are ways other than building it into the radio compartment to achieve this goal.

Fine, we found the essential requirement. It's what the principal really wants: operability while driving. If we continue asking for the Why, we can arrive at additional findings, such as the principal's goals. In this specific case, we find a cross-relationship to a requirement on the same level. Why do drivers have to be able to operate the on-board computer while driving? This is not required for picking up and returning cars—our system's core functions. The reason is that the principal wants to offer comfort functions, such as the navigation system or a possibility to make phone calls.

We are now ready to model the findings we won. We use the *derive* relationship between the technical requirements and the essential requirement that belongs to them.[7] We use *containment* for the cross-relationship to operate the on-board computer while driving, and the comfort functions, because this operability

[7]The containment relationship would be the better choice for this requirement decomposition. However that relationship also implies a nesting of namespaces. The requirement *Radio* could not be located in the package *Technical requirements*. Using the containment relationship the requirement would have the qualified name *Essential requirements::Convenience functions::Radio*. This problem is a current issue of the SysML working group.

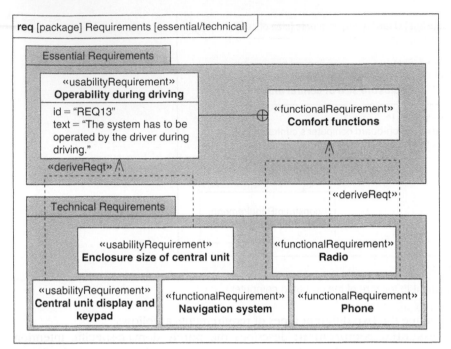

FIGURE 2-10

Relationship between essential requirements and technical requirements.

requirement is not needed without the comfort functions requirement. It is existentially contained in the requirement. You can see the result in Figure 2.10. This figure already gives a hint to an important fact that further modeling will confirm: If our contractor eventually decides to do without the comfort functions, then this will have only a minor effect on the core function, namely picking up and returning a car. There is an enormous cost savings potential in this fact.

The separation of essential from technical requirements corresponds to the differentiation between user specification and system specification. A *user specification* contains the principal's requirements from the user perspective. A *system specification* is prepared by the contractor. It contains details about the requirements from the user specification, further enhanced by requirements that refer to concrete solution approaches [10].

PROJECT DIARY

Project Time 5735

I have to be careful in this early project phase that my team won't fall into the feared analysis paralysis.

If a team gets infected by this illness they will add requirements and analyze and analyze and analyze and ... The question is how much requirements analysis will be sufficient. When is the analysis complete?

We will start early to create the design for these requirements to check the feasibility, recognize possible risks, and find changes to requirements that may be necessary. "Early" means as soon as we will have added the first bunch of requirements.

We bring this issue up regularly in our team meetings, trying to focus on our goals, our time, and the costs. The more we analyze the lesser the risk that the finished system might not meet the requirements. But the more we analyze the higher the costs. Little analysis at low cost increases the risk. We have to find a good trade-off between risk and time or cost.

2.3 Modeling the System Context

Rather than fulfilling an end in itself, the system supplies services to its environment. Vice-versa, it can also request services from its environment if it needs them for its own functionality. It is therefore important to know the system's environment.

There is manifold interplay between the system and its environment. We therefore have to analyze the type of embedding to ensure that the finished system will integrate into the environment nicely without negative surprises later on.

The system context model represents the direct environment of the system and gives initial information about the communication flowing from and to the system. The external interaction partners are the system actors. The communication itself is described by information flows.

The system context diagram is not a predefined SysML or UML diagram, but part of the SYSMOD approach. It is formally and correctly composed of standard elements and can be modeled using any SysML/UML tool. You would select the block definition diagram or the internal block diagram here as your standard diagram form.[8]

Figure 2.11 shows the details of the approach step *model system context* from Figure 2.1. You can see that, starting with the general requirements, there are three steps to model the system context. I'll explain each of these steps in detail in the following sections.

2.3.1 Identify System Actors

Identifying system actors is shown in Table 2.6.

Systems consist of several units that work more or less autonomously and, together, form the entire system as a network of communicating units. Since the single system is, in turn, part of a larger system, we speak of an embedded system. Note that for my definition of *embedding* it doesn't really matter whether the single system is a simple 8-bit processor or a complex aggregate, such as an automobile,

---

[8] Or accordingly the class or composite structure diagram in UML. You can also use the use case diagram instead of the class or block definition diagram.

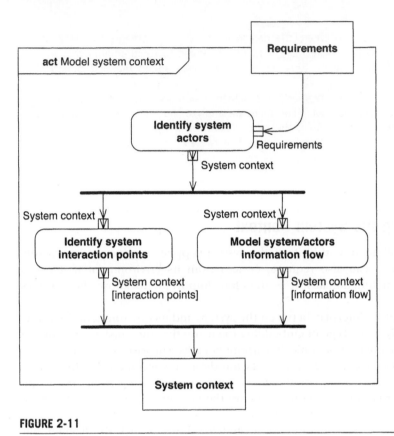

FIGURE 2-11

The approach model for modeling the system context.

for example. The underlying aspects that have to be taken into consideration in the system development are the same.

I've used the word "system" several times in the last short paragraph above. You may not have noticed it. But I still haven't even mentioned what I mean by a system. This is one of these trivial terms that are used all the time but hardly ever defined or examined. The term "system" is relative and varies with the onlooker's standpoint. For a software developer it means a software application that may have a few hardware artifacts. For a hardware developer it means the exact opposite. A systems engineer or customer usually has a rather holistic view. I myself take the view based on the *INCOSE* definition of a system [45].

A **system** is an artifact created by humans and consisting of system blocks that, together, pursue a goal. A block can be software, hardware, an individual, or any other unit.

The system under development interacts with individuals and other systems. Its boundary is an important piece of information: What belongs to my system and what's outside of it? This question can be answered in an early project phase—at least in part. We already know who will interact with the system. That's the nature

Table 2.6 Summary: Identify system actors.

Reference card: Identify system actors.	
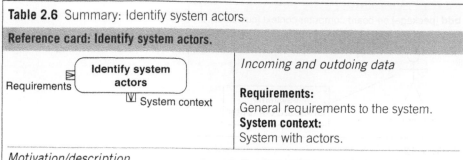	*Incoming and outdoing data* **Requirements:** General requirements to the system. **System context:** System with actors.

Motivation/description

Why? The system actors are direct interaction partners, for which services and interfaces have to be developed. They describe the system boundaries.

What? All users and systems that will interact with the system under development are identified and their roles are modeled.

How? The system actors are primarily derived from the requirements and modeled in the system context diagram.

Where? The services and interfaces for the system are identified on the basis of the actors.

Guiding questions
- Who or what belongs to the system?
- Who or what interacts with the system?
- What communication partners do you want to focus on?
- What aspects do you want to emphasize with an actor category?

SysML elements
Block definition diagram, internal block diagram, SYSMOD: system, actor (SYSMOD: actor categories, e.g., environmental effect), association, role, connector.

of the matter: I'll hardly have an idea or even a concept for a system unless I know who will operate it.

It is basically clear to all project participants what belongs to the system and what doesn't. However, these views can blur directly at the system boundary. What clearly belongs to a system for some parties could be seen as external interaction partners by others.

The system context diagram shows the system's environment and thus the system boundary. It is not a predefined diagram of SysML or UML, but a variant of block diagrams.[9] In the center of the diagram is the system under development. It is a block with the stereotype *«system»*. This clearly distinguishes this block from other system blocks yet to be identified. All currently known interaction partners are denoted all around the system and associations are used to connect them.

---

[9] In UML class or composite structure diagrams. The use case diagram can also be used for the simple variant.

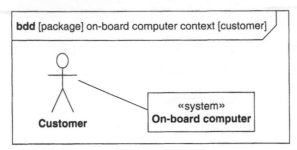

FIGURE 2-12

A user "customer."

The system's interaction partners, i.e., elements outside of it, are called actors. An *actor* is not a concrete system or a concrete individual, but a role, e.g., "operator" instead of "Miss Gabi Goldfish" or "temperature sensor" instead of "XY sensor article number 4711."

The model element *actor* is too general for our purposes. We need a rough categorization of actors and distinguish, e.g., between user, external system, mechanical system, environmental effect, actuator, and sensor. This differentiation helps us better understand the system and makes it easier to describe its services later on. For example, a user has clearly different requirements than a sensor. The categories are represented by different actor symbols.

A user is a human actor. When a human emerges as a direct interaction partner with the system we need to provide a user interface within the system, e.g., the GUI[10] of a software application, or the HMI[11] of a technical system, such as a dashboard.

A user can and should be asked directly about their requirements to the system. The success of our project depends on their acceptance. Unfortunately, it is not always possible to ask our future users directly. In this case, we try to find a suitable substitute, e.g., somebody in product management or marketing.

We use the standard symbol for actors—the stick man—to represent users (Figure 2.12).

An **external system** is a system that interacts directly with the system to be modeled. In its role as an interaction partner, the external system is seen merely as a black box. This external system can be the system under development in another project, and our system would then assume the role of an external system from their point of view.

An external system is denoted as a box (Figure 2.13).

A **user system** is a type of external system that serves as a medium for a user to interact with our system. Typical user systems are keyboard, display, and dashboards.

Whether we model the keyboard as an interaction partner or the user directly as an actor depends on the project. It can be useful for technical systems to

---

[10] *Graphical User Interface* for user–system interaction. The term refers to software systems.

[11] *Human Machine Interface*—a man-machine interface, e.g., key buttons, levers, light-emitting diodes.

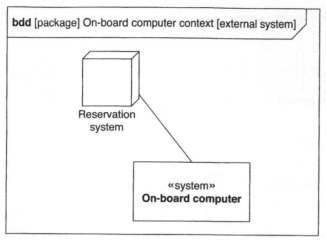

FIGURE 2-13

External system: reservation system.

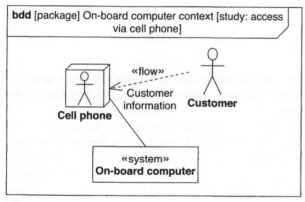

FIGURE 2-14

The user system "cell phone."

describe user systems as interaction partners, since they could be more important than the users behind them from our system's perspective.

Similar to an external system a user system is denoted as a box, but additionally with a user symbol (Figure 2.14).

We can additionally model the individual who operates the user system. For formal reasons, you cannot draw a solid line (association) between a user and a user system, i.e., between two actors. The relationship between any two actors is represented by means of an information flow.

A **boundary system** is a special external system that provides an interface to another external system. For example, this can be a sender that enables contacting another system. It is comparable to a user system, except that a boundary system is a mediator for another system rather than for a human.

A boundary system is only used if it has a special modeling significance. Otherwise, the external system is a direct actor.

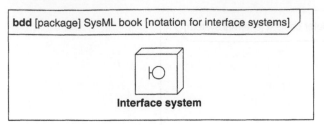

FIGURE 2-15

The notation for boundary systems.

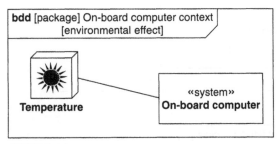

FIGURE 2-16

An environmental effect "temperature."

Similar to an external system, a boundary system is denoted as a box with an additional fish symbol (Figure 2.15). The fish symbol is also known as a *boundary* symbol in software class modeling.

Several factors from the environment influence the system without directly interacting with it. This includes environmental effects such as temperature, precipitation, or oxygen. Only relevant environment effects are of course considered. We don't generally have to model the fact that most systems won't survive umpteen degrees Celsius or total flooding. An environmental effect is denoted as a box with a sun symbol (Figure 2.16).

An **actuator** is a special external system that serves our system in influencing its environment. In contrast, a **sensor** is a special external system that accepts information from the environment and passes it on to the system.

Similar to an external system, an actuator is denoted as a box with an additional cogwheel symbol, while a sensor is denoted with an additional symbolic dial gauge (Figure 2.17).

Actuators and sensors are special categories for technical systems. Other categories can be introduced as needed by the project. For example, the sender and receiver categories with their respective symbols are more suitable than actuators and senders in a communication environment.

A **mechanical system** is a special external system that has only mechanical aspects from our system's view. In particular, it does not include calculation resources, and no data is exchanged, but there may be an exchange of forces, for example.

Similar to an external system, a mechanical system is denoted as a box with an additional tool symbol (Figure 2.18).

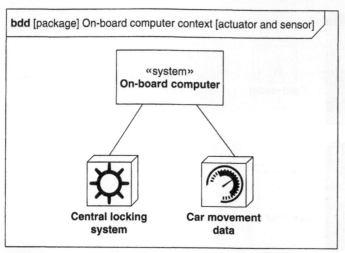

FIGURE 2-17

Example for an actuator and a sensor.

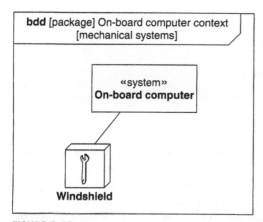

FIGURE 2-18

Example for a mechanical system.

You should be careful not to define too many categories, though. Here too, less is more. Think carefully about the goals you want to achieve with a new category before you introduce it. Will it make the diagrams easier to understand and improve the communication? Will it help winning more information or focus on an important fact? How would you model the actors if you were NOT to introduce a new category?

The system context diagram may make a trivial impression. In practice, however, searching for actors can lead to difficult discussions. For example, we modeled the actor *customer* as a user of our system. Would you have chosen the same actor? Or perhaps opted rather for the *card reader*? Or the *customer card*? (Figure 2.19).

The customer is just the one who holds the card in front of the card reader, and the card reader is just the mediator between the customer card and the on-board computer control.

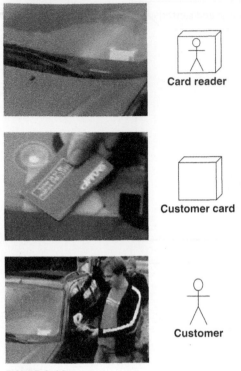

Card reader

Customer card

Customer

FIGURE 2-19

Searching for a matching actor.

And what about the processors in the card reader, or the cable between the card reader and the on-board computer, or …; are they all actors?

There can be good reasons to model each of the solutions mentioned above. You can surely imagine the kind of workshops where all these are discussed. There is no single recipe for finding the best solution. So every workshop participant would be right. Selecting an actor or the system boundary is a pure project decision.

What interaction partner do you want to focus on? And which blocks really belong to your system or project? Information about other potential actors won't necessarily be lost. If this is the information you think is important, then you should document it, e.g., in a comment.

Figure 2.20 shows you a different way. The relationship marked as *flow* between the actors *car service employee* and *car management system* represents an information flow. The car service employee transmits a *status request* to the car management system. Notice that you are outside the system under development. Your modeling focus is within the system boundaries. So don't invest too much work into modeling relationships between actors.

If you do have a bigger modeling need between actors it might be a good idea to move the system boundary further outward. The actors would then become part of the system and fall within the modeling focus.

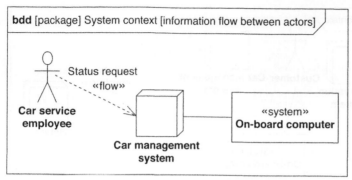

FIGURE 2-20

Information flow between actors.

But let's go back to our selection of actors in Figure 2.19. We decided to use *customer* which means, e.g., that *card reader* and *keyboard* are part of the system. In terms of systems engineering, we take a holistic view of the system. This allows us to then derive requirements for the card reader, which is to be purchased from a third party, or evaluate other conceivable access systems, such as a cell phone (see Section 2.8.1). Altogether, we now have the system context model fully worked out, as shown in Figure 2.21.

When searching for actors we normally run into elements that are not outside but inside our system. Now, what do we do with this information? We cannot model these elements as actors, since actors are outside the system by definition.

Of course, we won't discard this information for the only reason that it is not needed in this work step; instead, we add it. Model an element found as a so-called *block* and use the *composite* relationship to connect it with the entire system (Figure 2.22). Blocks are a concept of the SysML language. We will be looking at blocks more closely in Section 4.5.

PROJECT DIARY

Project Time 5942

We managed to excellently use the system context diagram in a workshop with the domain experts. Though not all of the participating domain experts came from the engineering field none of them had trouble understanding and commenting the diagram. That's very beneficial for our project, since we can coordinate the models directly with the principal, who will now be jointly responsible.

In contrast, there were fierce discussions about the planned navigation system. Though they considered it a very good service, they feared, on the other hand, that customers may feel they are being watched, because SpeedyCar would be technically able to determine the current position of a car at any given time. We will consider it secondary for the time being until there will be a final decision either for or against the navigation system.

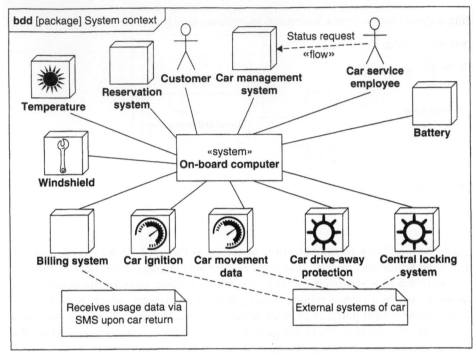

FIGURE 2-21

The system context model for the on-board computer.

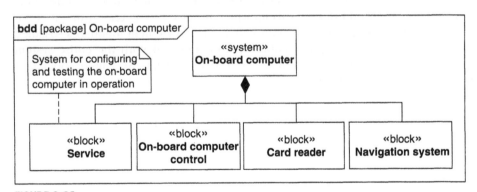

FIGURE 2-22

Structure of the on-board computer.

2.3.2 Model System/Actor Information Flow

Modeling the system/actor information flow is shown in Table 2.7.

Based on the system context diagram we now look at the incoming and outgoing information for our system. The fact that an actor is connected to the system means that they supply information to the system, or obtain information from our

Table 2.7 Summary: Modeling the system/actor information flow.	
Reference card: Model system/actor information flow.	
System context ⊽ ┌─────────────────┐ │ **Model system/actors** │ │ **information flow** │ └─────────────────┘ ⊽ System context [information flow]	*Incoming and outgoing data* **System context:** System with associated actors. **System context [information flow]:** System with information flow from and to the actors.

Motivation/description

Why? The system's information flow with its environment is required for a clear understanding of the system embedding.

What? Describe the information that the system will exchange with its environment.

How? Relevant information that actors send to or receive from the system is documented for each actor. Focus on the direction of the information flow from an actor to the system.

Where? The information flows are used in the analysis to identify and describe use cases. In the system design these information flows have to reflect within the system and correspond to the system interfaces.

Guiding questions
- What information will the actors send to the system?
- Does the information have domain relevance for our system?
- How does the system integrate itself into its environment?
- What information does the system send to its actors?

SysML elements
Block definition diagram, internal block diagram, block, actor, association, role, connector, information, information flow.

system, or both. The type of information exchanged here, and who participates in the exchange, is well known in this early project phase. Though you may be frowning now, it is not a matter of saying how the exact protocol to the external systems should look like. The information we look for is initially much more abstract. What sort of information does the on-board computer get from the customer? Right, card data or a PIN, for example.

We want to write this information down at this point, at which it isn't a matter of achieving completeness. It's rather a matter of documenting the knowledge the participants have gained so far and improving the understanding of the way our system is embedded in its environment. During the subsequent steps within our approach we will use this information to add details to our model and to further complete it (see Section 2.4.1).

The system context model with its information flow essentially serves two goals:

1. The information flow leads to a better understanding of the domain. We are interested only in domain-relevant information and not in technical details.

The diagram gives us a good insight into how the system is embedded in its environment. The meaning of the term *domain* is relative. What is domain-relevant depends on the type of system. If the system is very technical, such as an engine control, then domain-relevant things would be much more technical than in our system.

2. The information flow serves as basic information to determine the services demanded from the system—the use cases (see Section 2.4.1). The information flowing toward the system are potential requests for services from the environment. We therefore focus on this information flow direction.

The information flow is a new concept of UML 2. It is in principle a kind of data flow modeling. That's a technique many had missed in UML 1. The data flow modeling is an integral part of the structured analysis (SA) [8], which is also used in systems engineering, though it is primarily a software development technique. However, it wasn't really fitting for a purely object-oriented notation like UML to support techniques from the procedural world. Fortunately the times when the procedural world and the object-oriented world were enemies and excluded each other are mostly overcome. Today, proven techniques from the procedural world are not rejected in object orientation, but further developed and integrated in the paradigm.[12] The object-oriented concepts from the field of software development do not play a dominant role in systems engineering. In fact, SysML suppresses them, in part intentionally. For example, there are no classes and objects in SysML.

Now, take a look at our system context model. We think about the information flow actor by actor. We are primarily interested in the direction from an actor to the system. We want to find out what kind of services the actors request from our system. If you can't think of any meaningful information just omit the information flow. We don't have to do guesswork.

You can see the result of our thoughts in Figure 2.23. The information flow between the actor and the system is denoted by a black triangle on top of the actor/system relationship. The triangle shows the information flow's direction. Next to the triangle is the type of information, e.g., card data.

In our considerations about the information flow we found a new system actor. We found that vibration forces from the moving car can affect our system. This clearly shows us two things: First, SysML considers not only classic IT information, but also physical objects. Second, immerging into detailed levels leads to new findings about the next higher level.

Also, the information itself is explicitly modeled. UML knows the model element *information*. It is denoted as a frame with the name of the information in the center and a black triangle in the upper right corner (Figure 2.24). We distinguish explicitly between information and its flow.

If you want to document that a flowing piece of information consists of different units you can use the UML relationship *representation*. For example, Figure 2.24 documents that the very generally formulated information *user input* represents

---

[12] That's something you would call progress.

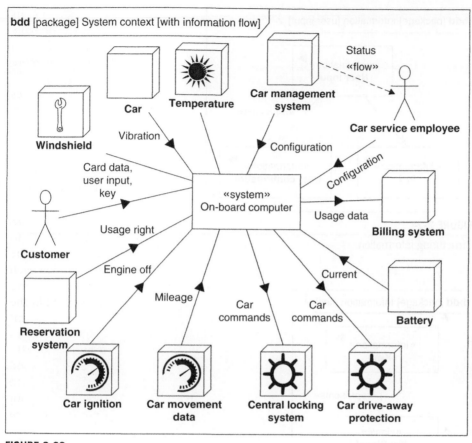

FIGURE 2-23

System context with information flow.

two pieces of information: *PIN* and *user confirmation*. In general, however, I'd go about this matter very carefully. I suggest you model this only provided you really see an immediate benefit in it. Modeling should never become an end in itself. SysML allows you to describe many different facts from your system's real world. However, the decisive question is not what can be modeled, but what benefit you'd have from it.

You can use the same relationship in a later point within the approach to connect a piece of information with concrete design elements. In the design, e.g., we model a signal called *KeySignal*, which describes the communication object that the on-board computer control receives from the key holder. In the system context model the signal is represented by the information *key* (Figure 2.25). Altogether we obtain traceability of this fact in the model.

Alternatively, you can tackle this matter much more directly. SysML extends the UML information flow by a property you can use to transport concrete objects rather than abstract information. These objects are described in more detail and they can

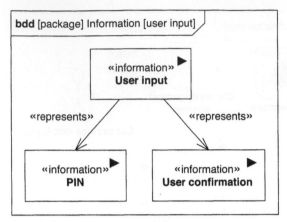

FIGURE 2-24

Structuring information.

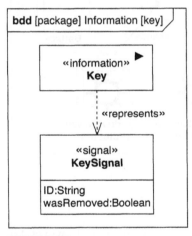

FIGURE 2-25

Information as a representative of design elements.

be present in this form directly in the design models. However, this extension is applicable to the internal block diagram only. We should switch to this diagram form at the latest when identifying the system interaction points (Section 2.3.3). If you include this step in your approach, then it would be a good idea to model the system context diagram as an internal block diagram right from the outset.

Figure 2.26 shows the system context in the internal block diagram. In what block are we, internally? We have to introduce a context element that encompasses the system and all actors. This element is denoted with the stereotype «*systemContext*». You can see in Figure 2.27 how this context element is modeled; note that this diagram does not show all actors.

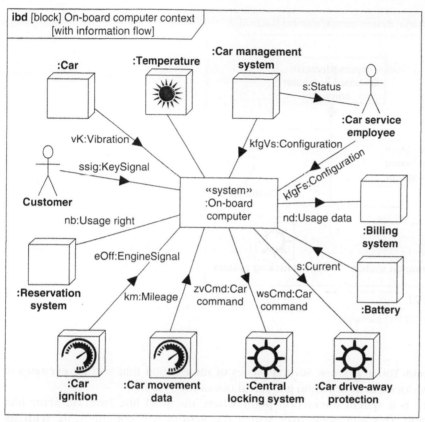

ibd [block] On-board computer context [with information flow]

FIGURE 2-26

A SysML information flow.

This modeling offers no more than a small benefit without system interaction points: real objects instead of information can flow between actor and system. Relationships between actors can be modeled using connectors where, in turn, other object can flow (see *car management system* and *car service employee* in Figure 2.26).

At this point it is a good idea to think about the required depth of details in your information flow modeling for your project. Are the pieces of information, i.e., simple names, sufficient? Or should they be detailed using the *representation* relationship? Or do we have to use the SysML extension of the information flow to model objects directly? In case of doubt we model less for the time being.

2.3.3 Identify System Interaction Points

Identifying system interaction points is shown in Table 2.8.

You know the actors who interact with our system from the previous results. This is modeled in the system context diagram by a relationship from an actor to

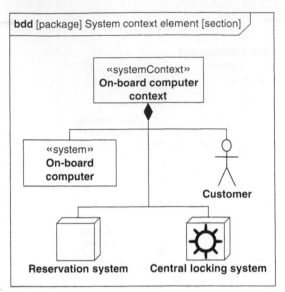

FIGURE 2-27

A system context element.

the system. You also know several pieces of information that will be exchanged. But how does this information get in and out of the system?

There is a system interaction point where the solid line from an actor hits the system. This is a point over which the system will communicate with its environment.

Imagine your system is a black box. This box has to provide interaction points for the actors to be able to communicate with the system. These can be connections for external systems or special clients, Web access for users, switches, displays, and so on (Figure 2.28).

We have to be careful not to confuse interaction points with interfaces. Interfaces and interaction points are different concepts. Unfortunately, the two terms are often used synonymously. On the other hand, the two terms are not totally unrelated either, as we will see later on.

UML lets you model interaction points with ports. They had been added to the modeling language with UML Version 2.0. In the diagram, ports are denoted as small rectangles on the edge of a class.

Though the concept of a port is new to UML, it hasn't been invented from scratch for UML. In fact, the concept roots in a notation and methodology called *ROOM (Realtime Object-Oriented Modeling)* [42].

ROOM doesn't depend on UML. The concept was first introduced to UML by Bran Selic and James Rumbaugh as a profile by the name of *UML-RT* in 1999 [39]. The ROOM modeling tool *ObjecTime* became *Rational Rose RT* when the firm was taken over by Rational Software. That sealed the end of ROOM as a notation and tool, but the concepts are still valid today.

Table 2.8 Summary: Identifying system interaction points.

Reference card: Identify system interaction points.

System context ▼ ┌─────────────────────┐ │ **Identify system** │ **interaction points** │ └─────────────────────┘ ▼ System context [interaction points]	*Incoming and outdoing data* **System context:** System with associated actors. **System context [interaction points]:** System with interaction points.

Motivation/description

Why? Interaction points describe the interfaces to the system environment and are responsible for successful system integration.

What? Describe the points of your system over which information will be exchanged with the environment.

How? Think about a relevant interaction point for each actor. Bear in mind that one single point could be used by several actors.

Where? The interaction points will then be specified in more detail in the design.

Guiding questions
- What paths will the system use to exchange information with its environment?
- Are your interaction points conceptual or physical?
- What interaction paths for actors can be merged?

SysML elements
Block definition diagram, internal block diagram, block, actor, association, role, connector, standard port.

FIGURE 2-28

Interaction points.

Interestingly, ROOM does not know interfaces in the sense UML does. The two concepts of *port* and *interface* have both been part of a language only since the introduction of UML 2.0. It is then a task of the approach models to cleanly separate the two concepts.

SysML distinguishes between a standard port and an object flow port. A standard port is used to supply or request services. Such a port normally has synchronous character, i.e., it is a point over which a request is started and where the sender of the request waits for the result from the receiver. In contrast, object flow ports transport information to and from the system. They often have asynchronous character, e.g., information from external sensors. We don't want to look at these details in this early stage of our approach. We will use only standard ports that comply with the UML-2 ports for now, and do without modeling interfaces for the sake of simplicity, since we are currently interested only in the interaction points themselves. We will differentiate port types later on in the system design, as described in Section 2.7.3.

A system port describes a point in the system that is used to exchange information with actors. Such a port can be a virtual, conceptual point or an object existing in the real world.

Now, how do we find the ports in our on-board computer? We look at our system context model and try to find out what interaction point each single actor may have to the system. There may be more than one. It could also be that the communication of an actor with the system does not flow over a port. For example, we won't model a port for the environmental effect *temperature*. In this case, the exchange doesn't occur over a designated point.

It is not a good idea in this early project phase to anticipate design or implementation decisions, or only to a very little extent. Use conceptual names for your ports, such as *ServerPort* for SMS communication with the SpeedyCar server in our system example. You can see our result in Figure 2.29.

You cannot connect actors directly with ports even if it may look enticing and useful from the graphical perspective. The following box describes the formal rationale.

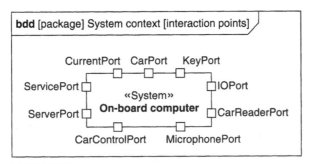

FIGURE 2-29

System interaction points for the on-board computer.

WHY ARE ASSOCIATIONS NOT PERMITTED ON PORTS?

It is often very enticing to connect an association with a port, e.g., in the system context diagram or in the block definition diagram. Though this is in fact supported by several SysML/UML tools, it is formally illegal. And a closer look reveals that it doesn't make any sense. A port is a property of a block and has a rank similar to that of an attribute. Attributes must not be connected with associations either.

The internal block diagram looks at more detailed structure aspects than the block definition diagram. For example, you could model how the properties of a block—ports and attributes—relate. You could then use a connector which, in turn, can have an association as its type, to connect a port.

The block definition diagram describes the type level, while the internal block diagram describes the role level.

To connect actors directly with ports, we have to switch over to the internal block diagram. I wrote in Section 2.3.2 how a system context element (Figure 2.26) can be used for modeling. It means that this is where we leave the type level and continue working on the role level. This level allows us to connect actors—more specifically, the roles—with ports. These connections are then formally connectors rather than associations. You can see the result in Figure 2.30.

PROJECT DIARY

Project Time 6137

I asked Klaus, our tools specialist, to expand the modeling tool accordingly to keep technical modeling details out of our daily project work. Luckily, our tool can be individually expanded over a programming interface. That way we can develop little helpers that will do several modeling details for the developer automatically and transparently. This includes, e.g., the system context element, which can be thought of as a sort of wrapping around the system and the actors, so that we can conduct a detailed environment analysis. The tool can create all model relationships of the context element automatically.

Ivar Jacobson founded Jaczone; one of the company's products is an intelligent agent that guides the developer through the modeling process [26]. Unfortunately, that doesn't correspond to our project requirements, so we cannot use the agent, but the concept is great.

2.4 **Modeling Use Cases**

Use cases represent the services provided by our system, which means that they are the central elements in our requirements analysis. The services a system provides determine that system's meaning and purpose. This means that all functional requirements of the use cases have a high priority. All other requirements, such as response times, weight, or size are of qualitative or supportive nature. That doesn't

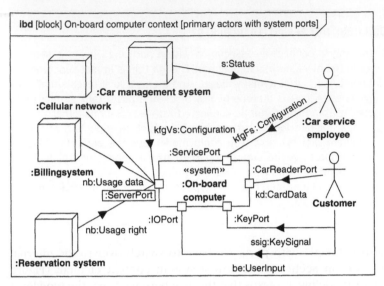

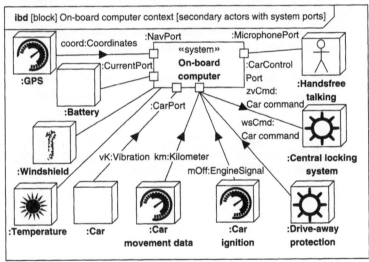

FIGURE 2-30

System context with ports.

mean that these requirements could not be important. An airbag that unfolds several minutes after its triggering is absolutely useless.

We've already collected requirements, including functional requirements, such as *rent car without staff assistance*. Use cases help us refine these requirements and describe them in greater detail. A use case itself is not a requirement.

Ours is a top-down approach, which means that we can achieve a broad collection of requirements in an early project phase. It also helps us obtain a full picture rather early. This provides us with a good basis, e.g., for cost and time estimates, in an early project phase [57].

One of the most important benefits of our approach is scalability. The depth of details of our model can be adapted to the project. Each step is realizable and achievable, from a superficial analysis to get a rough insight, e.g., for a feasibility study, to very detailed executable models. This allows us to further detail a superficial analysis model at a later point in time. And a very detailed model can appear like a superficial analysis model in suitable diagram views. If there is an interest in the details of a model element we simply "zoom in." This way we can make complex models manageable. The modeler won't be overwhelmed by the model's intricacy and they won't get lost in the details either; instead they can work on the details level they need for their current task. Grady Booch calls this *Illusion of Simplicity* [6].

In Sections 2.4.1–2.4.6, we will identify use cases, immerging into each of them, and then analyze them from the superficial use case essence all the way to the detailed flow description. The individual steps involved in use case modeling are shown in Figure 2.31. It is the detailing of the step, *model use cases*, from Figure 2.1.

2.4.1 Identify Use Cases

Identifying use cases is shown in Table 2.9.

Our approach is service-oriented, which means that we first look for the services our system is to provide. The only thing of interest for the actors is actually what functions the system offers or the services that will be requested from the system. The structures required for all of these are secondary for now. It is a "side product" that emerges when we describe and realize the services.

By way of example, we will briefly look at another system: a soft drinks vending machine. What does the actor *customer* want of this system (Figure 2.32)? They are not interested in the structures of the system, but in the services only. They want to *buy a soft drink*.

The services a system offers, i.e., its functionality, are described in UML by means of use cases. A use case is denoted as an ellipse, and the actors participating in the use case are connected to the ellipse by solid lines (Figure 2.32).

A **use case** has always at least one actor; it is started by a domain trigger, and it ends with a domain result. The flow between the trigger and the result has a time coherence, i.e., no domain interruption is possible.

The metaphor of a "service provider" is helpful to ensure that we won't lose sight of the important things. The system exists to render services to others. It has no end in itself. This perspective can get lost in the large number of (technical) details an engineer has to deal with, especially in later project phases. However, all use cases have to have been realized when the system is shipped. You can think of use cases as the "lighthouses" of your project, which you always have to have in sight to ensure that you reach your goal straight on in the secure groove.

This is the approach that's also behind the catchword "use case-driven," used in many process models or software development architectures (including, e.g., the *oose Engineering Process (OEP)* [35], the *Rational Unified Process (RUP)* [31], and the *4+1-Architecture* [30]). It means that the use cases are always kept in focus in the individual system development phases.

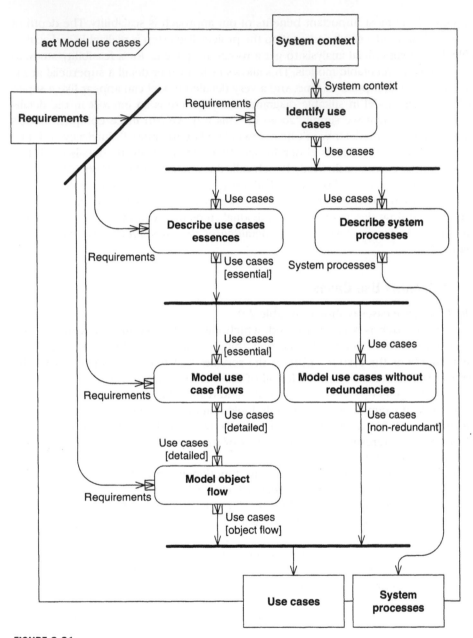

FIGURE 2-31

The approach model for use cases.

To identify services, we first of all look at the system context model and ask ourselves what the actor wants of our system, especially with regard to incoming information flows. Does the information flow trigger a new use case flow, or is it part of another flow? In case of doubt, we assume for now that a new flow is triggered.

Table 2.9 Summary: Identifying use cases.

Reference card: Identify use cases.

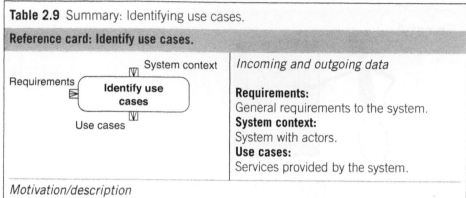

	Incoming and outgoing data
	Requirements: General requirements to the system. **System context:** System with actors. **Use cases:** Services provided by the system.

Motivation/description

Why? Use cases describe the system's services that are perceived and requested from the outside, which means that they are an important view on the requirements.

What? Use cases are identified and allocated to the participating system actors.

How? Use cases are elaborated systematically based on the requirements and the system context.

Where? Use cases are completed with a flow description and then serve as a starting point for deriving the design.

Guiding questions
- What can the system do for a specific actor?
- What incoming information is at the beginning of a flow?
- What services does each of the actors require from the system?
- What results do the services supply to the actors?
- Is the use case described from the actors' view?

SysML elements
Use case diagram, package diagram, use case (SYSMOD: continuous use case), actor, package, requirement, association, information flow, refine relationship.

Each newly found flow is a use case for our system. The categories we have grouped our actors in are helpful in this step.

When the actor's end, where the information flow starts, is a user we have to ask ourselves what the user wants of our system. The information flow is part of a dialog between a user and the system. The important thing is to find out whether the information starts the dialog, or whether the information is transmitted in the course of a dialog. If the user started the dialog, we have found a new use case. Otherwise, we track back the dialog to find the trigger.

The use case name is formulated from the user's view. Imagine you are supposed to mark a button at your system that triggers the use case for users to understand what the button does.

Though the naming is often independent of a direction, verbs like *buy*, *sell*, or *enter*, actually imply a direction. It is important to understand whether the actor or the system buys or enters something. From the triggering actor's view a

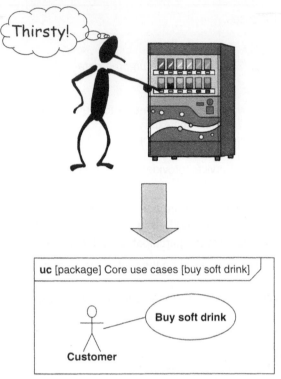

FIGURE 2-32

Describing use cases for services.

sentence in the form "<actor> wants <use case>" must sound meaningful. For example, "customer wants to buy soft drink." From the system's view, a sentence like "system wants to buy soft drink" doesn't make sense.

We proceed in the same way if the actor is an external system. Only this time we take the view of the external system.

If the actor's end from where the information flow starts is a user system we take the view of the user behind the user system and proceed similarly to user actors. From this modeling view, the user system itself does not have an interest, apart from the data transfer between a user and the system.

Similar to user systems, we describe the use cases for boundary systems from the view of the external system that communicates over the boundary system.

Actors representing environmental effects don't have to be considered as we look for use cases. They are the only actors that are not necessarily participating in use cases.

If the actor is an actuator, then it participates in some part of a flow, but it is not the trigger of a use case. A situation where an actuator sends domain-relevant information to the system is rather unusual; and it would be even more unusual if

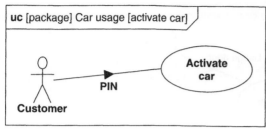

FIGURE 2-33

A potential use case called "activate car."

this information triggered a use case. The direction of the information flow is normally from the system to the actuator. Look for the start of the flow in which the actuator participates. If you find it you've found the pertaining use case.

If the actor is a sensor, it can be the trigger of a use case. However, the sensor is not interested in the result of the use case. This means that we cannot describe that use case from the sensor's view. Look for the actor or stakeholder that is interested in the result, and formulate the use case from its view. If you can't find anything or anybody, you can omit that use case. Nobody will notice it's not there. Or will they? If so, you've found the interested party.

We now want to apply these heuristics to our system. We find the information flow *PIN from customer to system* (Figures 2.23 and 2.24) in the system context model of our system. Does the PIN input trigger a new flow in the system? We will just assume it does in case of doubt. Why does a customer enter their PIN? The goal is to deactivate the electronic drive-away protection. Formulating it from the customer's view, we call this use case *activate car* (Figure 2.33). As seen in the figure we can also show the information flow in the use case diagram.

Next we look at the information flow *usage right* from the reservation system to the on-board computer. We recognize that it merely responds to a request of the on-board computer, but doesn't start a new flow. But who or what started the pertaining flow? In an attempt to trace back the flow, we hit the customer who started the flow by placing their customer card on the card reader. The result is the car being unlocked. Describing it from the customer's view, we call the use case *unlock car* (Figure 2.34).

You will notice at the latest when getting to the detailed modeling of your use case flows (see Section 2.4.5) that the flow after the one called *unlock car* is not yet complete. After this flow there is only a predefined time interval available for entering the PIN and removing the car key from the holder. Only then will the customer have started using the car. Beginning of the usage is stopped if either the PIN is not entered or the key is not removed within this time window. In this case, the car is automatically locked again. The business terms and conditions of SpeedyCar say that a car is deemed to have been officially given to a customer upon removal of the key.

This means that the use cases *unlock car* and *activate car* are one single use case. The trigger, *apply customer card*, normally leads to the result that the car

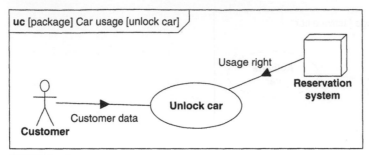

FIGURE 2-34

A potential use case called "unlock car."

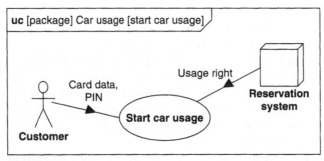

FIGURE 2-35

A use case called "start car usage."

usage has begun. Accordingly, we call the use case *start car usage* (Figure 2.35). There would be no negative effect if you were not to yield this finding in this phase; it would be perfectly alright if you were to find it later when you look at the details of your use cases (see Section 2.4.5), or if you were never to merge your use cases. The flows are the same, only their distribution across the use cases would differ. It is absolutely normal that new information is won as we work on the details which affect the previous modeling steps in arrears. Your modeling can be only as exact as the current abstraction level permits.

The information flow *mileage* from the sensor *car movement data* participates in a special use case. Use cases that are triggered by a sensor information often "feel" a little strange.

The information *mileage* seems to trigger a new flow. The system determines how many kilometers have been done and how much time has elapsed since usage started; then it compares the current time with the scheduled reservation end, and finally shows the result in a display unit. The party interested in this result is the customer. From their views let's call this use case *show car usage data* (Figure 2.36).

Do you think your use case has a strange look and feel? No? In that case you can skip the following lines. Yes? Then the reason is probably that the described flow represents only a traversal of a continuous flow. Such a flow does not correspond to the standard definition of a use case. It has no external trigger and no

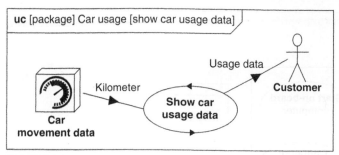

FIGURE 2-36

A use case called "show car usage data."

defined end result, but supplies results continually. So, if you want to describe a continuous flow rather than just a traversal, you should use a continuous use case.

When does the use case *show car usage data* begin? What we need is mileage information in order to determine the car usage data, which will form the basis for customer billing later on. To ensure that customers can keep themselves updated on the current state of costs incurred, this information is presented regularly on the display unit—similar to a taximeter. The display of usage data additionally includes the usage time currently run up, and it will be shown even while the car is not moving. We know from the person in charge at SpeedyCar that the first display appears immediately upon the beginning of the car usage. That is, before the engine is started and before any kilometer has been driven. The use case is triggered by an internal state transition. As soon as the system changes to the usage state, the display starts showing usage data. Leaving the usage state causes the use case to end.

I'm sure you would have noticed that we are in the middle of analyzing potential use cases. We normally don't start identifying use cases on our own hidden in our closets. We identify our use cases in a workshop. The participants are chosen such that we obtain as much knowledge about all disciplines involved in the system as possible. We then determine potential use case candidates in small groups. We write our use cases on metaplan cards. Such cards are also available fittingly in the form of use cases, i.e., ellipses. We can optionally note the pertaining actors, the information flow, open questions, and other information on the back of the cards. However, the focus is clearly on the identification of use cases. This means, for example, that we won't especially determine pertaining actors, but only add them if we already have this information.

In the plenum, we collect the use cases on a metaplan board. This helps us discover duplicate use cases, synonymous terms, use cases not clearly formulated, and use cases that are too abstract, too granular, or simply wrong.

We will keep only one card each of the duplicate or synonymous use cases. We will staple the duplicate cards to the main card each if the cards have additional information on their back. Otherwise, we can discard them.

A use case that is too granular is part of a larger use case. Again, we will staple the card to the larger use case if it contains additional information.

A use case that is too abstract can initially be used as a heading for a group of use cases.

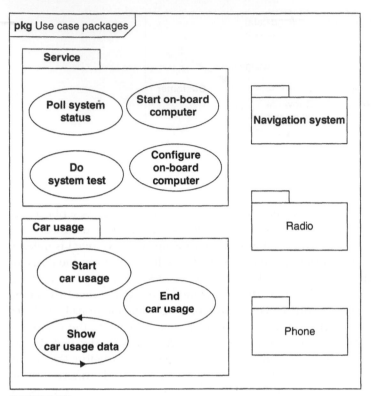

FIGURE 2-37

Model showing the results of the use case workshop.

We then take all use cases found and put them into domain-motivated groups on the metaplan board. We name these groups accordingly.

Next we use a digital camera to capture the result. We can transfer the use cases to our model later on. In the model the use case groups become packages. Since we want to concentrate only on the core functions of the on-board computer for the time being, we move the contents of the packages, *navigation system*, *phone*, and *radio*, to the side in the diagram (Figure 2.37).

There is normally other information that belongs to a use case, but for which there are no meaningful model elements in SysML. This additional information includes short descriptions, references to external documents, open issues, or management information like priorities and cost estimates.

We can normally accommodate this information in fields available to describe the use case in the modeling tool or as a comment in the diagram. We can of course create a description in a text document outside the SysML model as an alternative. If you opt for this alternative you have to make sure that the data stored separately—the model and the document—are maintained consistently.

Use cases also have the roles of functional requirements. How does this harmonize with the requirements we determined in Section 2.2? A use case is a

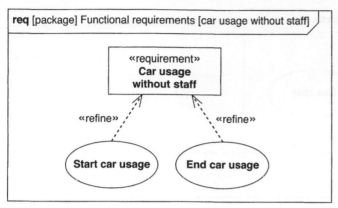

FIGURE 2-38

Refining use cases, requirements.

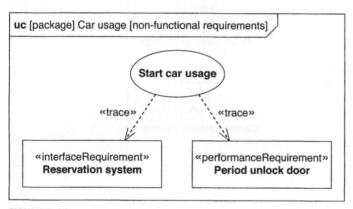

FIGURE 2-39

Relationship between a use case and a requirement.

refinement of a functional requirement. It fulfills further criteria, such as domain trigger, result, and time coherence. It has actors associated with it, and an activity describes the flow in detail (Section 2.4.5).

Functional requirements are more general in nature and are not subject to side conditions. The *refine* relationship (Figure 2.38) describes how a functional requirement and a use case relate. It could easily be that several use cases refine one single requirement, just as well as one single use case can have refine relationships with several requirements. A use case is an element of the analysis, but not a requirement.

Non-functional requirements can describe qualitative aspects of use cases, e.g., agreed system response times during a flow. This type of relation is modeled by means of a *trace* relationship (Figure 2.39).

So far we have been concentrating more on the identification of use cases and less on the allocation of actors. We'll catch up on this right now. You can find

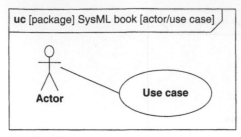

FIGURE 2-40

An actor and a use case.

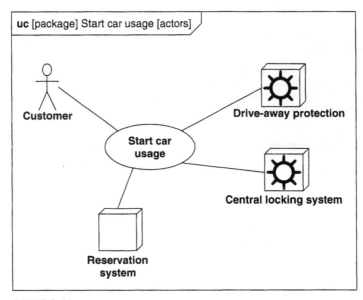

FIGURE 2-41

Actors and the use case "start car usage."

examples like the one shown in Figure 2.40—an actor denoted as a stick man, connected with a use case, in the UML literature.

However, use case diagrams for embedded systems look totally different. Embedding means that the system will interact with many other (external) systems. Consequently, many external systems are actors participating in the use cases. The pertaining diagram has a Star pattern, which we already know from the system context diagram (Figure 2.41).

We are now ready to assign actors to the use cases identified so far. We have actually done some when we identified the use cases. We try to find the actors that participate in each use case. Each actor also has to appear in the system context model. Since we are now looking closer at the details of our system it is absolutely normal to discover new actors. We extend the system context model accordingly.

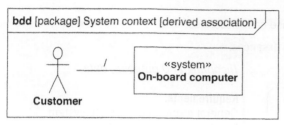

FIGURE 2-42

A derived association.

The dependency on the system context arises from the fact that we have redundant information in the model. Each use case actor is also a system actor. We could calculate most of the associations between the system and the actors from the use case model. To this end, we can use the UML construct of a *derived association*, which is denoted by a slash (Figure 2.42).

Unfortunately, in practice we often have to deal with the problem that derived associations are poorly or not at all supported by modeling tools. On the other hand, since the redundancy is controllable it is not dangerous to leave it in the model. Bear in mind that redundancy occurs in the model only later. We don't have use cases yet in the first step of modeling the system context.

In Section 3.5 you will find more techniques for actor modeling, such as generalization of actors, the OR relationship, and multiplicities in the actor/use case relationship that we haven't used here.

PROJECT DIARY

Project Time 6269

We can communicate directly with the domain experts about the use cases just as we do about the system context model. The simple representation of the use cases and the pertaining actors is easy to understand even for people who are not from the engineering environment. This helps us continue coordinating our model directly with the principal. Great!

We discussed the possibilities of the communication unit with the domain experts in a workshop. They consider data transmission via SMS as the cheapest variant. But the system has to be flexible to ensure that another communication technique could perhaps be used in the future.

The domain experts require that a so-called *emergency driving* be allowed. What they mean by that is a way for a customer to start using a car even if no connection to the reservation system can be established. For example, some rental stations are located in underground parking floors where it is often impossible to reach a cell network.

2.4.2 Describe Use Case Essences

Describing use cases essentially is shown in Table 2.10.

Table 2.10 Summary: Describe use case essences.

Reference card: Describe use case essences.

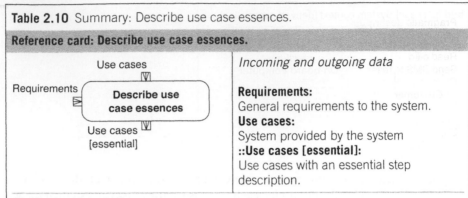

	Incoming and outgoing data
	Requirements: General requirements to the system. **Use cases:** System provided by the system **::Use cases [essential]:** Use cases with an essential step description.

Motivation/description

Why? We need an overview of the system's services that can be determined quickly and which is independent of technical solutions.

What? Describe the domain intention for the use case in the form of essential steps that don't consider technical details and concrete flows.

How? Think of the steps involved in the standard flow of a use case and remove the technical details that are contained in the standard flow so that they will no longer be present in the result.

Where? The essential steps give you the structure for the next level of details. The description is stable and can be reused for subsequent or similar systems, e.g., in a product family.

Guiding questions
- What is the domain intention for the use case?
- Does the essential description contain technical solutions?
- Is the name of an essential step identical with that of the use case?
- Is the essential description easy to understand for a domain person who doesn't know anything about the project?
- Does the use case have 2–8 essential steps?

SysML elements
Use case diagram, use case, comment.

We are now ready to deal more closely with each of our use cases. If you dive into the use case by one detail step deep you get to the essential use case description. It describes the flow of a use case in general and independent of any specific technology. This description is purely textual and is initially not modeled with special model elements.

While this description looks extremely easy it can be rather difficult to create it. The essential description omits a lot of details, doesn't consider exceptions but only the standard flow, and contains no technology and design decisions. The targeted omission of information is called *abstraction*. Abstraction at this point may prove to be difficult especially for engineers, since they normally have to consider every detail and every exception.

Pragmatic description

Apply customer card
Read card
Send SMS to reservation center
Receive SMS reply
Check usage right
Unlock car doors via central locking system
Poll PIN
Enter PIN
Verify PIN
Deactivate electronic drive-away protection
Remove key
Display customer welcome message

FIGURE 2-43

Pragmatic flow description for "start car usage."

A helpful path toward our essential description leads across a pragmatic process. Write down the standard flow of a use case freely out of your gut feeling. For example, this could look like in Figure 2.43 for our use case *start car usage*.

The pragmatic use case description corresponds to the explanations we obtained from the domain experts. The essential description we are looking for has a higher degree of abstraction. We want to detach from the technical realization and limit ourselves to the domain core—the essence.

As an example let's look at the first step of our pragmatic description. We discover a technical detail: the customer card. Inserting and reading the customer card are not the domain intention. These two steps are not the goal of the on-board computer. From the domain perspective what these two steps do is they identify a customer. We could easily think of a different technical implementation.

We similarly proceed step by step in the use case and distill the essence out of it. Since the description is more abstract it won't come as a surprise that it is much shorter than the pragmatic description. You can see the result in Figure 2.44.

Essential steps are denoted as comments in the model (Figure 2.45) or in the documentation field of the use case, provided the SysML/UML tool supports this.

It is mandatory in both cases to be able to generate the essence in the form of a report from the modeling tool; otherwise you won't have a clear description, and the information might go under in the depths of the modeling tool.

The sequence of the use case steps is not yet relevant at this point. We naturally write them down in a meaningful sequence. However, the sequence often depends on technologies and doesn't play a particularly important role on the domain level. For example, we don't want to think about the sequence of the PIN input or the key removal now. Of course, we will think about these things a lot later on when we will describe the use case in detail and with the respective technologies in mind (see Section 2.4.5).

The essence we found is not the only possible solution. You can see two alternative essences in Figure 2.46. Alternative 1 involves the same number of steps as

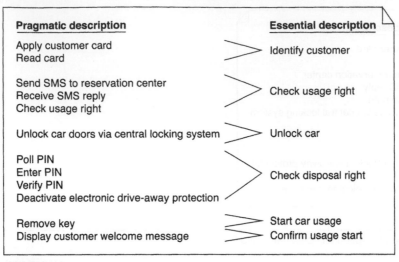

FIGURE 2-44

Essential flow description for "start car usage."

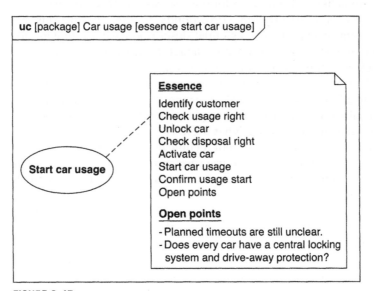

FIGURE 2-45

The essence of "starting car usage" as a comment in the model.

our solution. Taking a closer look reveals, however, that the steps are formulated in more concrete terms. For example, the last step is *remove key* rather than *start car usage*.

The phrase *remove key* is undoubtedly catchier. But it doesn't follow the pure theory of an essence since it includes a technical detail: the key. I recently rented a

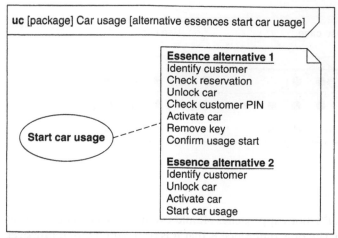

uc [package] Car usage [alternative essences start car usage]

Start car usage

Essence alternative 1
Identify customer
Check reservation
Unlock car
Check customer PIN
Activate car
Remove key
Confirm usage start

Essence alternative 2
Identify customer
Unlock car
Activate car
Start car usage

FIGURE 2-46

Alternative essences for "start car usage."

car and noticed that they've started offering rental cars that must be started with a chip card and by the push of a button. There was no car key. Of course, this can lead to an important discussion about terms. Is a chip card a type of key? You find a broad description of terms in Sections 2.5 (domain knowledge) and 2.6 (glossary).

The phrase *start car usage* is more essential and has the benefit that the name of the step and that of the use case are identical. This shows clearly that we are looking at the core of the use case. A use case often follows a certain structure: first the preparation, then the core, and then perhaps some touchup steps. The removal of the key is the formal consignment or delivery of a car to a customer based on the terms and conditions of SpeedyCar. So this is the domain core of the use case.

The second alternative essence is shorter than the other possibilities. It consists of only four steps. It is more abstract and omits more information. The best way to find out whether or not this is still sufficient are the reactions of the other project participants. Do they all understand the essence, or do you have to explain what is meant every time?

The way between the purely essential description and a more pragmatic description, which is normally sprinkled with technical details, is a tightrope walk. If you move too sharply to one side you risk "falling down." Once you've understood the degree of abstraction and the benefits of an essential description you will easily find the right way.

The number of essential steps naturally depends on the domain situation and cannot be universally stated. As a heuristic: there are at least two steps and at most eight steps in most cases. You should review the essence if your number differs a lot.

You will describe each of the essential steps in more detail later on in the approach. If you have few essential steps you will have to supply more information. If you have many essential steps you won't have to go much into breadth any

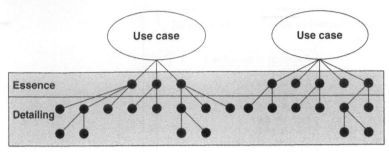

FIGURE 2-47

Number of essential steps.

more later on (Figure 2.47). Both approaches should eventually yield a description of the same information. The only difference is that it is distributed differently over the abstraction levels. I tend to prefer the approach with many essential steps.

It's easy to create essential descriptions as soon as you have developed a feeling for the abstraction required. It is generally not a good idea to conduct long academic discussions in an effort to obtain the perfect essence. You cannot transfer the above discussion about alternative essences in this form to your practical project. It is much too "finicky." Its purpose here is to help you understand the different aspects of essential descriptions.

Altogether, this gives you a compact domain description of the services provided by the system. The fact that technologies and details are not considered makes essences well suited for successor versions or related systems and keeps them open for different solution approaches.

PROJECT DIARY

Project Time 6429

Essential descriptions represent a major benefit for our project. The initial startup difficulties have been overcome and all participants, including our principal, can now work on this abstract level. This is extremely effective since it spares us from cumbersome discussions about details, which cannot be conducted in a meaningful way in this early project phase. We will examine the details later in an environment where we will have sufficient information and structures to analyze them productively.

2.4.3 Describe System Processes

Describing system processes is shown in Table 2.11.

As we identified our use cases we noticed that there can be dependencies between use cases with regard to their sequence of execution. That is, only once a

Table 2.11 Summary: Describing system processes.

Reference card: Describe system processes.	
Use cases ⩔ (**Describe system processes**) ⩔ System processes	*Incoming and outgoing data* **Use cases:** Services provided by the system. **System processes:** Holistic flows, consisting of use cases, in a domain-logical sequence.

Motivation/description

Why? Complex flow sequences between use cases have to be dealt with and modeled explicitly.

What? Describe the flow dependencies between use cases and group-related flows into system processes.

How? Study the flow dependencies of domain-related use cases based on your pre- and postconditions and describe them in an activity.

Where? System processes have to be considered in the design, and they may have to be implemented by blocks of their own.

Guiding questions
- What flow dependencies are there between the use cases?
- Which use cases have an important domain proximity?

SysML elements
Use case diagram, activity diagram. SYSMOD: system process, include relationship, activity, action, edge, control node (e.g., initial node, decision), composition.

certain use case has been fully traversed can other use cases be executed. We use system processes to describe this relation.

A **system process** describes a flow that extends over several use cases. It consists of a set of use cases that have a domain-logical flow sequence.

A system process is a special use case with the stereotype *«systemProcess»*. We use a different notation (Figures 2.48 and 3.87) to better distinguish it from system use cases. Its name is a noun without verb.

Not every use case belongs to a system process; only the ones with a flow dependency to other use cases do. These are often use cases that are in the same package, all belonging to a system process.

System processes serve two distinct purposes. First, they document flow dependencies in a compact and clear way. Second, you can use them to describe holistic behavior, which has to be explicitly considered in the system design and implementation.

System process information is implicitly included in the model. For each use case we can formulate a postcondition that, in turn, could be a precondition of another use case. This means that there is a domain-logical sequence between use cases. A system process represents this dependency explicitly.

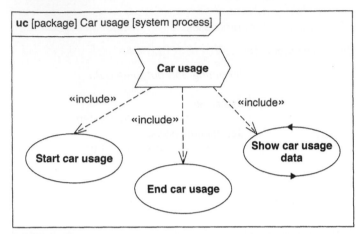

FIGURE 2-48

A system process with use cases.

We model the fact that a use case belongs to a system process by means of an *include* relationship. Its notation is a dashed arrow pointing from the system process to the use case and marked with the keyword *«include»* (Figure 2.48).

We use activities to model the flow sequence of system processes. Exactly one activity belongs to a system process. This relation cannot be represented in the diagram. SysML and UML know only few notations that combine two diagram types. But the *system process/activity* relationship exists in the model.[13]

The pertaining use cases are represented each by an action in the activity. The action is denoted as a rectangle with rounded corners. The name of the action— that is, in this case the name of the use case—appears inside the rectangle. The small fork in the lower right corner shows that this action invokes an activity. It is an activity that describes the flow of the corresponding use case (see Section 2.4.5).

Our next job is to connect the actions, i.e., to arrange them in some sequential order or flow. The flow begins at the initial node, which is a black circle, followed by the actions, and ends at the activity final node, which is also a black circle with an encompassing circle.

We define a system process called *car usage* and then continue modeling the dependencies of the use cases *start car usage*, *end car usage*, and *car usage data*. You can see the result in Figure 2.49. Displaying the usage data and ending the usage can happen independently of one another.

Independent flows are expressed by a fork node in activity diagrams. A fork node is denoted by a black bar at which one flow ends, and from which an arbitrary number of flows start. The incoming flow is "forked."

---

[13]For those who are well familiar with the UML metamodel: It's the composite relationship between *BehavioredClassifier* (in this case the use case or system process) and *Behavior* (in this case the activity).

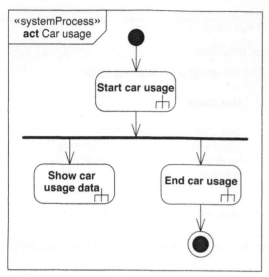

FIGURE 2-49

The activity of the system process "car usage."

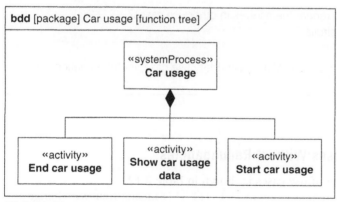

FIGURE 2-50

The function tree for the system process "car usage."

The display of usage data is a continuous use case. It is no longer exited in this system process. When the use case *end car usage* is completed, the entire system process and with it the usage data display are terminated over the activity final node.

You will learn other description elements that are possible in activity diagrams in Sections 2.4.5, 2.4.6, and 3.6.

You can just as easily represent a system process in the form of a function tree (Figure 2.50). This figure is a static view of Figure 2.49. The dynamic information about the flows is lost in this representation (Figure 2.50).

Table 2.12 Summary: Non-redundant modeling of use cases.

Reference card: Model use cases without redundancies	
Use cases Model use cases without redundancies Use cases [non-redundant]	*Incoming and outgoing data* **Use cases:** Services provided by the system. **Use cases [non-redundant]:** Use cases with generalization and include relationships for non-redundant flow description.

Motivation/description

Why? Redundant model information can cause serious problems if their consistency is violated.

What? Identify common things between the use case flows and model these areas in isolation to avoid redundancies.

How? Common things between use case flows are described in secondary use cases and embedded into the primary use cases by means of the include relationship.

Where? The non-redundant use case structure supplies useful hints for optimized, non-redundant system design.

Guiding questions

- Which use case steps repeat themselves in other use cases?
- Which use cases are similar?

SysML elements
Use case diagram, use case, SYSMOD: secondary use case, include relationship, generalization.

2.4.4 Model Use Cases Without Redundancies

Non-redundant modeling of use cases is shown in Table 2.12.

This step is used to refactor our model [16]. This means that we change the structures of the model without adding new domain information. The model is cleaned up, so to speak, to create a better basis for expansion.

As soon as we have finished creating essential use case descriptions we have a possibility to detect redundant flows. These are identical flows that occur in several use cases. The earlier we detect them the easier it will be to avoid multiple analyses, designs, and implementations. This will be particularly helpful later on; otherwise there could be a risk that a desired change is not made to all flows involved, causing the model to become inconsistent.

The essential description allows us to see the top level of our use case flows and to start refactoring. Since the essential description does not contain any technical aspects, we can discover even flows that are identical from the domain perspective, and which differ only in their technical implementation.

Several common flow steps between the use cases are very easy to find since the names of the respective steps are identical. However, if the essences had been created by several people, which is normally the case, we have to deal with synonyms and similar things. The same steps do no longer have the same names now.

This is where a glossary comes in handy, since it encourages the use of a uniform project language. For example, we added to our glossary that our principal uses the term *car* rather than *auto*, *vehicle*, or *rental car*. Accordingly, we called an essential step *unlock car* and not *unlock auto* in the use case *car usage*.

We can formalize our search for identical flows by means of pre- and postconditions as well as incoming and outgoing data. This information can be modeled as we will see later on in Section 2.4.5. And we can use query scripts to access it from within the model. A script can create a list of use case steps that have the same pre- and postconditions or the same incoming and outgoing data. These are potentially identical steps. Most SysML/UML tools allow you to develop tailored model query scripts.

However, there are neither pre- and postconditions nor information about incoming and outgoing data on the essential level yet. We can apply this technique only to more detailed use case flows later on.

A use case step that occurs more than once or related use case steps are modeled as one single new use case. However, since the criteria for a fully fledged use case—no trigger, result, or actor—are not met,[14] we denote it with the stereotype *«secondary»* or as a dashed ellipse. This is only one use case fragment, a so-called *secondary use case*. We use the *include* relationship to embed it in the primary use cases.

We find only one common step in the package *car usage*. We need to determine the usage data for two reasons: first, for continuous usage data display, and second, when the car usage ends to be able to forward the data to the billing system (Figure 2.51).

We need to be careful not to model routinely every step that occurs more than once as a secondary use case. Bear in mind the triple heuristic, which says that one thinks about resolving a redundancy only in its third occurrence. If so, we wouldn't have had to define the secondary use case *determine car usage data*. On the other hand, heuristics don't apply routinely either. We have to weigh each concrete case to find out what is more valuable: either no redundancy or redundancy with the benefit of having a less complex model, since we omit another model element and its relationships.

If you search your use cases for common things you may find that some use cases are pretty much alike. Not necessarily in the number of common steps, but in the flows themselves. The use cases of our system's navigation system are a good example: A customer can define a new route, or change or delete an existing route. This means that we found three use cases: *add route*, *modify route*, and *delete route* (Figure 2.52).

---

[14]This would violate the use case criteria of the SYSMOD approach and not the formal SysML criteria, which would be illegal.

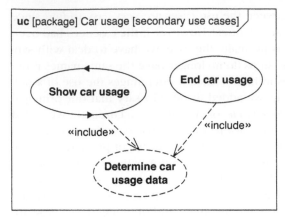

FIGURE 2-51

Use case relationships.

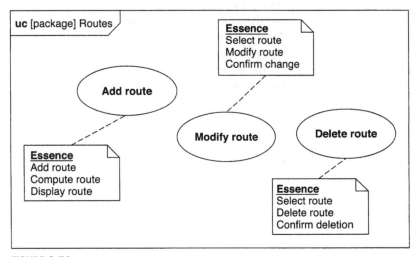

FIGURE 2-52

Use cases for "route."

Two use cases, *modify route* and *delete route*, are very similar. Nevertheless it is necessary to list both use cases, because they concern two different system services. You can document their similarity in another use case. The two flows will become identical if you move one abstraction level up.

The abstract flow is described by an abstract use case. SysML lets you denote the property *abstract* by writing its name in italics and optionally adding the word {*abstract*}. The relationship to the concrete use cases is a generalization, which is denoted by an arrow with a solid line and closed arrowhead (Figure 2.53).

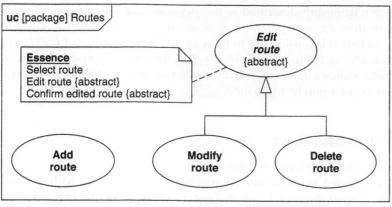

FIGURE 2-53

Use case relationships for "route."

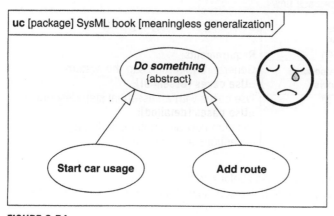

FIGURE 2-54

Too abstract!

The use case generalization is meaningful only provided that the relationship can be read in the direction of the arrow to say: "<use case> is like <use case>," or, in this specific case: "*modify route is like edit route.*" Sounds perfectly alright! Though this is not a 100 percent rule it covers most cases. Moreover, the abstract use case should be only slightly more abstract than the concrete use cases. Otherwise, they would have to become more and more abstract in order to always find a common "master" use case for two arbitrary use cases. Grossly exaggerating, this would mean that if we used a use case *do something*, we would have found a master use case for all our use cases. Obviously modeling such a use case doesn't make sense (Figure 2.54).

The *include* relationship described at the beginning of this section is much more important than the generalization. It is always a good idea to follow the guideline "the include relationship has to be searched for while the generalization relationship is found" in the modeling process. This means that you should search for potential redundancies in a targeted way, while you should model a generalization only if you found it purely "by chance."

2.4.5 Model Use Case Flows

Modeling use case flows is shown in Table 2.13.

The steps completed so far in our approach have provided us with a broad overview of the system. We now know the system environment (actors, information flows) and the catalog of services, including essential descriptions (use cases).

Table 2.13 Summary: Modeling use case flows.

Reference card: Model use case flows.

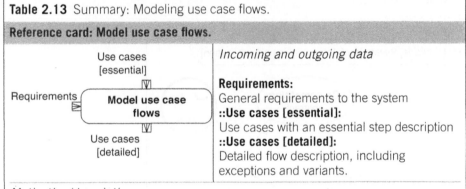

	Incoming and outgoing data
Use cases [essential] / Requirements → Model use case flows → Use cases [detailed]	**Requirements:** General requirements to the system **::Use cases [essential]:** Use cases with an essential step description **::Use cases [detailed]:** Detailed flow description, including exceptions and variants.

Motivation/description
Why? The flow descriptions of use cases belong to the core information of our requirements analysis. They provide a detailed view of the behavior required of the system.

What? Describe the use case flows, including all exceptions and variants, in appropriately detailed form.

How? The use case flows are described using SysML activities.

Where? The activities form a direct basis for the system design. Their clear representation in the activity diagram allows you to have the principal deeply involved in the system development process.

Guiding questions
- What steps are required for the use case?
- What exceptions and variants can occur during the flow?
- Is the use case sufficiently detailed and clearly described?

SysML elements
Activity diagram, activity, SYSMOD: essential/continuous activity, action, edge, control node (e.g., initial node, decision).

We achieved these results relatively quickly. Here, in this first round, the iterative-incremental approach does not demand completeness either. It is sufficient to have found the core use cases. As soon as their details have been analyzed we can also determine the remaining use cases easily.

In our analysis we normally spend the best part of our time describing detailed flows for use cases. We are ready to start this job now. Starting from the abstract essence description, we analyze and model flow details, exceptions, and variants. This requires many domain details. You will come across open issues that cannot be solved without the help of a domain expert. It is therefore always a good idea to have access to appropriate stakeholders in this phase to clarify detail questions in time.

We start our analysis by selecting a use case. If you haven't modeled use case flows for the system yet, you should select a use case that contains the central domain logic, and covers as large a system area as possible, and has a known flow. Let's select *start car usage* as our first use case.

When describing exceptions and variants of a use case flow, we quickly hit the limits of our natural language. It is normally easier to describe all these sorts of junctions, concurrencies, and terminations graphically. SysML and UML offer the activity diagram to graphically describe exceptions and variants.

First of all, let's look at the essential steps of our use case. A step becomes an action in the activity. It's now a matter of connecting the actions, i.e., putting them in a certain sequence. The flow begins at the initial node, denoted by a black circle, followed by the actions, and finally the activity final node, which is also denoted by a black circle with an additional encompassing circle.

We don't consider potential exceptions and variants just yet, which means that the result can be pretty trivial. Though the essential description does not dictate a fixed sequence, the steps are already listed in a meaningful order rather than meaninglessly mixed at random. In our use case, *start car usage*, this also applies to all the steps up to and including the step *unlock car* (Figure 2.45). However, the subsequent steps cannot be arranged in a fixed sequence. A customer can first remove the key and then enter the PIN, or vice-versa. The two steps are independent of one another. They can occur in an arbitrary sequence, perhaps even concurrently in case a customer is willing and able to go into contortions (Figure 2.55).

In activity diagrams we express independent flows by means of a fork node, which is denoted by a black bar at which a flow ends, and from which an arbitrary number of independent flows start. In other words: the flow is "forked" (Figure 2.56).

As soon as the independence is no longer desired, we have to synchronize the flows. The join node is also denoted by a black bar. In contrast to the fork notation, however, it has several incoming flows and only one single outgoing flow (Figure 2.56). The outgoing flow doesn't start before all incoming flows have arrived. So what happens here is a synchronization of the flows. In our case, we have to synchronize the independent flows before they reach the last action—*confirm usage start*. Otherwise, the faster flow part would trigger the confirmation before the other flow part has been fully traversed (Figure 2.56).

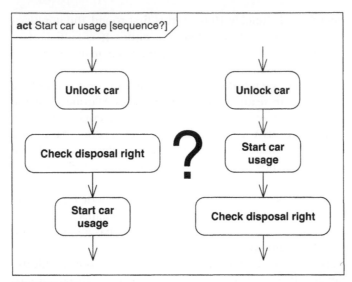

FIGURE 2-55

Arbitrary sequence?

Altogether, we obtain the result shown in Figure 2.56 for the use case *start car usage*. This result shows the standard flow without exceptions or variants, based on the essential steps.

Unfortunately, we have introduced some redundancy in our model. First, we denoted the essential steps textually near the use case. Second, exactly these steps are also described as actions in the activity diagram. If you were to change something in the essential steps as you progress, it would very likely lead to inconsistencies due to redundancy. It could easily happen that you change the textual description, but overlook the corresponding actions in the activity, or vice-versa.

To remove this redundancy we delete the textual essence description and add the stereotype *«essential»* to the actions in the activity (Figure 2.56).[15] This has the additional advantage that we see the essence in the activity directly. However, this modeling technique makes sense only provided that your modeling tool allows you to generate an essential description in the form of a text document from the activities. Otherwise, you'd lose the simple—purely textual—view of the essence. Many SysML/UML tools have interfaces to support such individual extensions, but they are not included in the standard product.

In the next step we look at the paths outside the standard flow. This means that we now take off our rose-colored spectacles and analyze what should happen if things are not "normal."

---

[15]As described further below and in Section 5.4, the action itself does not have a stereotype *«essential»*, while the invoked activity does. The stereotype of the activity is also represented in pertaining call actions.

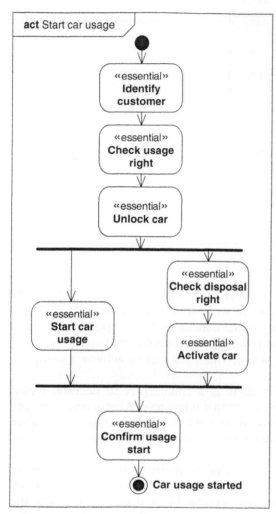

FIGURE 2-56

Standard flow for "start car usage."

We try to find possible exceptions and variants for each single action. We can often distinguish between successful and unsuccessful results after each action. Let's look at the first step, *identify customer*. The result can be either *customer identified* or *customer not identified* (Figure 2.57). The former result corresponds to the standard flow, while the latter requires more thinking. We ask the domain experts and learn that the system should terminate in such a case. If a customer cannot be identified, they shouldn't be able to access the car. Accordingly there is no flow variant where no customer has to be identified.

A flow can take different turns based on a decision. We use a *decision node* to model this in the activity diagram. The notation is a diamond with one incoming flow and an arbitrary number of outgoing flows, each fitted with a condition.

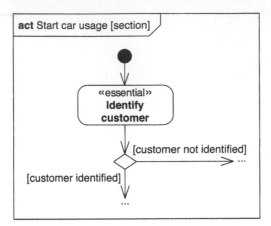

FIGURE 2-57

The decision "customer identified?"

These conditions have to mutually exclude each other to ensure that no more than one condition is met ever. Of course, we also have to ensure that one single condition is always met. If there are several conditions, i.e., no pure yes/no decisions, it is useful to add the keyword [*else*] to a flow, which will then be activated whenever all other conditions are wrong. This allows us to achieve a complete coverage of all possibilities.

Similarly to fork and join nodes, there is a counterpart to decision nodes. A *merge node* looks like a decision, except that it has several incoming flows and only one outgoing flow. No decisions are denoted. The only purpose of a merge is to unite optional flows to one single strand. It neither checks nor synchronizes anything (Figure 2.58).

A closer look at each of the use case steps reveals that one single step can, in turn, contain a complex flow. You can also use an activity that is invoked in that step to model this flow. To make sure this is visible in the diagram, we denote the calling action with a small fork in the lower right corner. This symbol represents a call hierarchy (Figure 2.58).

Many things happen in our second use case step, *check usage right*. A message is sent to the reservation center, a response is expected and received, and sometimes *emergency driving* (see Project dairy with Project time 6269 on p. 75) is triggered. We detail this step in a new activity of type «*essential*» (Figure 2.58).

First, we use the light-emitting diodes of the status display unit to show the customer that the system is on and that they should be patient. To this end, we send a corresponding signal to the status display unit. In the activity diagram we use a special symbol to represent this. Though the receiver of the signal is not denoted it is present in the model.

Note that we are no longer working on the essential level. The further we go forward in the detailing process the more specific we describe a flow. In contrast to the essential description, technical details are now not only permitted but desired. Try to knowingly draw a border between pure domain things and technical

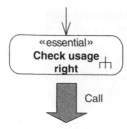

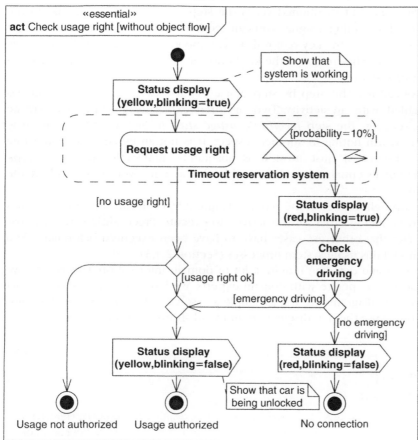

FIGURE 2-58

The detail activity for "check usage right."

solutions. We will be working exactly along this border in Section 2.8.1 to model technical variants.

In the next step, we send a usage right request to the reservation system and expect an answer. Of course, the waiting time has to be limited. We use an interruptible activity area to model this in the activity diagram. A dashed rectangle denotes the area within the activity that can be interrupted by an event. In our case it's a time event that we denote by a symbolic hourglass symbol. An edge with a lightning arrow begins at the event and leaves the interruptible area. Things continue at this point when the event occurs, at which time all flows within the area terminate.

There is yet another particularity at the interruptible edge: It states how likely it is that the flow will take this path. This construct is not specific to interruptible areas. It is an extension of SysML that can also be denoted, e.g., at outgoing edges.

You can see the entire flow of the use case *start car usage* in Figure 2.59. One particularity I haven't mentioned yet is the step *start car usage*. Similar to the symbol used for sending a signal, you can see here the symbol for receiving of a signal. This step hides the key removal. We can model it as a signal. This step waits until the customer has removed the key from the holder, which is perceived as a signal by our system.

We proceed like this step by step. Not every use case step has to be necessarily detailed with an activity. Two or three explanatory sentences may be sufficient; see, e.g., the step *terminate usage start* in Figure 2.59. By the way, this step is worth noting in another respect: It is not an essential step, but one that was "discovered" just now. It is absolutely admissible that new steps, which are not essential, are added on this abstraction level as we look at the exceptions.

In the top right corner in the activity (Figure 2.59) you can see a precondition that has to be met in order for the activity to execute. Preconditions result partly from the fact that other use cases have to have been executed beforehand. You can also model this using system processes (Section 2.4.3).

Exceptions and detailing require a lot of domain information. This is why we need to closely cooperate with domain experts. We have to be aware of the fact that the activity diagrams are not as simple as use case diagrams. You should nevertheless try to use them in discussions and workshops with stakeholders.

PROJECT DIARY

Project Time 6897

As we analyzed the use case *start car usage* Paul suddenly discovered the issue whether or not a customer who canceled but is still in possession of the customer card can access the car. Since access to a car is supposed to work even without connection to the reservation center (emergency driving, Project dairy with Project time 6269 p. 75) it's impossible to check such a case in their customer system. Should the on-board computer be fed regularly with a list of suspended cards?

2.4.6 Model Object Flows

Modeling the object flow is shown in Table 2.14.

You may have noticed as you have been dealing with use case flows that data or objects have not played a particular role yet. All our steps execute actions, but

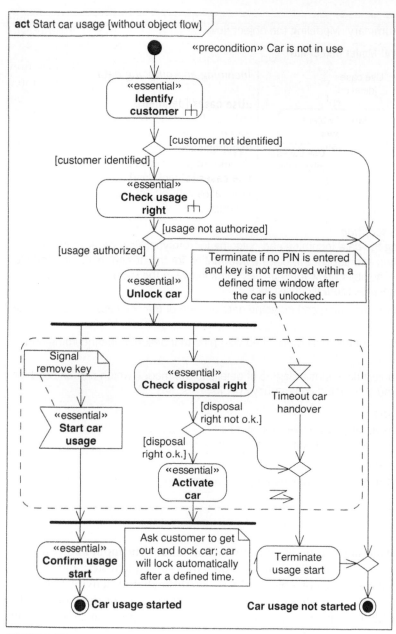

FIGURE 2-59

The flow diagram for "start car usage."

we haven't modeled yet what they require, or what they create or change. It's just as well we haven't looked into this until now, since we wanted to concentrate on the logical flow (called "control flow" in SysML/UML lingo).

Now—in a second step—we add information about this data. This is called "object flow" in the activity diagram. It represents how objects, i.e., data, "flow"

Table 2.14 Summary: Modeling the object flow.

Reference card: Model object flow.	
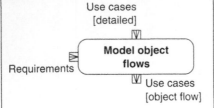 Use cases [detailed] ▽ Model object flows Requirements ▷ ▽ Use cases [object flow]	*Incoming and outgoing data* **::Use cases [detailed]:** Detailed flow description, including exceptions and variants. **Requirements:** General requirements to the system. **Use cases [object flow]:** Use cases with object flow in flow descriptions.

Motivation/description

Why? Studying the data incoming and outgoing to/from your flow steps sharpens your description and supplies important information for the design, e.g., for interface descriptions. The object flow functions as a link between the dynamic and static models and ensures mutual consistency.

What? Model the incoming and outgoing data of each of the use case steps and their relationships.

How? The actions of the activity are fitted with pins that describe the incoming and outgoing data.

Where? The object flow adds a degree of details to the model, which can be used for simulations and automated consistency checks.

Guiding questions
- What data is required by a use case step?
- What data is created or modified by a use case step?

SysML elements
Activity diagram, activity, activity parameters, action, pin, control node (e.g., initial node, decision).

---

across a flow. One step creates an object which is, in turn, the input information for another step, where it is modified and accepted by a subsequent step, and so on.

More specifically, it's not objects that flow through the activity, but object tokens. Think of the term *object* or *data* in the widest sense of the words. Either can be data within a software application, but also purely physical elements, such as liquids, electric current, gases, or forces.

We use pins in actions to model incoming and outgoing data. A *pin* is a small rectangle that is attached to an action. The name of the object is written next to the rectangle. We distinguish between input pins and output pins, depending on whether arrows point to the pin or away from it (Figure 2.60). Though the notation for pins is similar to that for ports, they have nothing in common.

We are now ready to add the object flow to our activity for the use case *start car usage*. We don't need an object or block model yet to do this. We define the

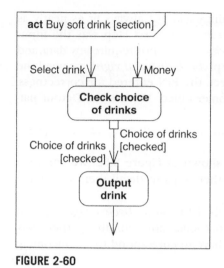

FIGURE 2-60

Example for input and output pins.

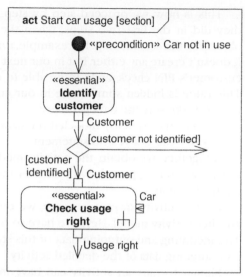

FIGURE 2-61

The object flow for "start car usage" (section).

object entirely intuitively. This means that we don't need object-oriented knowledge either. Just use the word "data" if "object" irritates you. We will turn to block modeling later in Section 2.5.

Look at the first use case: What result object will *identify customer* produce? Right—a customer. In the positive case, the next step will be *check usage right* (Figure 2.61). Within this step, an SMS with the authorization request is created and sent to the reservation center. Of course, the SMS also contains information about the customer, i.e., the customer object belongs to the incoming data of that step.

Moreover, the step needs information about the car in which the on-board computer is located, since this also has to be communicated to the reservation system. This information hides somewhere in the on-board computer. At this point we are interested only in the fact that we need it; we are not interested in the data source, since it has no effect on the flow. We use an input pin that is not connected to any edge to express this. To make sure the pin is recognizable as an input pin, we draw an arrow inside the pin (Figure 2.61).

At this point we should take a look at the car data from another perspective. From the finding that we need car data arise a few questions: How does the data get into the system? How will they be updated or removed? The answers to these questions mean that we found new potential use cases. We will name them *add car data*, *modify car data*, and *delete car data*.

It is generally a good idea with all kinds of data to take a look at their life-cycles. Where do they come from and where do they go? There are normally new potential use cases behind the answers to these questions. The term "data" is not limited to software; it also concerns physical things, like liquids or gases, for example.

This is how we proceed step by step. Things will not always fit as neatly as they did in the first two steps, when the result of the first step was the input object for the second step. For example, *unlock car* does not require any data, and it doesn't create any either. But in our next step, *check disposal right*, we need the customer's PIN check code to be able to check the PIN entered for correctness. This value is hidden somewhere in our customer object. We use the Detour pattern to make sure the data get there.

We haven't explicitly modeled the data outgoing from the step *check disposal right*, since this is a yes/no statement.

Altogether, we obtain the activity model shown in Figure 2.62. We continue using the same approach with each of the other steps to detail them by adding another activity.

In the activity *start car usage*, we described the step *check usage right* in another activity model. Here we have to pay particular attention to the transition. The incoming and outgoing data of this step have to correspond to the incoming and outgoing data of the detailed activity.

Similar to pins, an activity can have input and output parameters, except on the activity level. Input and output parameters are denoted as rectangles on top of the activity's encompassing rectangle (Figure 2.63). Inside the rectangle of a parameter there is its name, which normally corresponds to the parameter's type. An incoming activity parameter also assumes the function of an initial node. This is the point where a flow begins as soon as the activity has been invoked. In contrast, however, an outgoing activity parameter does not have the same function as an activity final node. It is the point where the flow that placed an object in the parameter node ends. This ends the entire activity only provided that this flow was the last within that activity. This means that the semantics is similar to that of flow final nodes.

You can see that both activity parameters and initial and final nodes are modeled in Figure 2.63. Invoking this activity causes three flows to start. The flows with the customer and car objects are initially blocked, because the target—the step *request usage right*—is not yet ready to accept these objects. The flow outgoing from the initial node sends a signal, *status display*. There upon, this flow visits the step *request usage right*. All start conditions for the step are now met, and customer and car objects can be consumed.

The activity is regularly terminated with an outgoing usage authorization when the outgoing activity parameter is reached. However, no usage authorization can be returned if the flow reaches the activity final node. Since outgoing activity parameters must not be empty at the end of the activity, we place a so-called *null token* into the parameter. The two possible results—*usage authorized* and *usage not authorized*—are taken into account in the calling activity, *start car usage*, in the subsequent decision (Figure 2.62).

In closing this section, let's have a look at the flow of another use case that introduces a new and important aspect. *Show car usage data* is a continuous use case. SysML extends the UML activity model by properties for modeling continuous systems. You can see several new SysML elements modeled in Figure 2.64.

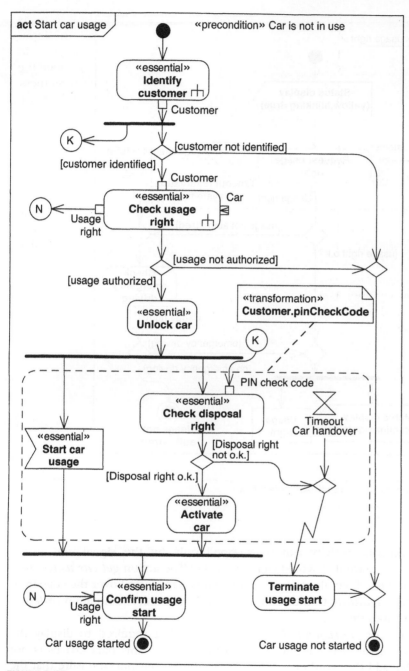

FIGURE 2-62

The activity "start car usage" with object flow.

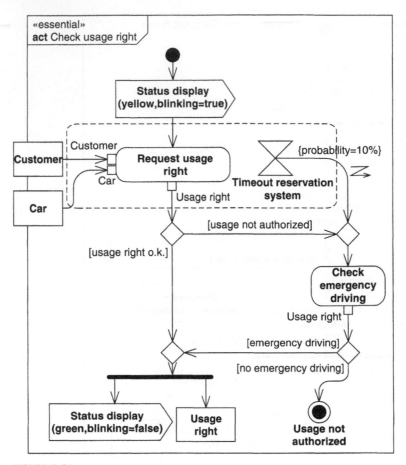

FIGURE 2-63

The activity "check usage right" with object flow.

The continuous activity can be stopped only by the signal *end usage*. Otherwise, once started, it would run continually. The action *get car usage data* has two incoming object flows. An object token is transported over the edge from the time event *updating* to the action once every minute. The notation *{rate=1/ minute}* describes the rate.

The signal *car movement data* supplies the data required to display the mileage since usage was started. The interval in which this data arrives is not described. We add the word *overwrite* next to the output pin to ensure that the action always processes the most current values. This means that the current token will always be the most recent.

The flow property is denoted by *{stream}* at the input pin of the action *show car usage data*. This causes the action to accept data over this pin "in active operation" rather than at the startup time.

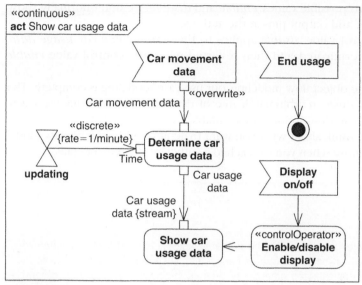

FIGURE 2-64

A continuous activity for "show car usage data."

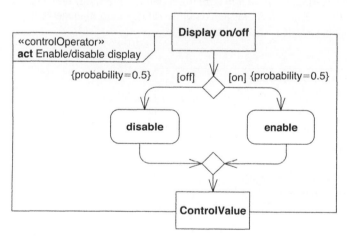

FIGURE 2-65

Detailing "display on/off."

But what if one of the subsystems for phone, radio, or navigation wants to use the usage data display? The signal *display on/off* switches the usage data display accordingly. More specifically, the subsequent action is responsible for this. This action is a so-called *control operator*, which means that it is capable of starting or stopping other actions.

To better understand have a look at the detailing[16] of this action in Figure 2.65. The action has an output value of type *ControlValue*. This type is defined in SysML

---

[16]We wouldn't need this detailing in practice; I'm only showing it here for better understanding.

and includes the two possible values, *enable* and *disable*. We don't normally show the pertaining input and output pins at the actions.

Now, if the control value *disable* applies to the action *show car usage data*, then this action is terminated, and then restarted when the control value *enable* occurs.

Together with the object flow modeling, our use case modeling is complete. The activities allow us to use an arbitrary degree of details to describe our use cases, from a superficial flow description to executable models. This is the reason why you should carefully think about what you want to achieve with your activity model to ensure you will know when you've reached a sufficient degree of details.

PROJECT DIARY

Project Time 7829

Today we were able, together with the domain experts, to clarify the question of whether or not the on-board computer can detect suspended customer cards in order to prevent unauthorized emergency driving. It should be possible to send data about suspended cards via SMS to the on-board computer. This means that we've found another use case, which we will call *add suspended customer data*.

Today is Mr. Speedy's birthday. I gave him a fountain pen for a birthday present. His reaction was somehow reserved. As far as customer relationship management is concerned I probably have to learn a thing or two yet.

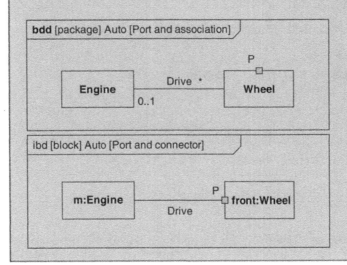

2.5 **Model Domain Knowledge**

Modeling the object flow is shown in Table 2.15.

The domain terms we are dealing with in our project are described in the glossary (Section 2.6). Some terms described there directly concern our system. The

Table 2.15 Summary: Modeling the domain knowledge.

Reference card: Model domain knowledge.	
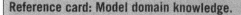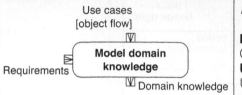 Use cases [object flow] Model domain knowledge Requirements Domain knowledge	*Incoming and outgoing data* **Requirements:** General requirements to the system. **Use cases [object flow]:** Use cases with object flow in flow descriptions. **Domain knowledge:** Structures of the system's domain terms.

Motivation/description

Why? The domain objects you are using in the object flow of activities have to be described in order to ensure that all stakeholders reach a uniform understanding and that they are used consistently in the model.

What? Model the structures of the domain-relevant terms from the system's view.

How? Model the terms and their structures as domain blocks in a block definition diagram.

Where? The domain knowledge model reflects the static view of the domain logic; it is well suited for coordination with the principal and as a design basis.

Guiding questions
- What domain terms does the system deal with?
- Are the terms known to the principal?
- Is a term important enough to justify being explicitly modeled?

SysML elements
Block definition diagram, SYSMOD: domain block, association, generalization.

system "knows" and uses the terms listed in the glossary. For example, a customer is known to our system. In the use case *start car usage*, the customer is identified. In the display unit, they are personally "addressed," and they are transmitted together with billing data to the billing system. This makes a customer a so-called *domain block*. Other candidates for domain blocks include, e.g., a phone call, the usage right, and usage data.

A domain block represents an object, a concept, a location, or an individual from the real-world domain. A domain block is directly known to the system.

To better understand what we mean by the term "domain block," let's take a brief look at a counter example. The term "customer billing" is a domain term from the glossary. But the on-board computer does not directly deal with customer billing. In fact, it doesn't know the term. So it is not a domain block. Other examples for non-domain blocks are normally the actors and objects our system is composed of, such as the card reader.

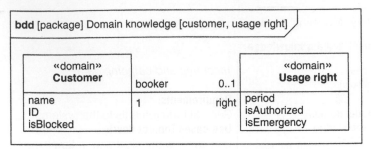

FIGURE 2-66

The domain blocks "customer" and "usage right."

These blocks are easy to find. Actually we've found them already. Look at the object flow in the activity diagrams of our use cases (see Section 2.4.6). The data we have denoted as incoming or outgoing data near the actions represent the domain information our system is dealing with.

We use the stereotype *«domain»* to denote domain blocks. Blocks do not normally have operations, and they have only few attributes. The types of attributes are generally not stated, because they are part of design or implementation details, which are not of interest in the domain knowledge model. Here it is irrelevant whether it's a *string* or *char[]*, an *int* or *integer*.

In our object flow model we have made assumptions about the structures of the objects. For example, the object flow in the use case *start car usage* implies that the object *customer* includes the PIN check code, or that the object *usage right* includes information about *emergency driving*, and so on. We can also derive relationships between objects.

These structures have to reflect in the domain knowledge model. We use the model element *association* to model structural relationships between blocks. An association is denoted by a solid line between two blocks.

Associations in the domain knowledge model are normally not directed, i.e., they have no arrowheads or, in SysML/UML lingo, no navigation direction. From the domain's perspective, either direction is both present and meaningful. For example, not only the customer as the booking party belongs to *usage right*, but also a usage right. Associations are denoted with role names (*booker, right*) and multiplicities (Figure 2.66).

Figure 2.67 shows the domain knowledge model of the on-board computer. The abbreviation *bdd* in the diagram header stands for "block definition diagram." The associations are read in the following pattern: "A <block> has <multiplicity> <block> in the role specified by <role name>." This sentence must be meaningful for the domain. Let's test it in a simple example: "A customer has null to one usage right in the role right." Though this sounds a bit clumsy it makes sense.

What makes sense and what doesn't will be decided by your principal or the domain experts in cases of doubt. The allocations of an association are not always unique. For example, there could easily be an association between *usage right*

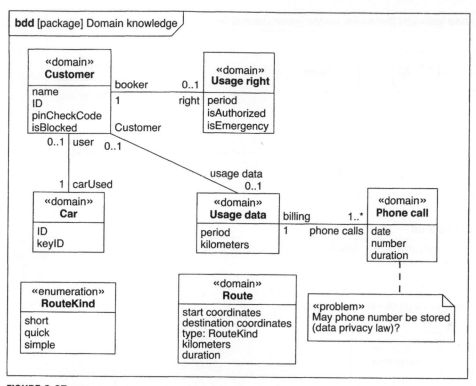

FIGURE 2-67

The domain knowledge model for our on-board computer.

and *usage data* rather than an association between a *customer* and their *usage right* (Figure 2.67). Bear in mind that, in the domain knowledge model, there is no right or wrong, only a better or worse.

The block *route* is a loner. That's possible too. Not every block has to necessarily participate in an association. In other words: We should never force a relationship onto something. The area around *route* is incomplete yet in our system, since we haven't analyzed the navigation system in depth yet.

The RouteKind is a so-called *enumeration* (Figure 2.67). We use this type if the number of values for an attribute is limited from the domain perspective. The attribute *type* in the block *route* is an example of this type.

A *generalization* is another possible relationship in the domain knowledge model. However, it is not required in our example. If you come across a potential generalization you should check whether or not the matter could be modeled more meaningfully with an enumeration type (Figure 2.68).

Eventually, what makes sense and what doesn't is largely decided by your environment: Which variant is better understood, especially by the domain people?

Multiple inheritances are absolutely legal and meaningful in the domain knowledge model, as opposed to the system design where they don't make sense.

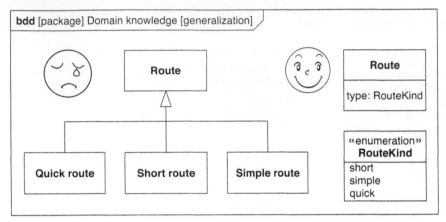

FIGURE 2-68

A generalization in the domain knowledge model.

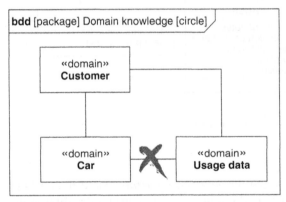

FIGURE 2-69

Circles in the domain knowledge model.

It means that a block has more than one generalization relationship with other blocks. Nevertheless, you should use multiple inheritance very sparingly.

Pay attention to circles in your domain knowledge model (Figure 2.69). They are not illegal, but they indicate that there is likely to be redundant information. In such a case you should check each association from the circle outward as to its importance. Try to do this by imagining you removed an association from the diagram and are trying to see whether or not your model lost some of its expressiveness. If you find an unimportant association, remove it.

Make sure your domain knowledge model doesn't turn into a design model. The primary goal is to describe the domain structures. Particularly software developers who are familiar with design patterns and various design tricks relating to class modeling have to be aware of this delimitation.

Table 2.16 Summary: Creating a glossary.

Reference card: Create glossary.	
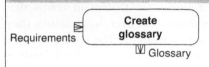	*Incoming and outgoing data* **Requirements:** General requirements to the system. **Glossary:** Description of domain terms for the project.

Motivation/description

Why? A glossary restricts the playground for free interpretations so typical of natural languages to avoid misunderstandings in the project.

What? Describe domain terms from the system environment.

How? Describe the terms in text form in the style of a lexicon. Long explanations and formal definitions do not belong to a glossary.

Where? A standardized project language that doesn't leave much room for all sorts of interpretations forms the basis for effective working and successful modeling.

Guiding questions
- What domain terms will be used in the project?
- Do all project participants have the same understanding of a term?
- Does every project participant have quick and easy access to the glossary?

SysML elements
None.

PROJECT DIARY

Project Time 7939

Similar to other diagrams used earlier, we can coordinate the domain knowledge model also directly with our stakeholders. They can read the diagram and reproduce the structures. That's great since it saves us the error-prone translation of our principal's wishes to our model.

2.6 Create Glossary

Creating a glossary is shown in Table 2.16.

Creating and maintaining a glossary are activities that continue during the entire project time. The glossary describes all domain terms from the project environment. Rather than defining terms, the glossary explains them briefly and clearly so that any project participant will understand the term unambiguously. It surely happened to you too during your daily project work that unnerving discussions or system errors emerged due to petty misunderstandings.

Our glossary should contain two types of terms: "real" domain terms that not everybody necessarily knows, and domain terms that everybody thinks they know. The second category is dangerous. Look at this example: The term *customer* is certainly known to all project participants. So hardly anyone will ask what is meant by it. Unfortunately, this domain term hides potential misunderstandings. Is a customer always an individual? Or are there corporate customers? If so, do all employees of a corporate customer have identical customer cards? Since the term appears to be trivial, it can easily happen that these questions will never be discussed. This means that the finished system is potentially faulty and might have to be corrected, probably causing considerable cost that hadn't been planned for.

Other good examples from a real-world project are the terms *configuration* and *parameterization*. Both terms had been used in that project, but they had different meanings for the project participants. The bad thing was that everybody had a different idea of what they meant. Many disputes were eventually clarified once the misunderstanding had been discovered. Yet another real-world project had used the term *printer*. It didn't mean the device, but the profession, i.e., an individual who was a user of the system. I could easily list many more such examples and you could probably add your own to that list.

WIKI

The official name is *WikiWikiWeb*, which means that it has the abbreviation *WWW*, which shows clearly what it is all about. Just like the World Wide Web, a wiki is based on an arbitrary number of Web pages that present information. The word "wiki" is not an abbreviation, but a Hawaiian-language word for "fast." Some busses or taxis in Hawaii are called "Wiki-Wiki." A Wiki can present information fast, where "fast" refers to the time from an idea to its presentation. For example, you read a Web page and have an idea about adding more information to that page. Using a wiki that can be done real quick. Each wiki Web page includes the function "*edit page.*" You select this function and start entering your new information. As soon as you finished typing, this information is available to everybody immediately. You do not have to know HTML. A wiki can be fed with (almost) normal text.

Wiki is not a commercial system, but a concept for which there is a large number of free implementations. A pretty extensive collection can be found on the pages of Ward Cunningham, the inventor of wikis, at *http://www.c2.com/cgi/wiki?WikiEngines*. In addition, there are public wikis that everybody can access or edit. One of the most popular wiki communities is the Wikipedia encyclopedia [62].

I strongly recommend you play with this technology and consider seriously using it in your project. It is free, simple, and effective.

Building a glossary is tied to a number of problems in practice. It is a cumbersome job that nobody wants to do, let alone being motivated to do it. That's no good news for a starter. You'll often see that the glossary disappears in a document

Table 2.17 Glossary entries.

Usage right	
Description:	A usage right describes whether or not a customer is entitled to use a car. It includes information about the customer, the booking period, and whether it is an emergency driving case.
Domain block:	Yes
Author, last change:	Tim Weilkiens, April 30, 2004
Disposal right	
Description:	The on-board computer grants a customer disposal right, if this customer has entered a correct customer PIN upon start of usage.
Domain block:	No
Author, last change:	Tim Weilkiens, April 30, 2004

that nobody reads. It is normally not updated as everybody shies away from the effort. I recommend to lay out your glossary in a pragmatic and simple way. An ideal medium for a glossary is a wiki (see box on p. 108 (previous page)). A wiki creates a platform where every project member can add entries and update information. The wiki is also generally suitable to be used as an internal communication medium in a project. Using a wiki means that your glossary stands a good chance to be "lived." And there won't be one or a couple members in the team who have to take care of the glossary while hating to even think about it, since a wiki is always a joint effort.

In our on-board computer project, there are mainly two terms that could lead to misunderstandings: *usage right* and *disposal right*. You can see the glossary entries in Table 2.17.

I'm giving a few rules for glossary entries that, when observed, will help you create them in an easy-to-understand way to avoid misunderstandings:

1. Write down entire sentences rather than headwords. This helps you avoid that important information will eventually be missing. For example, compare the entry in Table 2.17 with the following description of "usage right".
   - Customer
   - Booking period
   - Emergency driving

2. Try to write active sentences rather than passive ones. This helps you prevent that you inadvertently omit information. For example, use a style similar to the one in Table 2.17 instead of the following description of "disposal right."

   A customer is granted the disposal right if he or she has entered a correct customer PIN at the beginning of the usage period.

3. Write short, communicative sentences. Somebody who tries to look something up in a glossary doesn't expect long essays. Think of entries in a lexicon.

PROJECT DIARY

Project Time 7989

The marketing department of SpeedyCar expressed their concerns about the fact that the regular car radio has to be removed to make room for the on-board computer. Car radios have increasingly evolved into a multimedia center in cars. That's a development that the customer requires, but the on-board computer cannot catch up with.

For this reason, there may be a major concept change coming up. Luckily, this doesn't have an impact on our project in its current phase, since we haven't analyzed the radio subsystem of the on-board computer in detail yet. We've modeled the other parts independently of it. This shows once again that a good dependency management and a structured model pay in the end.

2.7 Realizing Use Cases

We have identified and modeled the requirements to the system in the previous steps in Sections 2.2 through 2.5. That's the area we generally call "analysis." We now dedicate ourselves to the design of the system. This means that we describe structures and behaviors that realize the requirements we identified and determined in the analysis.[17]

We now have to deal with the issue of how the results from the analysis should be transferred into the design in a structured and reproducible way. That's the only way to ensure that all results from the analysis will be taken into account, and that changes to the requirements will be made in the right places, or changes to the design will be harmonized with the requirements.

We are only looking at the abstract solution in this book, i.e., structure and behavior descriptions, excluding concrete implementations. This means that we do not take the technical aspects, such as concrete hardware, software technologies, and so on, into account. We will add these technical aspects later on when we'll be ready to take technological decisions on the basis of the abstract solution.

The most important thing about a system is the services it offers to its environment. A system is useless without them. I've emphasized this fact over and over again in the previous sections. Accordingly, we will now have a closer look primarily at the use cases as the representatives of services, and we will realize them systematically in our design.

Our approach is shown in Figure 2.70. We begin with an outer view and develop an interaction diagram of the system/actor dialog (Section 2.7.1). From there we can derive our system's interfaces (Section 2.7.2). We continue from the outer view toward the inside to model the system structures. We identify blocks, look

---

[17] Note that the transition from the analysis to the design is flowing. This is the reason why there are often discussions about the exact delimitation of the two terms that lead to no result. In fact, we already took solutions, such as the card reader, into account in the analysis.

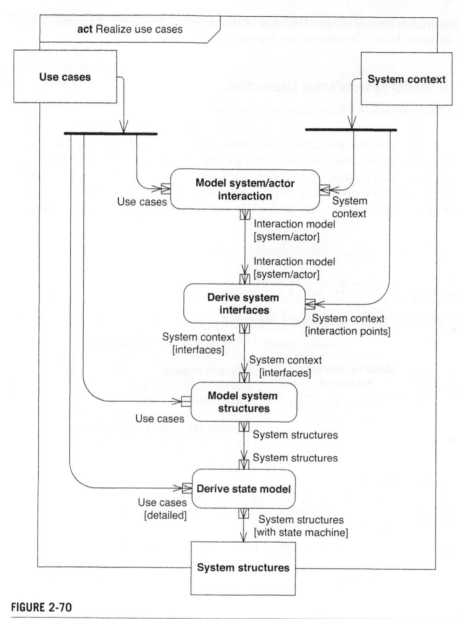

FIGURE 2-70

The approach model for "realizing use cases."

at the information flows between the blocks, and use interaction diagrams again to derive interfaces (Section 2.7.3). This time they are the interfaces of the blocks. The behavior of each of the blocks can be easily described in a state machine.

This approach will repeat itself if we want to detail a block. We treat a block as we treated the system in the approach described above, and so on, until we reach the desired degree of details. This way of doing things produces diagrams in various detailing levels—similar to our approach to the analysis.

2.7.1 Model System/Actor Interaction

Modeling system/actor interaction is shown in Table 2.18.

The first step where we map the required flows to the system/actor structure, i.e., the system context, takes us closer to our system design. We previously modeled the flows in the use case activities. These flows don't describe who executes the individual steps or who communicates with whom. To this end SysML offers the sequence diagram, which the interaction model is based on. It weaves elements together that we already have in our model—the system and its actors

---

Table 2.18 Summary: Modeling system/actor interactions.

Reference card: Model system/actor interaction.

System context → **Model system/actor interaction** → Use cases, Interaction model [system/actor]	*Incoming and outdoing data* **System context:** System with actors. **Use cases:** Services provided by the system. **Interaction model [system/actor]:** Interactions between the system and actors.

Motivation/description

Why? The system context and the use cases do not look at the interaction between the system and its actors in detail, which can lead to faulty estimates of the usability and system integration.

What? Describe the interactions between the system and its actors each with regard to a use case.

How? The interaction between the system and its actors is described in a sequence diagram for selected flow scenarios.

Where? The system/actor interaction supplies a template for the design, especially with regard to defining the interfaces.

Guiding questions
- What requests will the actors send to the system during a use case flow?
- What requests will the system send to the actors during a use case flow?
- Who will make which request when?

SysML elements
Sequence diagram, lifeline, message, interaction operator.

with the use case flows—and adds information about the communication between the participants.

Our interaction modeling effort has primarily the goal of identifying the system interfaces, which we will do in the next step (Section 2.7.2). In the step after that we will trace the messages arriving at the system and leaving the system, and we will build the required system structures.

How do we create a sequence diagram? First thing we take a use case, e.g., *start car usage*. The system and the participating actors are the interactions partners to be shown as lifelines in the sequence diagram. What we'll do is we model a concrete scenario only, excluding all exceptions and variants, as we did in the use case activities. We pick the standard flow—the positive case. We translate this flow from the activity to the sequence diagram. We draw messages that describe the communication between the lifelines. Interaction operators, denoted by boxes, influence the possible flow. The operator *par* is used in Figure 2.71.

You have to pay attention to obtain a meaningful degree of details for our messages. You have a certain degree of freedom depending on your goal. Do you want to describe conceptual messages and interfaces, or do you want to examine all technical details already in this step? We are moving on a more conceptual level in Figure 2.71.

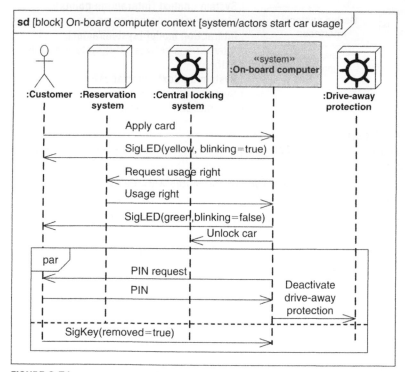

FIGURE 2-71

System/actor interaction for "start car usage."

A complete modeling process requires us to transfer all flow variants from the activities to a sequence diagram, regardless of whether we use an interaction operator for a variant or another sequence diagram. This is normally not meaningful, since the standard flow is sufficient. You should add variants only if they help you gain new findings. Otherwise, the modeling effort would rise out of proportion.

2.7.2 Derive System Interfaces

Deriving system interfaces is shown in Table 2.19.

From the interaction models in the previous step (Section 2.7.1) we can understand the kind of messages our system receives from the actors, and which messages it sends to them. This provides us with an idea about the protocols that each of the interaction points understands.

Table 2.19 Summary: Deriving system interfaces.

Reference card: Derive system interfaces.	
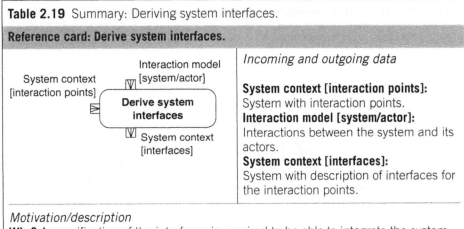	**Incoming and outgoing data** **System context [interaction points]:** System with interaction points. **Interaction model [system/actor]:** Interactions between the system and its actors. **System context [interfaces]:** System with description of interfaces for the interaction points.

Motivation/description

Why? A specification of the interfaces is required to be able to integrate the system with its environment.

What? Describe the system's interfaces versus the actors with regard to the individual interaction points.

How? Derive the interfaces from the system/actor interactions and model them at the system ports.

Where? The system interfaces represent "contracts" the system enters into with its actors.

Guiding questions
- What services are offered over the interaction points?
- What services are requested over the interaction points?
- What data flows across the interaction points?

SysML elements
Block definition diagram, interface.

We can see in Figure 2.71 that the system receives the message *apply card* from the actor *customer*. This means that the system offers a service to a customer. So, the interaction point from within the system context is a standard port. This service is described with an interface called *ICustomer* and denoted with the lollipop notation (Figure 2.72).

The customer is informed about the state of the on-board computer by means of light-emitting diodes over the same interaction point. This is a message from the system to an actor, i.e., a service requested by the system from a customer. The customer is expected to understand this message. The service is also described by an interface. The fact that the service is requested is denoted by the compact socket notation ("grabber" symbol) at the standard port.

In this way we proceed message by message across our interactions between the system and its actors. You can see our result from the sequence diagram from Figure 2.71 in Figure 2.72. Only the interfaces of the *CardReaderPort* are shown in detail. However, the entire picture remains the same: An interface contains only one operation, or an incoming signal. This is not the normal case, but only the

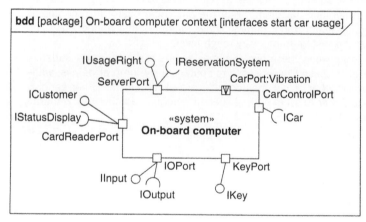

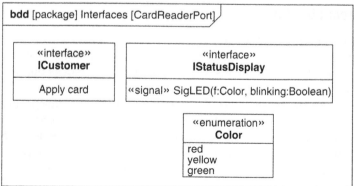

FIGURE 2-72

System interfaces of our on-board computer.

result at the beginning of our modeling work. As we look at other flows we will see that the interfaces will gradually contain more elements.

We also consider interaction points that are not used by messages in the sequence diagrams. There are vibration forces that affect the system over this port. This is not an interaction that could be meaningfully described by a standard port and interfaces. *CarPort* is an atomic object flow port, which transports objects of the type *vibration* to one direction—from the outside to the system.

A SysML design rule says that the interfaces of the standard ports should specify only operations. Signals and data flows run across object flow ports. The SYSMOD approach deviates from this rule with regard to the system ports if their interaction partner is a human user. In this case, we always have to use standard ports, and the interfaces may also contain signals.

PROJECT DIARY

Project Time 8042

The transition from the analysis to the design often leads to conflicting discussions in the team. Some members headjump from the analytical board into the depths of the design, arguing about minor details. Other members just mince along and continue looking at the system from a very rough level.

I think a way in between these two extremes seems to be the most suitable, as is often the case. It doesn't make sense to courageously jump at details, while we still don't know whether or not they are relevant at all. On the other hand, it doesn't make sense either to avoid getting specific and instead cowardly withdraw to the rough abstract levels.

We should keep these considerations in mind as we start working on the design.

2.7.3 Model System Structures

Modeling system structures is shown in Table 2.20.

In this approach step we want to describe the system's structures that are needed in order to realize the requirements. We are talking of the blocks our system is composed of eventually.

The domain knowledge model shows us the structures of the domain-specific objects that occur in the system. This model is primarily a model of terms and does not represent the system structures. Based on our top-down approach, we first start looking for the next level below the system, where we will develop the structures from the rough to the detail. What levels are there anyway? And how many? The scheme is shown in Figure 2.73.

A system consists of several subsystems and a subsystem, in turn, consists of several blocks. This scheme is only a rough rule though. If a system is small, e.g., it

Table 2.20 Summary: Modeling system structures.

Reference card: Model system structures.	
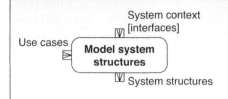	*Incoming and outgoing data* **System context [interfaces]:** System with interface description of the interaction points. **Use cases:** Services provided by the system. **System structures:** Description of the static structures of the system.

Motivation/description

Why? The system structures form the static design of the system.

What? Model the blocks and their relationships in sufficient depth of details as required by the entire system to meet the project requirements.

How? Determine the required blocks and structures for each use case or requirement, and model all these in block diagrams.

Where? The blocks of the system design can, in turn, describe the system in a discipline-specific development project, e.g., a software application or a hardware component.

Guiding questions
- What blocks are required to realize the use cases/requirements?
- How is a block composed?
- How are the blocks interconnected?
- What interaction points and interfaces do the blocks have?

SysML elements
Block definition diagram, internal block diagram, block, interface, association, connector, port, information object flow.

---

may not have a subsystem level at all. Such a system would then be composed of blocks only. On the other hand, there can be blocks on subsystem level.

We will now start looking for the structures of our on-board computer. I'm drawing a naïve approach here, which would probably not be used in this form in practice. But it is suitable for showing the relations that should be present in any arbitrary approach.

We first take a use case. The services represented by use cases have to be offered by the system. Their realization is the primary goal. In working toward this goal, we also have to take the requirements that somehow relate to a use case into account, e.g., a defined system response time. Depending on how complete the requirements are covered by use cases (refine relationship), we also have to directly select a requirement instead of a use case.

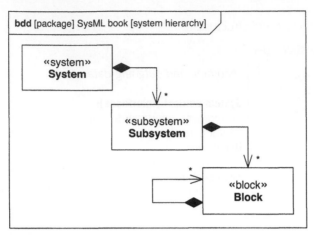

FIGURE 2-73

Hierarchical view of the system structures.

In the first step, we will be looking for a central use case. A good candidate for our system would be *start car usage*. We pick this use case and select its standard flow to develop a system structure that supports this flow.

The pertaining system/actor interaction from Section 2.7.1 shows the flow on message level (Figure 2.71). Since we are now interested in the system structures and not in the actors, we zoom in to that system element in the sequence diagram. This "zooming" is formally modeled with a *part decomposition* (Figure 2.74). The interaction partners in the detailed sequence diagram are the blocks we are looking for.

What happens when the first message, *apply card*, arrives at the system (Figure 2.74)? The customer card is part of our system, as is the card reader. The latter reads data from the customer card, but it won't process the data; it will pass it on. To whom? Our on-board computer will be equipped with a central control unit. This control unit receives card data, controls the light-emitting diodes at the card reader, sends and receives SMS for usage rights, unlocks the central locking system to open the car doors, and so on.

We track identified messages between the system and its actors all the way into the system. This sounds trivial but requires many design decisions in practice. We document our considerations in a sequence diagram (Figure 2.75). This diagram shows us the blocks that are connected (exchange of messages), so that we can model the structures in an internal block diagram (Figure 2.76).

The message *apply card* gets into the system over *CustomerPort*. At the customer card, we model another (conceptual) CustomerPort as an interaction point. Together with CardReaderPort, this new CustomerPort stands for the interaction with customers. In the following, we model the structures to read customer data from the card.

The card reader emits an energy field. The customer card feeds itself with electric power from this energy field if it is near enough to the card reader. The

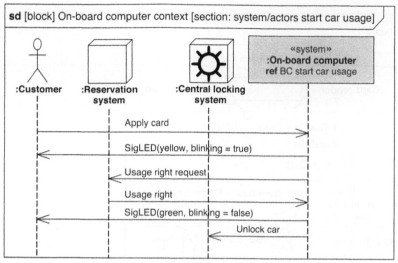

FIGURE 2-74

Using a part decomposition to trace messages.

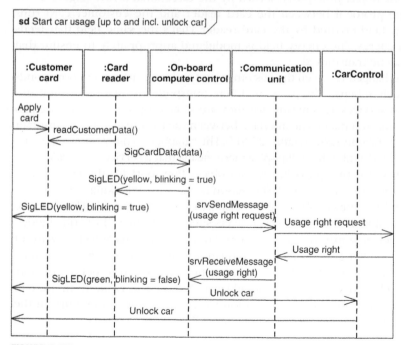

FIGURE 2-75

Interaction between the on-board computer structures.

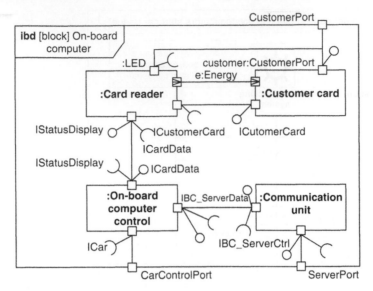

FIGURE 2-76

System structures of the on-board computer.

pertaining ports transport only one object (energy) in one direction. They are so-called *atomic object flow ports*, shown by the directional arrow (Figure 2.76). Technically the protocol between the card reader and the customer card runs over an energy field emitted by the card reader. That's the same field that feeds the card with energy. The energy field is modulated appropriately to ensure that information can be transmitted.

The data exchanged between the customer card and the card reader corresponds to a request/reply scheme. The ports used here transport not only data—they also offer or request services. This means that they are standard ports that are specified in more detail over interfaces. The interface between the card reader and a customer card is called *ICustomerCard* (Figure 2.76).[18] The "grabber" symbol shows that the service is requested, while the "lollipop" symbol means that a service is provided.

We have modeled two ports in total: an object flow port for the energy flow and a standard port for the protocol. The reason is that we are looking at two layers, the application layer (protocol) and the transport layer (energy field). There can be more layers, e.g., if you think of the seven layers specified in the OSI layering model.

It makes a lot of sense to look at several layers. But you have to be aware of the difference, and you have to model the relations. Above all, you should be careful not to mix the layers. The *allocate* relationship allows you to define relationships between elements of different model layers. We use this relationship here to allocate the standard port of the application layer to the object flow port on the transport layer. You can see the result in Figure 2.77.

---

[18] The "I" stands for "Interface." It is a common naming convention to use the type of model element as a prefix.

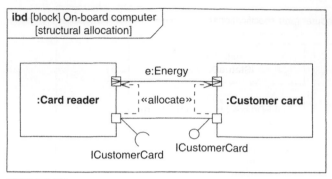

FIGURE 2-77

Using a structural allocation.

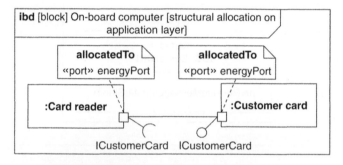

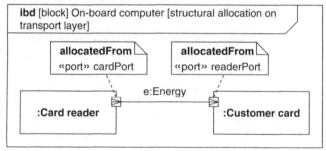

FIGURE 2-78

Using the callout notation for structural allocation.

It is usually a good idea NOT to show model elements of different layers in one diagram to prevent aspects from being confused. I recommend to use the callout notation shown in Figure 2.78 rather than the direct representation shown in Figure 2.77.

Similar to the system/actor interactions, we can derive the interfaces from the interaction between the blocks. The messages become operations and signals, which are meaningfully grouped into interfaces (Figure 2.79). Each of these interfaces is then either a providing interface or a requesting interface and allocated to the respective port of the block.

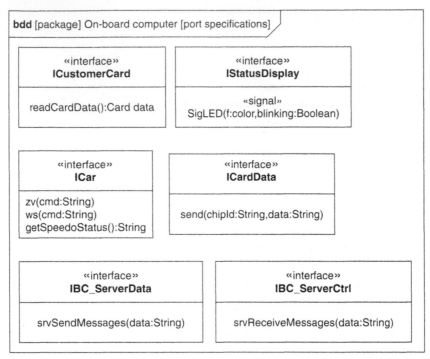

FIGURE 2-79

Specifying the identified ports.

The sequence of flows shown in Figure 2.75 takes us to the structure of our on-board computer, which is described in the internal block diagram in Figure 2.76. The picture will naturally change as we look at more flows. There will be new blocks, ports, and connections to be added, and existing ones will be modified or removed.

The resulting picture has to make sense, of course. For example, may block *X* communicate with block *Y*? If we find an undesirable connection we must search for the reason why it's there. Is the exchange of messages between the blocks concerned really necessary? Where does the requirement come from? Are all necessary infrastructure elements, e.g., power supply, available?

These decisions are not hewn in stone. Considerations like the ones mentioned above form a good starting point that, in turn, can change later on. It may well happen that blocks are merged, removed, or newly shaped. You can also experiment with alternative designs and compare them. Models provide an excellent vehicle for this sort of studies.

We can derive the definitions of the blocks used from the internal structure of our on-board computer and describe them in a block definition diagram (Figure 2.80). Figure 2.80 shows the relationships between several blocks. In contrast, Figure 4.29 (p. 244), e.g., shows the detailed definition of a single block, *card reader*.

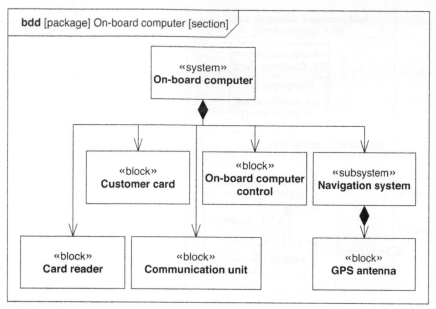

FIGURE 2-80

Block definition diagram for our on-board computer.

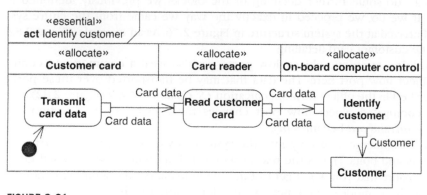

FIGURE 2-81

Allocating a flow to system structures.

By way of example, we have added the navigation subsystem in Figure 2.80, which we would normally find only later when looking at the pertaining use cases. We have described the domain flows in activity diagrams. We have now identified the system structures and modeled them in block diagrams. The *allocate* relationship brings the two models together and answers this question: Which action of an activity is executed on which block?

There are several possibilities to visualize this relation. You can see an *allocate activity partition* in Figure 2.81 and other ways of using an *allocate* relationship in Section 4.4.

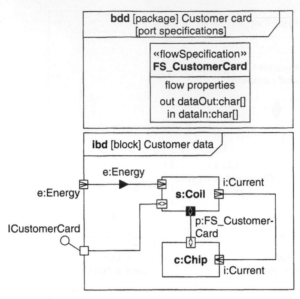

FIGURE 2-82

Structures for "customer card."

We can do some further detailing of the blocks we previously identified if needed. If we do, we proceed in exactly the way we came from the entire system and arrived at the system structure in Figure 2.76. As an example, Figure 2.82 shows the customer card detailing.

In addition to atomic object flow ports, we also used a common and conjugated object flow port here. The data that may be transported over these ports are described in the object flow specification *FS_CustomerCard* (Figure 2.82).

The conjugated object flow port changes the data transport direction (*in* becomes *out*, and *out* becomes *in*).

You can immerge as deeply into the system as you want, until you arrive at single nuts and bolts. This is the reason why it is important to set yourself clear limits to ensure that you won't get lost in the modeling depths. What do I want to achieve with the models? For whom is the information useful?

In closing I want to show you how we produce a reference to the requirements set forth in the beginning. It can easily happen that we forget looking at our requirements as we proceed in our work, but only they determine what the system is to perform. SysML offers the *satisfy* relationship, which can be used to connect a model element, e.g., a block, with the requirement that is realized by this element (Figure 2.83).

The relationship doesn't state whether or not the requirement is fully realized by the design element. This would require that the requirements and the design models had identical granularities. Apart from the fact that this is not practically feasible, it would result in an undesired dependency of the requirements on the design. As a pragmatic approach, I recommend to use a comment to document completeness of the realization (Figure 2.83). A good alternative would be a suitable

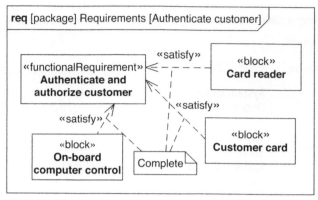

FIGURE 2-83

Fulfillment of requirements to the card reader and the customer card.

stereotype with a property that describes the degree of realization, e.g., 60 percent. Before you start using comments or stereotypes, you should of course think about whether or not you need this information in the model at all. You could run a model request to determine whether all requirements have at least one model element that realizes them, and vice-versa, whether each model element is based directly or indirectly on a requirement.

Modeling these relations is costly. While it's easy to model the relationships, it is costly to maintain them. The benefit is higher than the cost if many changes are made to the model during the course of the project, or if the model is used for subsequent projects. A good traceability of the relations is then very important. It is also possible that your principal or standards you have to comply with dictate the traceability of the requirements all the way to the design or the finished system.

PROJECT DIARY

Project Time 8152

The good preparation and coordination with the customer in the analysis now pays. The domain issues and insecurities have been clarified largely, so that we can fully deal with the technical challenges in the design.

There are still white spots in the analysis model, which we will now examine in the further course of the project. Of course, we haven't started with the pertaining design yet. Also, there will surely arise new domain issues that will have to flow back into the analysis. The consistency of the model facilitates an iterative adaptation and prevents consistency errors.

The principal is happy, our development processes are doing fine, we are within the time plan... I'm confident that we will successfully complete the project.

2.7.4 Derive State Model

Creating a state model is shown in Table 2.21.

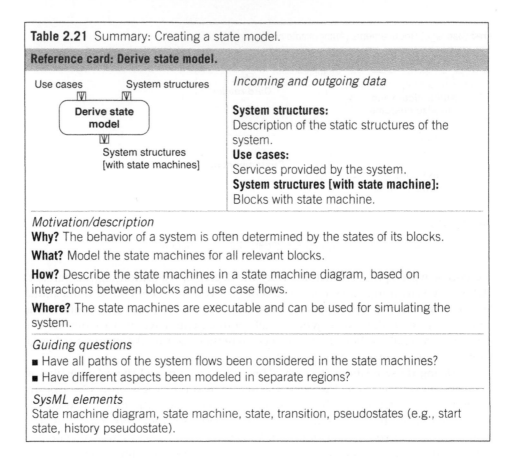

Table 2.21 Summary: Creating a state model.

Reference card: Derive state model.	
Use cases System structures **Derive state model** System structures [with state machines]	*Incoming and outgoing data* **System structures:** Description of the static structures of the system. **Use cases:** Services provided by the system. **System structures [with state machine]:** Blocks with state machine.

Motivation/description

Why? The behavior of a system is often determined by the states of its blocks.

What? Model the state machines for all relevant blocks.

How? Describe the state machines in a state machine diagram, based on interactions between blocks and use case flows.

Where? The state machines are executable and can be used for simulating the system.

Guiding questions
- Have all paths of the system flows been considered in the state machines?
- Have different aspects been modeled in separate regions?

SysML elements
State machine diagram, state machine, state, transition, pseudostates (e.g., start state, history pseudostate).

The states of the system change when something happens in the system, i.e., when behavior is executed. Vice-versa, the system states influence the behavior. So far, the activity diagrams with our use cases and the sequence diagrams with our blocks describe the behavior of our system. We use this information to derive a state model.

To this end, we select a use case and take the pertaining sequence diagram that describes the standard interaction between the blocks (Figure 2.75). Our goal is to derive state machines of the blocks that occur in the interaction we are looking at.

We think along the lifelines to see what state that block is in at the respective position. The state could theoretically have changed after each event that occurred on that lifeline, e.g., when the block received a message and responded to it. We can denote the current state as a state invariant directly on the lifeline in the appropriate position (Figure 2.84).

In the next step, we use the states we found to describe a state machine for each block, which may be very trivial. However, we have looked at only one flow of a use case so far. So we will take more interactions and the activities of that use case and extend the state machine accordingly. Each flow variant has to reflect in

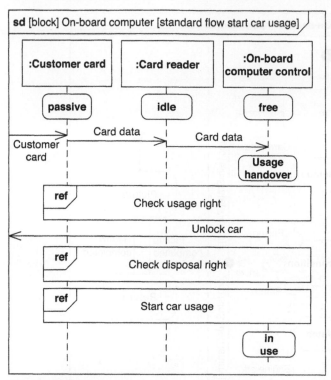

FIGURE 2-84

A sequence diagram with states.

the state machine in some form or another. You can see the on-board computer control in Figure 2.85.

The state machine starts in the state *free*. It changes to the composite state *usage handover* as soon as the signal *card data* arrives. The internal view of the state is not shown. It has a special exit point. The exit point *cancel* is selected when the usage handover is canceled, e.g., due to an invalid PIN. The on-board computer control is then in the state *free* or *in use* again.

The state *usage handover* is internally terminated (final state) in the positive case. This causes the transitions outgoing above and below to activate immediately, because they may not have triggers. Instead they have conditions that check the state the right-hand region is currently active in. In our case, that's the *handover* state, and we switch to *in use* state. During the transition we send the signal *pickup completed*. This sets the state *return* in the right-hand region. This region serves as a sort of knot in the handkerchief to remember the direction in which the next usage handover should occur.[19]

---

[19]This corresponds to the *State Latch pattern* in [12].

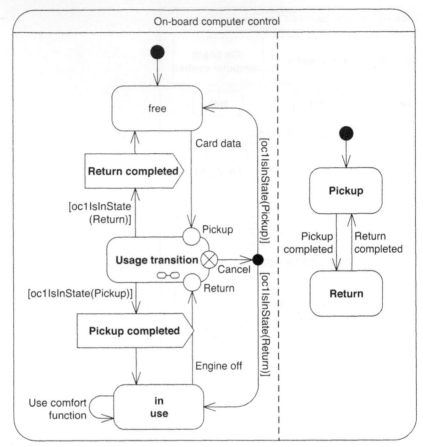

FIGURE 2-85

A state machine for the on-board computer control.

Only little is missing now to take this machine to execution in a modeling tool with the corresponding capabilities. Simulating the system behavior is a fascinating aspect. However, before you get to work you have to define the goals you want to achieve with the simulation. These goals determine the system areas you are looking at in the simulation, and the kind of state modeling.

2.8 Marginal Notes

Marginal notes complete the approach chapter. This final section discusses a few topics that support our modeling effort, including variant management or modeling patterns, and topics such as testing that should not be left unmentioned, but which would go beyond the scope and volume of this book if I were to discuss them in detail.

Missing a topic? Or should I actually deal with a topic in more detail? I'll be happy to receive your suggestions. Please write to me: *twe@system-modeling.com*.

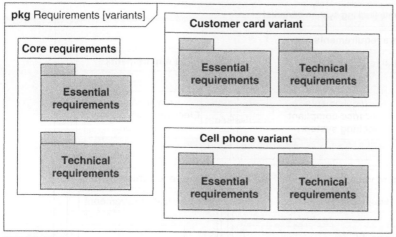

FIGURE 2-86

Package structure for requirements variants.

2.8.1 Variant Management

We have quickly opted for one specific solution to the requirements of our principal in our example project. The blueprint came from the principal themselves, which is absolutely the norm. The road we took makes itself notice in the model early on, e.g., in the project context or the list of stakeholders. As for the requirements, we have put in some effort to separate the purely domain-specific and essential requirements from the technical requirements (Section 2.2.2). In this section you will learn how different solution variants can be modeled. You obtain several variants if you create a model for a product family, or if you want to evaluate several solution alternatives for one system to identify the best one.

Let's begin with the requirements from the status quo where the essential requirements are separated from the technical ones. We put both areas into a package by the name of *core requirements*. Next, we determine the requirements that are NOT valid for all variants. If you are just looking for solution variants, you should limit your search to the technical requirements. If you are looking at a product family, you should be aware of the fact that essential requirements too can belong to the variants.

A **core requirement** refers to the entire system and is independent of the particularities of system variants. A **variant requirement** refers exclusively to a variant and is valid only for the system design of that variant.

Put one package for each variant on the level of the core requirement package and then, in each of them, create subpackages for essential and technical requirements. We pick up the ideas we had at the beginning of our project (see p. 32) and look at alternative access systems for our on-board computer. You can see the structure of the requirement model with variants in Figure 2.86.

The requirements to the on-board computer with the access system variant *customer card* are all in the packages *core requirements* and *customer card*

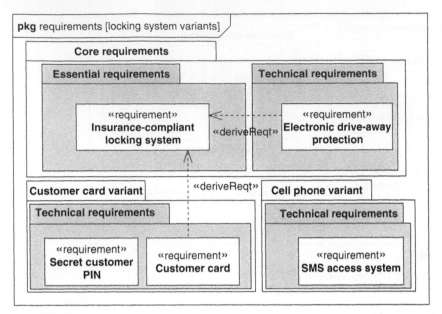

FIGURE 2-87

Variants for modeling requirements.

variant. Accordingly, the requirements to the access system *cell phone* are all in the packages *core requirements* and *cell phone variant.*

You can see the relationships between the core requirements and the variant requirements in Figure 2.87. Model views can be used to zoom in and out of variants.

Except for the requirements, a generalization is essentially the relationship used for variant modeling. For example, Figure 2.88 shows the variants for the customer identification feature in the domain knowledge model, which are required because we have different access systems. If you compare this version with the model in Figure 2.67 in Section 2.5 you will see that it involves some work to create the model structures required. In fact, an independent domain block came into being from the *pinCheckCode* attribute.

You also have to find suitable abstractions in the design in order to be able to map your variants. This means that you describe the things that vary versus a common basis. If you enrich the model elements by adding information, such as cost, time, performance, and so on, you can compare your variants in different perspectives. This allows you to achieve a good information basis for your decision in favor of the solution that best meets your goals (Figure 2.89).

2.8.2 Model Simulation

SysML offers a rich choice of elements to support an executable model. What we need are structures (block diagrams), behavior descriptions (activities, interactions, state machines), and elementary instructions (action model). Tools provide runtime environments so that you can execute the model to simulate and test your system.

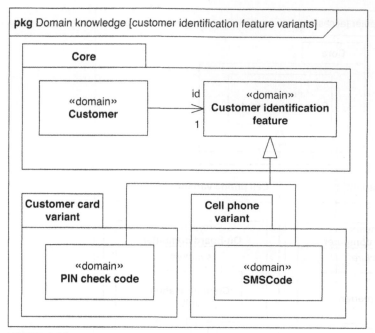

pkg Domain knowledge [customer identification feature variants]

Core

«domain»
Customer

id

«domain»
**Customer identification
feature**

1

Customer card
variant

«domain»
PIN check code

Cell phone
variant

«domain»
SMSCode

FIGURE 2-88

Variants for domain blocks.

This is an excellent way to discover wrong or unfavorable analysis or design decisions. The earlier we discover that there is a problem the easier and cheaper it will be to solve it.

Of course, this benefit comes at a price. We have to describe the model in its very details to be able to execute it. This means a lot of work, which translates in time and money. This is the reason why you should think carefully what the benefit of an executable model is worth. However, you normally won't have to execute the entire model. Of utmost importance are the critical areas, including complex and error-prone flows, or the analysis of design alternatives.

There is currently no literature available on executable SysML models. Executable UML models are described, e.g., in [32] and [11]. *ARTiSAN Studion* and *Telelogic Rhapsody* are SysML/UML tools that support model simulations.

2.8.3 Testing

Testing is a highly significant issue in development processes, especially for system engineers. Nevertheless, it landed in the marginal notes in this book. The reason is that it is far too complex to be discussed in detail within the scope and volume of this book. I'll just highlight a few points in this section.

A test verifies the requirements for correct and complete realization or fulfillment. SysML lets you also create a test model. Block diagrams are used to describe the required test structures, while behavior diagrams, such as activity or sequence

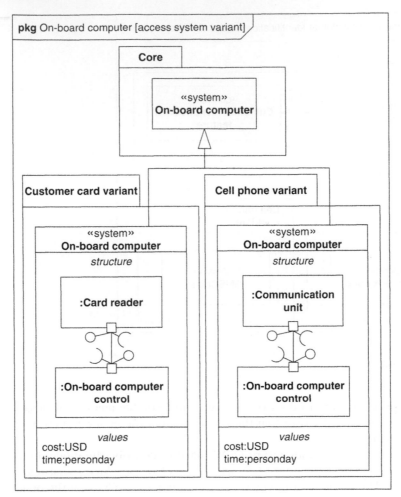

FIGURE 2-89

Two access system variants, customer card and cell phone.

diagrams, are used to describe the test processes themselves. SysML knows a model element called *test case*. This model element produces a connecting link to the *UML testing profile* [53], which defines additional model elements like *test context* and *test components*.

You can start very early to build your test model. As soon as you have finished identifying the first bunch of requirements, you can think about the pertaining test cases. This highlights the fact that it must be verifiable whether or not a requirement is satisfied. The further you detail your requirements, the more details of your tests you can describe. For example, every possible traversal through a use case activity is a potential test case (Figure 2.90).

The test model grows in parallel with the system model. The relation—the test model verifies the requirements to the system—is modeled explicitly. To this

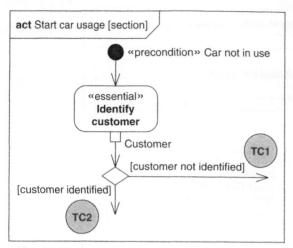

FIGURE 2-90

Deriving test cases.

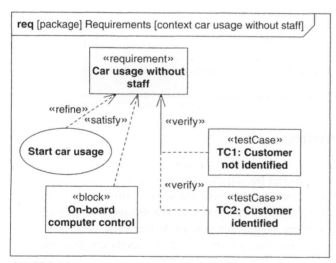

FIGURE 2-91

Using a verify relationship.

end, SysML has a *verify* relationship that allows you to connect a test case with a requirement to be verified (Figure 2.91).

Part of a test specification is a description of the test environment. The internal block diagram is a suitable form for this description. You can see in Figure 2.92 that values have been assigned to some of the block attributes. For example, the ID describes the concrete block that has to be used in this test environment. Together with these values, the blocks deviate from their original definition. This is the reason why we model these blocks as property-specific types.

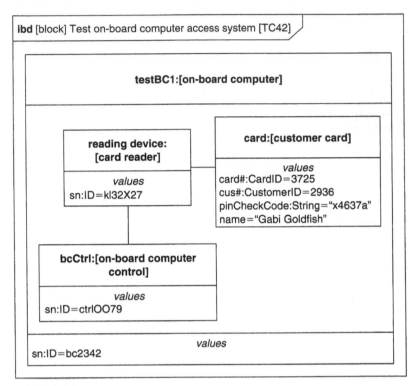

FIGURE 2-92

A test environment.

2.8.4 The System of Systems

If you want to consistently model systems that, in turn, consist of systems, you have to pay special attention to the model transitions. The reason is that, in this case, the model of your entire system consists of fragments which form an independent model from the view of other projects. What you have is a *model of models (MoM)*.

What may be an independent system for you from the view of your project may be "only" one block out of many for another project. This means that your system is part of another system—a *system of systems (SoS)*.

The elements at the model transitions may play various roles. For example, the block *card reader* of our on-board computer system could be an independent system from the view of another project. In this case, it plays two roles that are both realized by the same model element—the block. This means that you can simply model both roles by using two stereotypes («*block*» and «*system*»), which are shown or hidden, respectively, in the respective context. Things are a bit harder for the *on-board computer control*, which is a block in the *on-board computer* system and an actor in the *card reader* system. These are different model elements. This means that the on-board computer control exists twice in the entire model. We use the trace relationship to ensure that we won't lose sight of the difference of these elements.

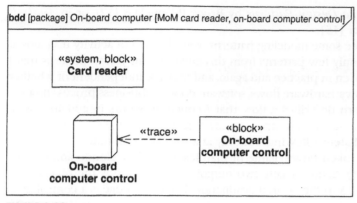

FIGURE 2-93

Model relations in the MoM.

The relationships in the model are shown in Figure 2.93. I'm presenting the diagram in this form here only to show you the model relations. You wouldn't use such a view of your model in practice.

2.8.5 Modeling Patterns

Have you ever heard of modeling patterns or design patterns? Even if you don't know what patterns are, you can rest assured that you have worked with patterns. If a known problem arises during your daily work, you will most likely solve it by the same pattern you used the previous times, provided, of course, that your solution was successful. A pattern is a proven solution.

Modeling patterns are proven and documented solutions from the practice to frequently recurring problems. They are often very simple. Their major benefits are that they are for sure proven solutions, and that the solutions have names. Modeling patterns facilitate the communication among modelers. For example, "I have an idea of how to solve this: model an abstract block and derive your block from it. Give those blocks that can be nested an association relationship to the basic block with a multiplicity of infinite. As unusual as that may sound, I assure you that it works. I've solved many problems like the one you're trying to solve successfully that way." That's harder to understand than "I'd use the composition pattern."[20] The fact that patterns have names makes it much simpler to communicate about them as long as the communication partner knows the pattern by content and name.

I intentionally omit design patterns for class modeling, or block modeling in SysML lingo, at this point. First of all, they focus on software development problems rather than on the things we are doing here. Second, there is extensive literature that deals with this issue. The book *Design Patterns* by E. Gamma et al. [18] is considered the seminal work in this field. Special patterns can be found, e.g.,

---

[20]A well-known design pattern from [18] used to model tree structures.

in the book *Real-Time Design Patterns* by Bruce P. Douglass [12], or in *Analysis Patterns* by M. Fowler [15].

I'd like to introduce some modeling patterns from the area of activity diagrams at this point. There are only few patterns from this environment yet. All patterns that I will present have proven in practice and again, and they are independent of whether you model system flows, hardware flows, software flows, or business process flows.

The Detour pattern describes a flow that frequently occurs in activities with object flow. An action, *A*, has an output pin for object *S*. The object is not required by the action immediately following, but only at a later point in time.

The rules of the token flow ("game of marbles") enable a simple and elegant solution (Figure 2.94). Action *A* gets two outgoing edges. One is the object flow that transports object *S* to the desired destination. The other edge is a control flow, which is responsible for the flow sequence. In our flow pattern in Figure 2.94, action *B* starts after action *A*. The object token, *S*, remains in the output pin of *A*, because action *C*—the target node of *S*—is not ready yet. Action *C* starts only once action *B* has terminated, since there are now tokens present at both incoming edges. In total we have the execution sequence *A*, *B*, *C*, and object *S* is transported by *A* past *B* directly to *C*.

Turn to page 99; you will see that we used the Detour pattern in Figure 2.62.

After most actions in an activity there is some checking as to whether or not they were successful. The decision after an action is based on the outgoing object flow: The object is either present or not, or the action was successful or unsuccessful. The fact the no object is present doesn't mean that there is no object flow. What flows here is a so-called *null token*—an empty object. The UML specification says that the edge must go to and end in an object node. This means that the action following that action needs an input pin for formal reasons although it may do without input data. A zero token is not very informative.

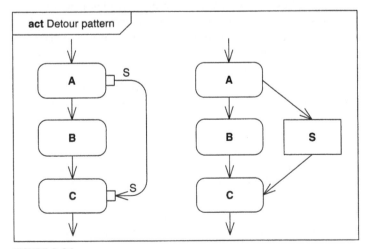

FIGURE 2-94

Using a Detour pattern.

UML knows so-called *control pins*, which accept object tokens, so that they can cause an action to execute, but without passing the object on to the action. This means that the action cannot access the object itself. The object token plays the role of a control token. Control pins are often not shown in the diagram. Figure 2.95 shows a control pin for better understanding. If you want to have a model that is 100 percent formally correct you sometimes have to use such modeling tricks. Normally the information is only in the model and not in the diagram.

We used a Success pattern in Figure 2.58.

The Termination pattern helps activities that have a decision to take after each action to check whether or not it is necessary to terminate (Figure 2.96). For example, these can be flows that can be terminated by an event, such as an emergency-off event of a machine, or a termination due to expiry of a given time interval.

The region concerned is modeled with an *interruptible activity region* all around it, which can be exited by a termination event (Figure 2.97). If the entire flow, i.e., the complete activity, is to be terminated by the event, then the interruptible activity region is omitted (Figure 2.98). The Termination pattern simplifies the activity and maps the reality more exactly.

We used a Termination pattern in Figure 2.64.

In contrast to the pure control flow, an object flow adds important information to an activity. On the other hand, it makes the model more complex, e.g., due to additional edges across the Detour pattern. The Indirect object flow pattern describes how information on incoming and outgoing data can be completed without modeling the actual object flow.

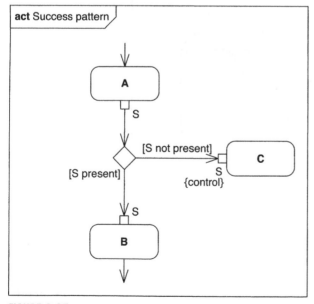

FIGURE 2-95

Using a Success pattern.

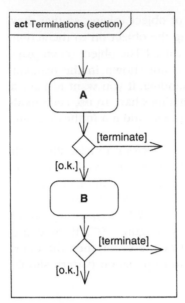

FIGURE 2-96

Terminate?

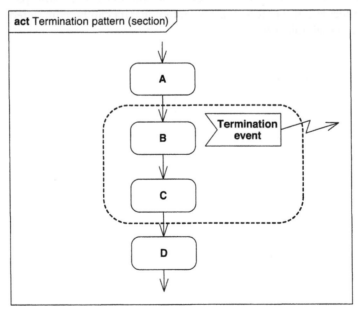

FIGURE 2-97

Using a Termination pattern.

Input and output pins are denoted near actions for data. Since we do not represent the Object Flow, omitting the edges between pins, we need a feature to distinguish between input and output pins. UML uses a small arrow, which is drawn inside the pin rectangle (Figure 2.99). The model is not exact, because there is no explicit

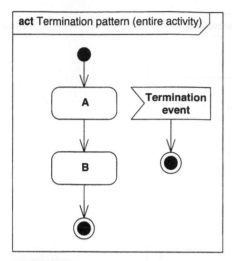

FIGURE 2-98

A Termination pattern without interruptible activity region.

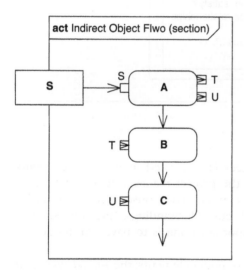

FIGURE 2-99

Using an Indirect Object Flow pattern.

connection between the output pins and the corresponding input pins. This means, e.g., that it is not defined that input pin *T* accepts the object token from output pin *T*.

One restriction is the activity parameters. They have the role of initial or final nodes and have to be connected with an object flow edge.

2.8.6 Model Views

A large number of individuals normally participate in a system development project. Depending on their role within the project, each individual has a certain

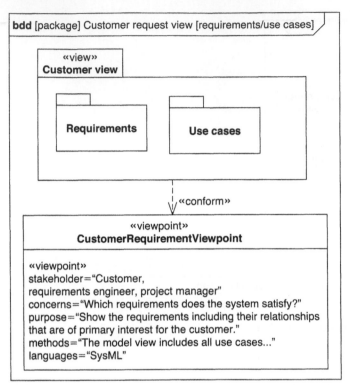

FIGURE 2-100

Example for a model view.

view of the system model. A test engineer is interested in different elements and relations than a system engineer or the project manager. It would be fatal if each of these roles created their own model. The consequences would be high redundancies, inconsistencies, and misunderstandings, and the success of the project would be at stake. The important thing is to have one model for everybody.

To solve this problem SysML offers two model elements: the *model view* and the *viewpoint* (Figure 2.100). The model view presents only a certain selection of model elements and diagrams, so that they meet all needs of, say, a test engineer. It realizes exactly the viewpoint that describes the stakeholders and their interests, and includes rules as to how the pertaining model view is to be created.

Model views and viewpoints are easy to describe and use in theory. In practice, they represent a challenge for the manufacturers of SysML modeling tools to ensure that both model elements can be practically realized.

It is a common concept in architecture and process descriptions to provide special model views for different stakeholders (e.g., [30]). SysML refers to the definition of IEEE standard 1471, and defines both the model view and the viewpoint in compliance with this standard.

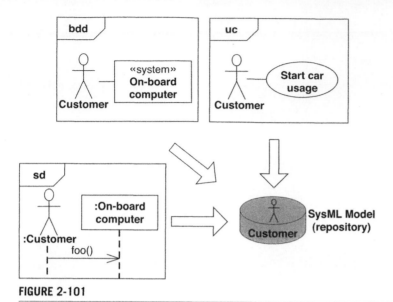

FIGURE 2-101

The diagrams/model relation.

Another way to emphasize different aspects of a model is the diagrams themselves. Each diagram always shows only a section of the model, i.e., the section that represents certain aspects, rather than all information stored in the model (*repository*). You can see in Figure 2.101 that a customer appears in three diagrams in a different context each. However, this customer is present in the model only once as a model element; see also Section 3.2.

UML—Unified Modeling Language

If language is not correct, then what is said is not what is meant.

(Confucius)

UML had originally been developed to create models for software systems. The word *unified* stands for the claim that the language can be used for software systems of a large number of different domains—from business and economics systems to the development of standard software products to technical systems, such as an airbag control. The language uses controlled extension mechanisms (stereotypes) to let you adapt it to your domain, so that UML actually lives up to that claim.

At the latest since the introduction of Version 2.0, the term *unified* has had a more ample meaning. Since then, the target groups include not only the large number of different software development domains, but also neighboring disciplines, such as business process modeling [33] and systems engineering. Again, UML lives up to the claim to be truly *unified*. Of course there are limits. For example, UML is suitable for systems engineering. However, Systems Modeling Language (SysML) is much more closer to systems engineering, as you will see further on in this book.

UML is not a Babylonian language. You shouldn't give in to your inclination to try expressing everything in UML. However, to make sure you can maintain a complete model altogether, for example, you can integrate a general element—a "placeholder"—in your model. The details of this placeholder are described outside the model. One good example is requirements that are usually described in detail outside the model in requirement management tools, such as Telelogic DOORS™ (Section 2.2.2).

UML is a worldwide industry standard. The software consortium *Object Management Group* (*OMG*), which has about 800 members, is responsible for the language. But only 20–30 corporations actively participate in the development of UML, including modeling tool vendors, such as IBM, Telelogic, and ARTiSAN Software Tools, and other corporations, such as Motorola, NIST, and oose Innovative Informatik GmbH. The language is subject to continuous further development. When UML 2.1.1 was finished, work had been started on UML 2.2 right away.

This development effort lives from users' feedback. Please notify OMG if you find errors or irregularities in UML, if you think something should be clarified, or if you have a suggestion for improvement. You don't have to be a member to do this. You can find the online form on the pages of OMG at *http://www.omg.org/technology/issuesform.htm*.

In contrast to SysML, there are a large number of books on UML. This is why you won't find a full description of all model elements; I'll describe only the areas that are really part of the SysML language. I recommend "*The Unified Modeling Language Reference Manual*" by the "Three Amigos" [41] for a full description of UML.

You can find detailed information about the UML grammar in my preparatory book for the UML Certification [61]. The UML specification is freely available. You can find it on the Internet pages of OMG [48].

The class is a central element of UML. The SysML language uses a different term for it: block. I use the UML vocabulary in this chapter. If you want to read this chapter through SysML spectacles, simply replace the word *class* by *block*. All content items described in this chapter apply to SysML too. If there are differences I'll say so in the appropriate places. I've used the SysML vocabulary in all the other chapters of this book. Over and above, SysML is fully described in this chapter and the specific SysML extensions are discussed in Chapter 4.

3.1 History

UML has its roots in the software development domain. The language is a logical consequence of the fast pace progress that has been made since Konrad Zuse took his first computer into operation. As the performance of hardware has increased software has become increasingly better performing too. This led to requirements for increasingly complex systems. Ensuring that developers can meet this challenge has meant that progress was also necessary in the area of their tools—the programming languages.

The original building blocks of software—zeros and ones—had quickly become too small. What was needed was a programming language that offered larger building blocks. And thus, development went on from assembler over macro-assembler and C to eventually object-oriented programming languages. The building blocks of which software is composed were no longer zeros and ones, but classes and objects.

The rise of object-oriented programming languages began in the 1980s with Smalltalk and particularly C++. The evolution of programming languages appeared to have hit its limits when it had reached object orientation. The class is the largest software building block still today. However, since the continued progress in hardware required more and more complex systems, a new path has emerged.

People had begun to graphically visualize software pretty early. In particular, algorithms were documented and specified in diagrams (e.g., the Nassi-Shneiderman diagram). This type of modeling intensified at the beginning of the

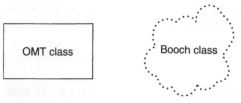

FIGURE 3-1

The OMT versus Booch class notation.

1990s. A large number of object-oriented notations emerged during that time. The most prominent representatives are *Booch* by Grady Booch [5], *Objectory* by Ivar Jacobson [25], and *Object Modeling Technique* (*OMT*) by James Rumbaugh [40]. In addition to the notation, a methodology was defined as well, which describes both the approach and the application of that notation.

The phase in the early 1990s is often referred to as a *blossoming of methods* or *war of methods*. The latter shows that there had been fierce disputes between the different camps. The issues had usually been hackneyed: Had I better denote a class as a rectangle (OMT) or a cloud (Booch) (Figure 3.1)?

The discussions showed that the different camps has basically been agreeable, and they eventually converged—something practice had desperately needed. The wide choice of notations would have caused just as large a choice of tools, training programs, and consulting efforts, which would have translated in considerable friction losses.

Grady Booch had been with Rational Software back then. He was joined by James Rumbaugh and together, in 1995, they presented the *Unified Method 0.8* (*UM 0.8*), a merger product of the notations and methodologies—*Booch* and *OMT*—at the OOPSLA[1] Conference 1995 in Austin, Texas. The discussions between the two had certainly been exciting. While Grady Booch is a pragmatist, James Rumbaugh is thought to be more of a theorist.

Neither of the two had the customer and user of the system in mind. This focus was introduced by Ivar Jacobson, who joined Booch and Rumbaugh.[2] In fact, use case modeling is the brain child of Ivar Jacobson. Since the methodology of the UM had still caused problems, while the notation was deemed to be mature, the three of them reduced the extent to the sheer language, and the *Unified Modeling Language—UML—*was born. From then on Booch, Rumbaugh, and Jacobson had been named "The Three Amigos." There's a lot of speculation about the origin of this name. The methodology re-emerged within the *IBM Rational Unified Process*™ (*RUP*™) later on.

In 1997, the responsibility for UML went from Rational Software to *Object Management GroupTail* (*OMG*). Since then UML has been further developed by this group. In 2005, a new generation of the language—UML 2.0—was officially published. The group currently works on UML 2.2.

---

[1] Short for *Object-Oriented Programming Systems, Languages, and Applications*.
[2] More specifically, his company, *Objectory*, had been taken over by Rational Software.

James Rumbaugh had also participated in the development of UML 2.0, while Grady Booch and Ivar Jacobson had taken different roads.

3.2 Structure and Concepts

UML is extremely extensive, which might overwhelm some people at first. However, once you know the basic structure and the concepts of UML, the mass of language elements do no longer represent a hurdle. Compare it with a natural language. You don't have to know the meaning of every word to have a talk with somebody, say, in German, Spanish, or Swahili.

You can see the rough structure of the UML language in Figure 3.2. There are two levels to be looked at. We can distinguish between structure and behavior elements. Structure elements include classes and components, for example. You use them to describe the structure of your system. Functions are described by means of behavior elements. They include activities, state machines, and interactions. The column "*Others*" includes elements that refer to both structure and behavior (cross-section functionality).

On the other level we distinguish between model and diagram. The model contains the full description of the system. In contrast, a diagram is only the visualization of the model with regard to a certain aspect. For example, there are class diagrams that show classes and their associations, but no attributes or operations. And there are other class diagrams that show all attributes and operations, but only few selected associations. Both diagrams are based on the same model. Figure 3.3 is a schematic view of this example.[3] All of this globally obeys the rule that the information represented in a diagram are incomplete, compared with the model. You could think of this as a spreadsheet: the table with the data is the model, while you find bar charts, line charts, and pie charts on the level of the diagrams.

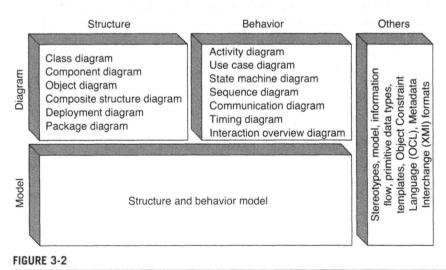

FIGURE 3-2

The structure of UML.

---

[3] The figure also shows the model as a diagram for better understanding.

The terms *diagram* and *model* are often generally used as synonyms. This hardly leads to misunderstandings as long as everybody involved is aware of the actual difference.

In contrast to UML 1, UML 2 includes not only one but four specification documents. The language is described in Superstructure [48]. It is based on a core that is defined in the infrastructure [51]. Moreover, UML includes another language—the *Object Constraint language* (*OCL*)—that has been described in a separate document since UML 2 [52]. And the XML Metamodel Interchange (XMI) Metadata Interchange format [64] has been around since UML 1. XMI allows you to exchange UML model between different tools. A new data format for diagrams (Diagram Interchange [50]) was introduced together with UML 2; it lets you exchange the diagram level, in addition to the model level, between different tools.

UML is defined in a modular way. You can work with parts of the language. For example, you don't have to deal with class modeling when all you want to do is an analysis of your use cases. The criticized point, that UML was too large and too extensive a language is unjustified. It is not necessary to realize all modeling possibilities UML offers in one project. And it wouldn't normally be meaningful. Also, you don't have to have a command of all language elements in order to work with UML.

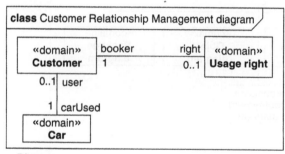

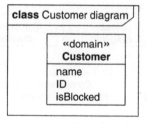

Diagram

Model

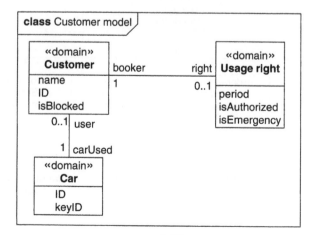

FIGURE 3-3

1 = model, 2 = diagrams.

UML is extensible to ensure that it is *unified* and, on the other hand, can offer useful model elements for specific domains and disciplines. Stereotypes and profiles offer a controlled extension mechanism that allows projects to define new modeling elements (i.e., new vocabulary for the language). At the same time, the models remain interoperable, so that they can still be exchanged between different tools.

Figure 3.4 gives an overview of all UML diagrams.

3.3 The Class Diagram

No doubt class modeling is currently the most popular use of UML. Many software projects have used UML for the only reason to model classes and to generate

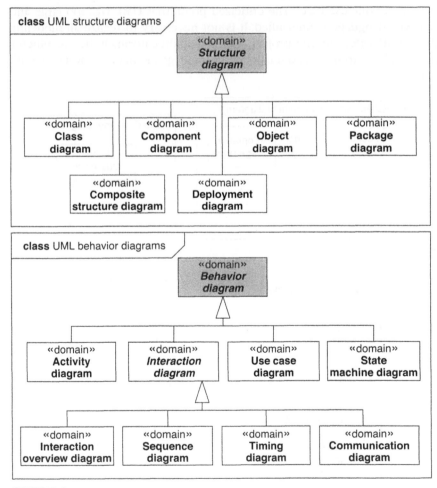

FIGURE 3-4

Overview of UML diagrams.

simple source-code scaffolding. Several integrated development environments support this approach by using UML as a graphical editor for the source code.

However, class modeling can also be used outside the software development domain in a meaningful way. Generally speaking, classes are used to describe structures and behaviors of virtual or real-world objects. Look at your current environment, for example. If you are presently in a room, then the class diagram in Figure 3.5 can be thought of as a simple model of your environment. A room can contain several tables, with up to two chairs at each table, where each chair has a defined number of legs. Chair and table are types of furniture.

Classes and objects represent the core in object orientation. A class is the smallest building block of an object-oriented system. Classes are interconnected by associations to form larger structures. Objects are concrete elements that are created based on the building plans of classes.

SysML does not know the term *class*, but calls it *block*. Everything I write about classes in this chapter applies just as well to blocks in SysML. You just have to swap the two terms in your mind. Instead of a class diagram, SysML knows the *block definition diagram*. Objects play a subordinate role in SysML. Over and above, SysML removes the software aspect from the UML class model, so that objects can be used in any discipline to describe system structures.

3.3.1 Class

Definition

A **class** describes structure and behavior of objects that have the same characteristics and semantics. The structure is described by attributes, while behavior is described by operations.

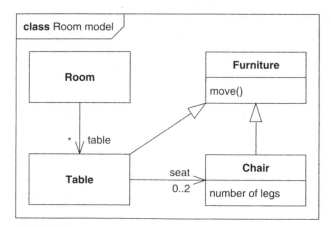

FIGURE 3-5

A simple class model.

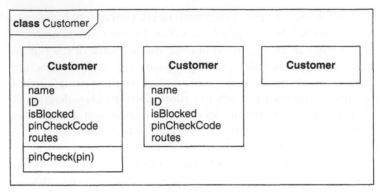

FIGURE 3-6

Example for class customer.

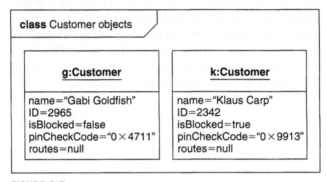

FIGURE 3-7

Example for objects.

A class is the building plan for similar objects. For example, the class *customer* in Figure 3.6 describes objects that each have a name, an ID, blocking information, a PIN check code, and personalized routes for the navigation system. Moreover, they are capable of verifying whether or not a PIN is correct. All customer objects meet this building plan. Other examples for classes are *car*, *braking system*, *current*, or *energy*.

Each object has a unique identity, regardless of its attribute values. This means that we can still distinguish two customer objects that happen to have the same attribute values. This is not the case with instances of data types.

We often speak of instances rather than of objects, and we say "instantiate objects" rather than saying "create objects." The formal name in UML is instance specification.

A class is denoted as a rectangle divided into several *compartments*: the name compartment, the attribute compartment, and the operation compartment. While the name compartment always has to be visible, the other compartments in the diagram can be hidden (Figure 3.6).

Objects are denoted in a similar way (Figure 3.7). A colon is used to separate the name of an object from its type. The text is underlined. The attributes contain concrete values. Operations are not represented.

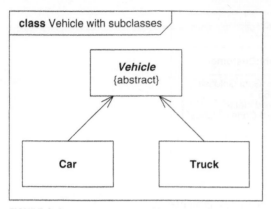

FIGURE 3-8

An abstract class and concrete subclasses.

A class can be abstract, and abstract classes can describe attributes and operations as well. However, objects cannot be created directly by this building plan; they can be created only by concrete subclasses. The abstract property is represented by writing the name in italics. In addition, we can optionally denote the adjective *{abstract}* next to the name (Figure 3.8). Abstract classes represent a superordinate term for concrete subclasses that are bound with the abstract class through a generalization relationship.

3.3.2 Attribute

Definition

An **attribute** defines a structural property of a class. The description is composed of visibility, name, type, and a multiplicity.

The structure of a class is defined by the sum of its attributes. Here the abstraction of the model compared to the real world plays an important role. The attributes reflect only the structure that is relevant for the model. For example, the class *customer* in Figure 3.9 has no attribute for the color of the customer's eyes, but it does have one for the name or the PIN check code. In another system the color of the eyes might indeed be a relevant attribute.

The type of an attribute is denoted behind the attribute's name, separated by a colon. Objects created on the basis of the class' building plan include one value of attribute type for each of that class' attributes. This type is often itself a class—the building plan of the attribute.

An attribute can also be defined such that it contains several values of the same type. The so-called multiplicity is denoted within square brackets behind the type. It describes an interval (Table 3.1) that defines the possible number. For example, a customer object can contain any number of route objects in the range 0–5 (Figure 3.9).

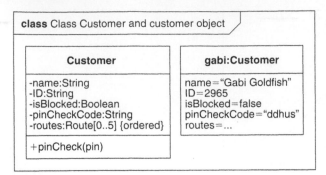

FIGURE 3-9

Example for attributes of the "customer" class and a customer object.

Table 3.1	Examples for multiplicities
Multiplicity	**Meaning**
0..1	The value is optional.
1	Exactly one value (default when no multiplicity is stated).
2..4	At least two values and at most four values.
0..*	None to an arbitrary number of values.
*	None to an arbitrary number of values (shortcut notation).

We can assign an initial value to an attribute right away as we define it. Each new object of the pertaining class will then initially have these values.

We can use property strings predefined in UML to specify an attribute more closely. For example, *{ordered}* specifies that a set-type attribute (multiplicity > 1) is ordered, or *{nonunique}* specifies that the set of attribute values may contain identical elements.[4] Several property strings are separated by commas within curly brackets.

The visibility of an attribute is denoted before the name. It states whether or not the attribute is visible for elements outside the class, which means that it can be read and written. UML defines four different visibility types:

1. *public* (denoted as +)—the attribute is publicly visible. Each element outside the class can access this attribute.
2. *private* (denoted as −)—the attribute is private. No element outside the class can see this attribute.
3. *package* (denoted as ~)—the attribute is visible to all elements located in the same package as the class.
4. *protected* (denoted as #)—the attribute is visible only to subclasses of the pertaining class.

---

[4] Mathematically, a set cannot contain identical elements.

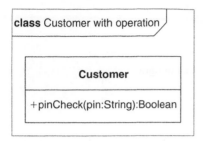

FIGURE 3-10

Operation of the class "customer."

Altogether, the syntax for attributes is:

```
<visibility><name>:<Type> [<multiplicity>]=<initial value>{property
string}
```

Visibilities do not play any role in SysML, where all attributes are public by definition. Visibility is not shown in the SysML notation.

3.3.3 Operation

Definition

An **operation** defines a behavior property of a class. The description consists of a visibility, a name, as well as parameters and a return type.

The behavior of a class is largely described by the sum of its operations. The class *customer* in Figure 3.10 has an operation called *pinCheck(/)* with an input parameter, *pin:String*, and a return type, *Boolean*. The input parameter passed on to this operation is a string (*pin:String*). It verifies whether or not the string corresponds to the PIN of that customer and returns a Boolean value (true/false) as the result. The actual verification of a PIN is part of the implementation of the operation, but you can't see it in the class diagram. Often it is not directly described in the UML model either. It is often described in mechanical or electronic components, for example, in a hardware development project. In the UML model itself we could use an activity, a state machine, or an interaction to describe the implementation.

Parameters are denoted similarly to attributes. Several parameters are separated by commas.

```
<name>:<Type> [<multiplicity>]
```

Similarly to an attribute, an operation has a visibility with the same meaning. All operations are public in SysML models. The visibility is not shown in the notation. The syntax of an operation is as follows:

```
<visibility><name>(<parameter list>):<Return type>
```

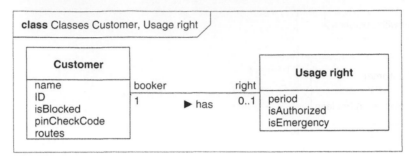

FIGURE 3-11

Example for an association.

3.3.4 Association

Definition

An **association** is a structure relationship between two classes.[5]

You can see an association between the classes *customer* and *usage right*. This association is a structure relationship, which means that the structure of the class *customer* includes not only the attributes listed in the class symbol, but also a property, *right*, of type *usage right*.[6] The multiplicity states how many values are included. In this case, it's one at most.

In contrast, the class *usage right* has a property, *booker*, of type *customer*. From a pragmatic perspective, there is not much of a difference between attribute and association. For example, the customer attribute *routes* can also be represented as an association to the class *route*. Looking at the details, however, there are differences between association and attribute. Rather than discussing them here I refer to further UML literature; see [61], and [41]. In SysML these differences reflect in values, references, and parts.

An association can have a name. If we use a name we write it centered at the association line. The name of an association often refers to a reading direction, which is stated by a black triangle in front of the name. In Figure 3.11, we read, "*Each customer has one or no usage right.*" Since only one association name is permitted we can state only one direction in this way, even though the other direction might be valid. You have to be careful not to confuse the triangle with the information flow.

In the above example, what if the class *customer* had a *usage right*, but no customer should belong to the class *usage right*? We would need a uni-directional association. This property controls the so-called navigation. We denote an arrow at

---

[5] We can actually model an association between more than two classes, but it is not customary in practice and not supported by SysML.

[6] Actually, this is a common but simplified view of an association. For details see [61].

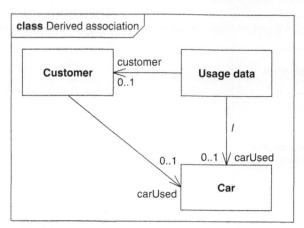

FIGURE 3-12

A derived association.

the association end to express that it is possible to navigate from one class to the other.[7]

If we continue thinking along these lines in our example, then we should actually denote an arrow at the other end too, since this direction is also valid. The question is then why we haven't used any arrows in Figure 3.11. The answer is that, by convention, both navigation directions are possible if no arrows are stated.

You can see a so-called derived association between the *usage data* class and the *car* class in Figure 3.12. You can recognize a derived association by the slash before the name of the association. This association is actually superfluous in this context because it results from the other two associations in the diagram. A *usage data* object can reach the *car* object through its *customer* object. This is the reason why the association is referred to as "derived." It emphasizes the indirect relationship between *usage data* and *car*. Derived associations are used mainly in analysis models, for example in the domain class model.

Associations are used not only between classes, but also between actors and use cases, or between actors and the system (Figure 3.13). We are talking about the same model element. The different forms of uses are supported in UML by default.

3.3.5 Aggregation and Composition

Definitions

An **aggregation** denotes an association end as an aggregate and describes a whole-part hierarchy.

A **composition** denotes an association end and describes a whole-part hierarchy, where the composite is existentially responsible for its parts.

---

[7]The concepts navigability and owning properties were split apart in UML 2.1.1 [48].

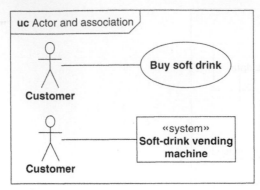

FIGURE 3-13

Association and actor.

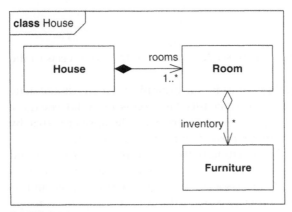

FIGURE 3.14

Example for a composition.

The meanings of aggregations and compositions can be best explained by using a simple example. Figure 3.14 represents one aggregation and one composition. Both are denoted by a rhombus at the association end. The composition as the stronger form has a filled rhombus.

The example class model describes that a house consists of between one and an arbitrary number of rooms, and that a room can contain an arbitrary number of pieces of furniture.

The aggregation underlines the whole-part relationship. The room is the whole and the pieces of furniture are the parts. However, the room is not existentially responsible for these pieces of furniture.

The relationship from the house to its rooms is different. The house is the whole and responsible for its parts, the rooms. If the house is removed, then all the rooms disappear, but not the furniture. The composite is here also referred to as the owner of the parts, since it is responsible for them.

Similarly to the real world, there can be only one owner for a part in a composition. The house/room example shows this clearly. A room of a house cannot

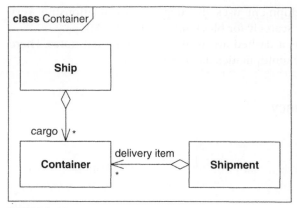

FIGURE 3-15

Example for an aggregation.

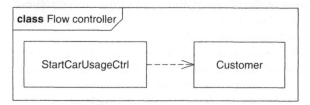

FIGURE 3-16

Example for a dependency.

concurrently belong to several houses. With an aggregation, in contrast, there can be several aggregates concurrently. They are merely referenced by the aggregate. For example, a piece of furniture can be assigned to several rooms. Another example from a port logistics system is shown in Figure 3.15. The containers are present both as cargo in the ship and as delivery item in the shipment.

3.3.6 Dependency

> **Definition**
>
> A **dependency** is a relationship between two elements, which describes that one element needs the other element for its specification or implementation.

In contrast to an association, a dependency can be defined not only between classes, but also between almost any model elements. This is the most common use in class modeling.

Figure 3.16 shows a dependency between a flow controller[8] and the class *customer*.

---

[8] Flow controllers are special classes with the primary task to control flows. In software development, use cases are often realized by flow controllers in the design.

The field of software development uses the dependency relationship very intensely, while it is used rather scarcely for block modeling in SysML.

A dependency is denoted as a dashed arrow without additional notes. There are no role names, nor are there multiplicities, as in associations.

3.3.7 Abstraction Dependency

Definition

An **abstraction dependency** is a mapping between model elements on various abstraction levels.

A design model is developed on the basis of an analysis model (specification). The test model verifies the correctness of the design with regard to the analysis. These relations are examples for relationships between various abstraction levels. The abstraction dependency allows us to explicitly model them.

The notation is a dashed arrow, similar to how we denote a dependency, except that it carries the additional keyword *«abstraction»*. The semantics of an abstraction dependency is often refined by a stereotype. In SysML we can use *«allocate»* or *«deriveReqt»*, for example. UML defines *«derive»*, *«trace»*, and *«refine»*.

Figure 3.17 shows an abstraction dependency between two abstraction levels—business process model and system model.

3.3.8 Generalization

Definition

A **generalization** is a taxonomic relationship from a special class to a general class.

Taxonomy is the division of things in groups. In software development it is common to use the term *inheritance* rather than *generalization*. In Figure 3.18, the class *Location* inherits all properties from the class *Waypoint*. This means that an object of type *Location* has an attribute *coordinates* in addition to the attribute *name*. Not only attributes are inherited, but also constraints and operations, if defined.

A generalization is denoted as an arrow with solid line and hollow triangle as an arrowhead. It is read as "is a kind of" in the direction of the arrow. In Figure 3.18, we read, "a location is a kind of waypoint."

The relationship forms a hierarchy. This is why we speak of superclasses and subclasses. The class *Location* is a subclass of the superclass *Waypoint*.

A generalization is also permitted between actors and between use cases. It's the same model element and the same concept in all cases. However, it must not

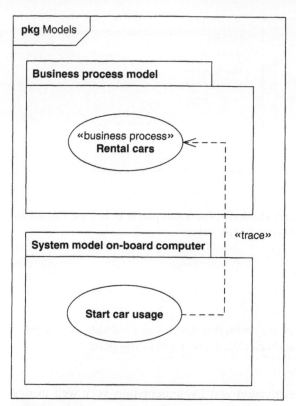

FIGURE 3-17

Example for an abstraction dependency.

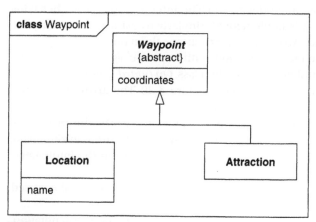

FIGURE 3-18

Example for a generalization.

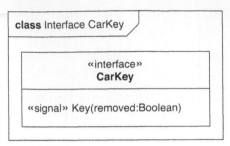

FIGURE 3-19

Example for an interface.

be mixed between different model elements. For example, it is not permitted to use a generalization between a class and a use case.

3.3.9 Interface

Definition

An **interface** specifies structure and behavior. It does not include any implementation, and no object can be created based on its building plan.

We know the separation of specification and implementation very well in our daily lives. Think of a socket, for example. It specifies the structure of the plug as well as textually the intensity of current and voltage. The implementation—electric power or mains supply—is not visible to the user. For the user, only the specification is important.

We use the same principle in modeling, too. The interface specifies a behavior without stating how exactly it is implemented. Similarly to classes, the notation is written with the additional keyword *«interface»* above the name.

Figure 3.19 represents the interface *CarKey* with a receive signal, *Key(removed: Boolean)*. The interface is implemented by the class *On-board computer control*. This relation is described by the realization in Figure 3.20. The arrow is denoted similarly to a generalization, but with a dashed line.

Together with the realization, the class is obligated to realize the properties of the interface. The interface is a contract that is fulfilled by the realizing class. Accordingly, the interface's receive signal shows up once more in the implementing class. The class *KeyDeposit* is a user of the interface.

Alternatively the realized (offered) interface is denoted as a *ball*, while a used (requested) interface is denoted as a *socket*.[9]

The realization also comes as a more general concept in the same notation. In that case, what is being realized doesn't have to be an interface; it can be any specification element. SysML uses this for the *«satisfy»* relationship.

Interfaces are very common in software development, while SysML uses them only for the specification of standard ports.

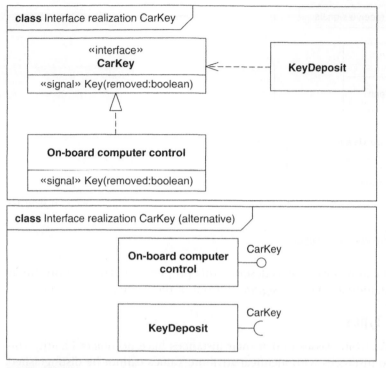

FIGURE 3-20

Example for an interface realization.

3.3.10 Signal

Definition

A **signal** describes the structure of a communication object.

UML knows two communication forms between objects: One form lets an object invoke an operation at another object. This means that the first object determines the behavior the second object should execute. In the second form, one object sends a signal to the other object.

The most important difference between these two forms is that, though both forms transmit information, the second form lets the receiver object decide how it will respond. When an operation is invoked, then the sender decides on the behavior to be executed.

The signal is a type and is written in a notation similar to the one for classes. In addition, the keyword *«signal»* is denoted above the signal's name (Figure 3.21). A signal has only attributes; it does not normally have operations.

---

[9] Within the *ball-and-socket notation*, the ball by itself is commonly referred to as *lollipop notation*.

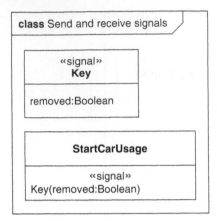

FIGURE 3-21

Example for send and receive signals.

Classes that can receive signals describe this property similar to an operation, but with the additional keyword *«signal»* in front of the name (Figure 3.21).

3.3.11 Data Types

Data types differ from classes in that their instances have no object identity. This means that two instances with identical attribute values cannot be distinguished. UML knows three forms of data types.

> **Definitions**
>
> A **data type** is a type the instances of which can be identified solely by their values.
>
> A **primitive type** is a special data type that has no structures worth mentioning.
>
> An **enumeration** is a special data type the value range of which consists of a limited set of defined literals.

Data types are used when we are interested only in a value but not in the object identity. Examples for data types are *period*, *date*, *current*. Two equal values cannot be distinguished. This is different with classes. Two objects with the same attribute values can be distinguished: they are equal but not identical.

Data types are denoted like classes, with the keyword *«dataType»* above the name (Figure 3.22).

A primitive type has no structures. For example, *date* is not a primitive type since it has structure elements like *day*, *month*, and *year*. UML has four predefined primitive types: *Integer*, *Boolean*, *String*, and *UnlimitedNatural*. *Unlimited Natural* is the value range for natural numbers, including zero and * as the symbol for infinite.

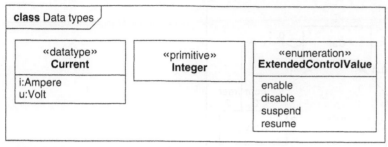

FIGURE 3-22

Example for data types.

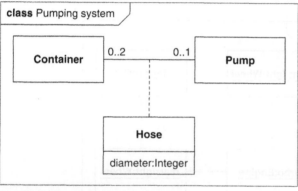

FIGURE 3-23

Example for an association class.

A primitive type is denoted like a class, with the keyword *«primitive»* above the name (Figure 3.22).

Another special data type is enumeration. Its value range consists of a limited set of literals, which have to be fully stated. Figure 3.22 shows an example of an extended control value with four literals.

3.3.12 Association Class

Definition

An **association class** unifies the properties of an association and of a class.

In UML, associations are more than people normally think. An association is not an alternative representation for attributes, but an independent element. An association as a relationship between classes can have properties itself. This is particularly striking with the association class.

An association class is denoted like an association and a class, where the class is connected with the association by a dashed line (Figure 3.23). The objects of

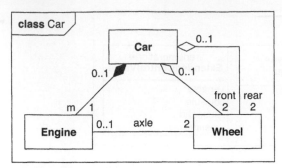

FIGURE 3-24

Simple class model for a car.

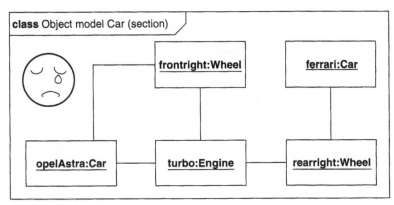

FIGURE 3-25

Undesirable object model "car" (section).

an association are called *links*. Accordingly, the objects of an association class are referred to as *link objects*.

3.4 The Composite Structure Diagram

This section discusses a diagram form of UML 2 that was not around in UML 1: composite structure diagrams. A *composite structure diagram* describes the internal structure of classes on role level. UML is a very extensive language already, so that you may ask, "Why do we need yet another diagram form?"

To answer this question, let's look at the class diagram in Figure 3.24. It is a simplified representation of things a car is composed of. The car consists of an engine that drives two wheels. In total, the car has four wheels—two front wheels and two rear wheels.

All of this looks pretty logical at first sight. But take a closer look at the section of the object model shown in Figure 3.25, which can result from this class diagram. The engine in the Opel Astra doesn't only drive the front right wheel,

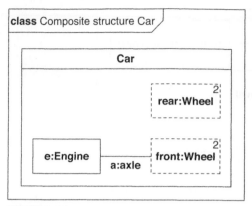

FIGURE 3-26

The composite structure diagram for "car."

but also the rear right wheel, but the latter is a wheel of a Ferrari. All objects correspond to the building plan that defines the pertaining classes from Figure 3.24. I leave it up to the playful reader to think of more unhappy constellations.

How can such a situation be prevented? How can a modeler express which object relationships are valid and which ones are not? Unfortunately, this is impossible in a class diagram, because it describes types, and with them all object relationships that are permitted in each context across the entire model. However, we want to describe that certain relationships are invalid while others are mandatory for an object, depending on the role it plays. This is where the composite structure diagram comes in handy.

The diagram and the underlying model close the gap between type level (classes) and object level. In between these two there is the role level. The engine plays a role in the context of the car. The four wheels can play two roles: Each can either be a front wheel or a rear wheel. The context-specific relationships between the roles and sets are defined in a composite structure diagram.

Figure 3.26 shows the internal composition of the class *Car*. The car has an engine, *e* that drives the two front wheels. Moreover, there are two rear wheels. In contrast to the rear wheels, the role of the front wheels has a relationship to the engine, *e*, in the context of a car. This role specification ensures that undesirable object constellations are prevented (Figure 3.27). Figure 3.26 shows the wheels in dashed notation, because the car doesn't own them any more; it uses an aggregation to merely reference them. The special designation of the objects with slashes in their names were be explained in Section 3.4.1.

3.4.1 Role

Definition

A **role** describes a structure in the context of a class.

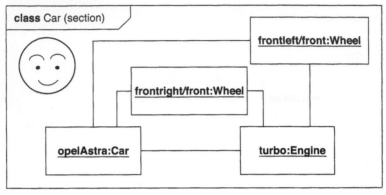

FIGURE 3-27

Desirable object model "car" (section).

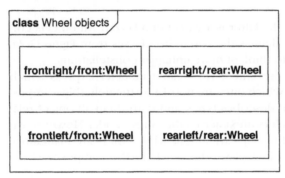

FIGURE 3-28

Wheel objects.

Attributes specify the structure of a class. An attribute's type is a class. This class describes the structure of the attribute. This description is independent of the class (i.e., the context) the attribute is in.

You can see in Figure 3.24 that an engine can belong to the structure of a wheel. Whether or not a specific wheel does really have a relationship to an engine depends on the role it plays. If it is a front wheel of a car, then it has a relationship to an engine (Figure 3.26). Relationships between roles are called *connectors*.

The role is within the context class and is denoted similarly to an object (i.e., as a rectangle) except that the name is not underlined and the multiplicity of the role is in the upper right corner. The rectangle is dashed if the context class references the role rather than owning it—association/aggregation versus composition (Figure 3.26).

Note that, on the object level, we can also state the role name. The object is written as follows (Figure 3.28):

```
<object name>/<role name>:<Type name>
```

You can omit single parts of this object notation. For example, the role names of *Car* and *Engine* were omitted in Figure 3.27.

3.4.2 Connector

Definition

A **connector** specifies a relationship between two roles, allowing these roles to communicate.

There are associations between classes, links between objects, and connectors between roles. They express that the roles can communicate. This is frequently the case since the classes belonging to roles have an association between them. In this case, the association is the type of the connector.

We can see in Figure 3.24 that the association between *Engine* and *Wheel* is named *axle*. The connector between the engine, *e*, and the role *front:Wheel* in Figure 3.26 has this association as a type. The syntax is the same as with other typified elements, namely <name>:<Type>.

When the connector is typified, then the desired multiplicity is written at the connector end. Of course, this multiplicity must not be in conflict with the multiplicity of the pertaining association end. The multiplicity at the connector end corresponds to the multiplicity of the role if none is stated at the connector end. For example, multiplicities of *1* and *2* are explicitly stated at the connector between *e:Engine* and *front:Wheel* in Figure 3.26.

3.4.3 Port

Definition

A **port** describes an interaction point at which a class uses interfaces to provide services to its environment, or to request services from its environment.

A class encapsulates structure and behavior. Encapsulation means that the inside is separated from the outside. However, the class has to communicate with its environment in order for the entire system to function. Ports describe the points at which the class can communicate. They are properties of the class, similar to attributes. A port has a name, a type, and a multiplicity.

The notation is a small square positioned on the edge of the class rectangle. Next to it is further information in the following syntax:

```
<name>:<Type> [<multiplicity>]
```

The type and the multiplicity are often not represented. The name of a port is normally written in lowercase letters. Ports can also be denoted on roles, if they belong to the class of a role (Figure 3.29).

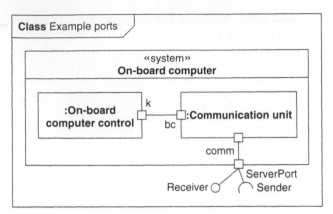

FIGURE 3-29

Example for ports.

The potential communication over ports is described by their interfaces. A port can have several interfaces, both requested and provided interfaces.

3.5 The Use Case Diagram

A use case model describes the services a system offers as well as the users of these services. In contrast to the other UML areas, the use case model elements are very vaguely defined, allowing us a large degree of freedom. An approach model is responsible for concretizing this degree of freedom. The SYSMOD approach in Chapter 2 describes how you find and model use cases for systems.

Use case diagrams look very simple. These diagrams are communication interfaces between system engineers and stakeholders, such as domain experts or future users of the system. Many stakeholders are normally not from the technical environment, but they can still be involved in the modeling, thanks to the simplicity of the use cases. This had been one of the goals of Ivar Jacobson when he invented use cases back then.

Use cases, actors, and the include relationship will be described below. We will not be looking at the *«extend»* relationship though. It is not used in the SYSMOD approach described in this book. I'm following Martin Fowler's recommendation for the extend relationship:"Just pretend it doesn't exist" [17].

3.5.1 Use Case

Definition

A **use case** describes a coherent and targeted interaction of an actor with a system, at the beginning of which there is a domain trigger, and at the end of which there is a defined result of domain value.

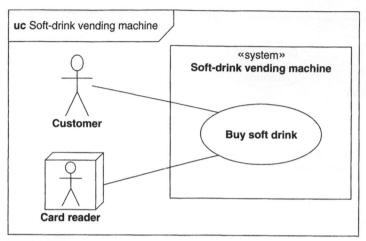

FIGURE 3-30

A use case with actor and system.

A use case describes a service performed by the system for its environment. The users of this service are actors. A use case is generally triggered by an actor. The result of a use case is normally significant for the triggering actor (see exceptions in Section 2.4). I intentionally chose these vague formulations because UML does not make any specific statement about the trigger and result of a use case. You'll learn how to handle exceptions in Section 2.4.

In addition to actors who are users, there can also be actors that a use case requires in order to perform a service. It is typical especially for embedded systems to have many actors connected with a use case.

A use case is denoted as an ellipse. The name of the use case is written inside or underneath the ellipse. The participating actors are connected with the use case by a solid line. Several actors being connected with a use case means that all of them participate in that use case (AND semantics).

The use case *buy soft drink* in Figure 3.30 has exactly two actors: a customer using the control panel to select a soft drink, and the card reader from which a chip card is read and written for payment.

The system the use case refers to can be drawn as a box around the use case, or use cases (Figure 3.30). Having a system boundary is important for use case modeling since it determines who the actors are and what execution steps the use case describes.

The solid line between an actor and a use case is formally an association. It means that the actor and the system communicate in the context of the use case.

A use case can also be abstract. It then represents common features with similar use cases. Similar to an abstract class, the name is written in italics, and it can be optionally completed by the adjective *{abstract}*. Concrete use cases are connected with the abstract use case by a generalization. This is the same relationship as between classes. Reading in the direction of the arrow, the sentence "*use case A is a kind of use case B*" has to make sense. Otherwise, there is a modeling error.

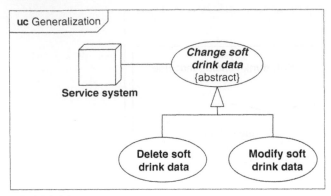

FIGURE 3-31

Use case generalization.

Let's test this on the example in Figure 3.31:

- *Delete soft-drink data* is a kind of *change soft-drink data*.
- *Modify soft-drink data* is a kind of *change soft-drink data*.

Bingo!

A use case describes only that a service is present. The service itself is described by an activity, for example. The relation between use case and activity cannot be represented in a diagram. However, the relationship exists in the model. It is up to the modeling tool you use to visualize the relation.

You do not necessarily have to represent the concept of use cases in UML. You can alternatively work with text documents (Table 3.2). The most important things are the concept and a standardized filing of information, and not the notation.

3.5.2 Actor

> **Definition**
>
> An **actor** is a role that interacts with the system. The role can be assumed by an individual or by an external system. An actor is outside the system.

Actors represent users of the system as well as users outside the system which are, in turn, used by the system.

The UML notation uses the stick man for an actor. Since not only humans can be actors, but also other systems, for example, UML allows us to use any other symbol for an actor. For example, a box is a common symbol for an external system that is an actor (see also Section 5.1).

An actor is connected with the use cases it participates in by an association. An actor can additionally be connected directly with the system class it interacts with. We use this property in the system context diagram.

The solid line is an association. It is the same model element that is used between classes. This means that we can also state role names and multiplicities. However, they are generally omitted in the diagram.

Table 3.2 The use case "buy soft drink".

Description of use case	
Name:	Buy soft drink.
Trigger:	A customer selects a soft drink at a vending machine.
Result:	The vending machine dispensed the selected drink and booked the corresponding amount of money.
Actors:	Customer, card reader, communication unit.
Short description:	A selected drink is dispensed. Payment is effected by a chip card that is read and rewritten by a card reader. Headquarters may be informed about the filling status of the vending machine via SMS.
Essence:	Select soft drink.
	Pay for soft drink.
	Remove soft drink.
	Transmit vending machine status.

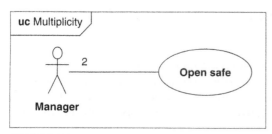

FIGURE 3-32

Example for multiplicity.

Multiplicity has the following meaning here: At the actor's side the multiplicity describes how many concrete individuals or systems participate in their roles as actors in the use case. The use case *open safe* in Figure 3.32 requires exactly two managers. Each of the two managers can deactivate part of the safe's security system to open the safe.

At the use case side, the multiplicity describes how often the use case can be executed concurrently by the actors.

Actors can have only few relationships among them. Since they are outside the system, which means that they are not within the modeling focus, there is little need to examine the relations between actors in detail.

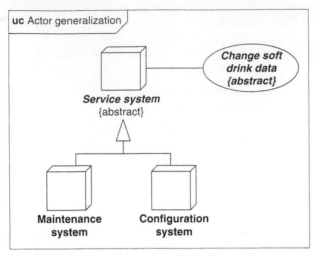

FIGURE 3-33

Example for an actor generalization.

Table 3.3	Description of actors.
Name:	**Customer**
Type:	User
Description:	An individual who buys a soft drink at a vending machine.
Example:	Train passenger.

A relationship that is permitted between actors is a generalization (a "is a kind of" relationship). This allows us to describe taxonomic[10] hierarchies between actors. They can be abstract, just like use cases and classes. In this case, the actor's name is written in italics. The adjective *{abstract}* can optionally be denoted behind the actor's name.

A generalization is also used to model an OR semantics between actors and a use case. The use case *change soft-drink data* in Figure 3.33 has only one actor, *service system*. More specifically, this is either the *maintenance system* or the *configuration system*.

An information flow is another relationship that is permitted between actors. You can use an information flow to describe the information your actors exchange.

Associations between actors are not allowed.

Actors can alternatively be described in text form, just like use cases (Table 3.3). This is a textual representation of the model, but it's not standardized in UML.

---

[10] Taxonomy means dividing things into groups.

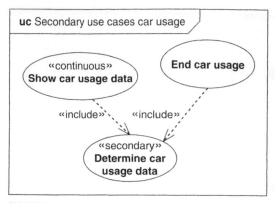

FIGURE 3-34

Example for an include relationship.

3.5.3 Include Relationship

> **Definitions**
>
> An **include relationship** describes that a use case is included in another use case.

This relationship is used to enable writing only once flows that occur in more than one use case. However, a flow occurring several times is hardly ever a fully fledged use case. In such a use case, the domain trigger, the result, or the actor do not exist or correspond to the use case definition of our approach. This is the reason why this type of use cases is marked with the stereotype *«secondary»*. This is an extension of UML introduced by the SYSMOD profile. UML itself does not know this differentiation.

An include relationship is denoted as a dashed arrow with the keyword *«include»*. The arrowhead points to the use case that's being included. For example, in Figure 3.34 the secondary use case *determine car usage* data is included in the use cases *show car usage data* and *end car usage*.

You use an include relationship to model a scenario that you would execute in exactly the same way if you weren't describing your use cases in UML, but instead just in text files. You'd swap common areas in a separate document, while only inserting references in the original documents.

3.6 The Activity Diagram

An activity diagram is used wherever flows have to be described. From business process modeling [33] to system use case flows to detailed descriptions of algorithms and operations.

This diagram represents a model that describes the sequence of elementary actions. This sequence can be split sequentially or into several flows, it can be

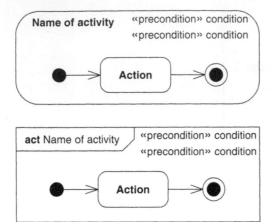

FIGURE 3-35

Notation of an activity with and without diagram frame.

concurrent, it can be synchronized, or it branches in various alternatives based on conditions.

The UML action model that describes the elementary and executable actions is integrated in the activity model. This includes, for example, simple actions that write or read a value, or actions that create or delete objects. All these actions together allow us to create executable flow models, for example, to be able to simulate the system in the model and test it at an early stage (catchword: executable specification). However, current modeling tools concentrate on state machines with regard to the execution of models.

3.6.1 Activity

Definition

An **activity** describes flows consisting of several elementary actions. A flow can be parallel or synchronized, or it can be forked and joined on the basis of conditions.

Similar to a state machine or an interaction, an activity is a complete behavior element. In contrast to other UML behavior elements, however, an activity has its own notation: a rectangle with rounded corners. Its name is in the upper left corner, and the upper right corner can be used to optionally write preconditions or postconditions. The remaining area is used to describe the flow, including nodes and edges. The activity rectangle is omitted in combination with the diagram frame (Figure 3.35).

A precondition begins with the keyword «*precondition*» and is written in the upper right corner of the activity (Figure 3.35). The condition itself can be an arbitrary Boolean expression (e.g., in OCL[11]) in a programming language, or in a natural language. The activity starts only provided that the precondition is met.

---

[11] *Object Constraint Language* [52].

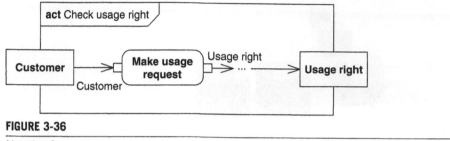

FIGURE 3-36

Notation for activity parameters.

A postcondition is preceded with the keyword *«postcondition»* (Figure 3.35). It is always deemed to have been met upon termination of the activity.

Input parameters are used so that the caller of the activity can initially transmit data. Output parameters are used so that the activity can return data outwards to the caller upon termination. These parameters are denoted as rectangles (without rounded corners) on the edge of the activity rectangle, and the name of the parameter is inside. This is normally the name of the parameter type (Figure 3.36). However, it is also possible to assign a name, regardless of the type. The syntax has the pattern <name>:<Type>.

One particularity is the possibility of a stream property for input and output parameters. If it is activated, then the activity can accept or supply new data through the parameters in running operation. Compared to an assembly line, this means that you can continually put new work pieces on the assembly line and have them transported in a machine (= activity). In the end, the finished elements come out of the running assembly line. Without flow property—the standard behavior of activity parameters—you would put a work piece on the assembly line, the machine (= activity) would switch on and produce a result, and switch off again. Subsequently, you could put the next work piece on the assembly line, and so on.

A stream property is denoted with the word {stream} on the parameter (Figure 3.37).

Playing marbles: The flow of an activity is determined by the so-called *token flow*. A token can be thought of as a marble that rolls along the edges through the activity. If it encounters an action, then this action can be activated.

"Playing marbles" begins as soon as the activity is invoked. One marble is placed on every initial node and every input parameter of the activity. More specifically, a control token each is put on the initial nodes and an object token each is put on the input parameters. An object token is a marble, which additionally describes that the specified object is present at the respective position within the flow. It can then be consumed, for example, by an action as an input object over a pin.

Two conditions have to be met in order for the marble to roll over an edge:

1. The edge has to be ready to transport the marble. For example, this can be influenced by a condition denoted at the edge.

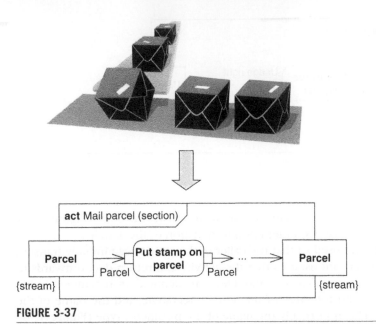

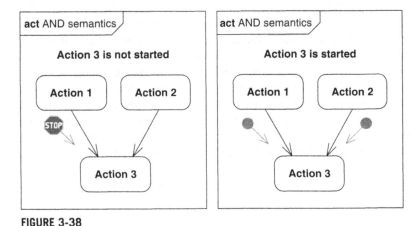

FIGURE 3-37

Example for the flow property of an activity parameter.

FIGURE 3-38

Token flow rule AND semantics.

2. The destination has to be ready to accept the marble. An action is only ready if marbles are available at all incoming edges of the action (AND semantics). In Figure 3.38, there is one marble ready on the left side after action 1. It cannot start rolling, because the target node, action 3, is not ready yet. For this to happen, action 2 also has to make a marble available. On the right-hand side, there are marbles available at both incoming edges, and action 3 can be started.

The AND semantics can easily lead to misunderstandings in practice. In other flow notations (e.g., activity diagrams in UML 1) the OR semantics holds when there are several incoming edges.

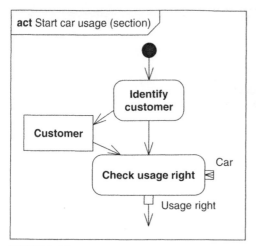

FIGURE 3-39

Example for input and output pins.

3.6.2 Action and PIN

Definitions

An **action** is an elementary executable step in an activity.

A **pin** is the connecting link between the parameters of an action and the object flow. We distinguish between input pin and output pin.

An action is elementary and executable. UML already defines all actions, so that they are independent of a special domain. Modeling tools can implement these actions and make them available in a runtime environment.

The notation for an action is a rectangle with rounded corners. It's like the notation for an activity, except that an action is not further decomposed. Several predefined actions deviate from this standard notation, for example, the action for sending a signal (see *status display* in Figure 3.42).

Actions consume data and can supply new data as a result. The data are transported from and to actions by object tokens. Pins function like buckets for object tokens and bind them to the parameters of an action.

The notation for pins reflects their name. It is a small rectangle that is pinned to the action from the outside. Depending on whether a pin is connected with incoming or outgoing edges, we distinguish between input pin and output pin (Figure 3.39).

Next to the pin is the name of the object that the pin can accept. This is normally the name of the object type. You can optionally add the state the object should be in within square brackets next to that name (Figure 3.40).

You can alternatively denote the input pin and the output pin between two actions as one single rectangle if they have the same object. This allows you to

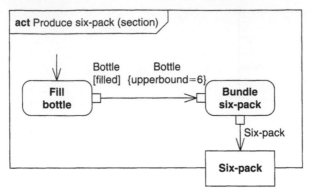

FIGURE 3-40

Example for limiting the pin buffer.

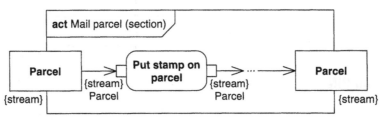

FIGURE 3-41

Example for the stream property of a pin.

visually separate the object flow stronger from the control flow (*Customer* in Figure 3.39).

Unless otherwise specified, a pin can accept an unlimited number of tokens. You can limit the number to *n* tokens by stating *{upperbound=<n>}* next to the pin (Figure 3.40).

Similar to activity parameters, pins can also have the stream property. This means that new data can be accepted over input pins, or previously created data can be passed on over output pins while the action is still active. Pins with this property are denoted with the keyword *{stream}* (Figure 3.41).

So-called control pins play a special role. A control pin is not a model element in itself, but a property of a pin (*isControlType*). An input pin with this property accepts object tokens, but it doesn't pass the object (i.e., the data) to the action. In this case, the object token has the same effect as a control token, except that control tokens cannot be buffered. SysML utilizes this property for the control operator and the control value.

Pins with this property are often not represented in the diagram. If they are, then they are denoted with *{control}* next to the pin name.

There are approximately 40 predefined actions in UML. This set includes actions that read and write values, actions that compare, create, and destroy objects, and actions that invoke a behavior or an operation. Each action is defined such that a modeling tool can make a runtime environment available. Describing each of these actions here would go beyond the scope and volume of this book. You find an extensive description of all these actions in [60].

I limit my discussion of these actions here to the so-called *CallBehaviorAction*, the *OpaqueAction*, and the actions used to send and receive signals (*SendSignal Action* and *AcceptEventAction*). They show the concept and explain why actions like *identify customer* are possible in use case flows, and what's formally behind it.

As its name suggests, the *CallBehaviorAction* invokes a behavior. This can be a state machine or an activity, for example. If there are input pins at the action, then they are mapped on input parameters of the behavior. Similarly, the output pins correspond to the output parameters. If the invoked behavior is an activity, then a fork symbol is denoted in the lower right corner of the action rectangle to symbolize the call hierarchy of activities (Figure 3.42).

OpaqueAction integrates an implementation in an arbitrary language in the model. This can be something executable (e.g., something written in a programming language) or a natural-language text that explains the implementation. The purpose of *OpaqueAction* is to formally embed such user-specific instructions in the entire model. For example, the step *check emergency driving* in Figure 3.42 is an *OpaqueAction*. You can't see this in the notation, but this information is stored in the model.

We even used the SendSignalAction twice in Figure 3.42—both times for sending the signal *status display*. The notation of this action differs of those of the other actions. It's a kind of arrow symbolizing that something is being sent. You cannot represent the receiver of the signal in the diagram, though this information is present in the model. Here the receiver is the card reader that switches its light-emitting diodes as a result of the signal (Section 2.4.5).

There is also an action to receive a signal—an *AcceptEventAction*—modeled in Figure 3.42. Here we receive the signal *timeout reservation system*. It is a timing signal, shown by a symbolized hourglass. The left-hand receive symbol from Figure 3.43 is used for all other signal variants.

The *AcceptEventAction* in Figure 3.42 is not within a flow, like *SendSignal Actions*, which is also permitted. In this case, it plays the special role of receiving a signal to terminate the interruptible activity region.

The action concept is not only known in UML. There are a number of textual languages that map elementary actions and support a runtime environment. The *Action Specification Language* (*ASL*) was developed in the early 1990s. Later versions of the language consider the action model of UML 1.5. Development tools for ASL are available from *Kennedy Carter*.

The *Object Action Language* (*OAL*) is used as a language for the action model of UML 1.5 in the *BridgePoint* development tool by *Accelerated Technology*.

3.6.3 Parameter Set

Definition

A **parameter set** is a complete set of input parameters or output parameters of a behavior exclusively selected instead of other parameter sets of that behavior.

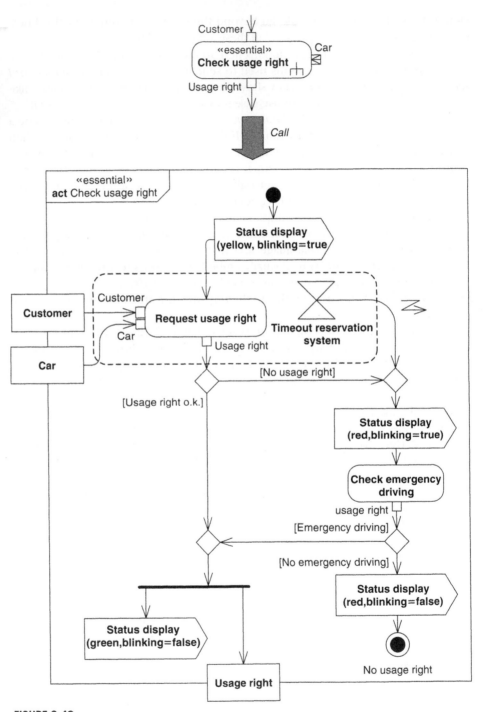

FIGURE 3-42

Check usage right.

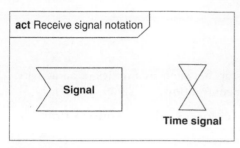

FIGURE 3-43

Notation for AcceptEventAction.

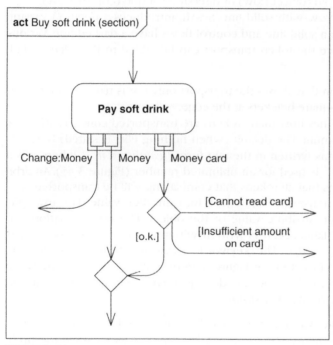

FIGURE 3-44

Example for parameter sets.

A parameter set is always used in combination with other parameter sets that mutually exclude each other. They each contain all input or output parameters a behavior requires. This allows you to model behavior that requires alternative inputs or produces alternative outputs. Two parameter sets may have common parameters, but they must not be fully identical.

The pins that belong to a parameter set are enclosed by an additional rectangle (Figure 3.44).

3.6.4 Activity Edge

Definitions

An **activity edge** is a directed relationship between two nodes of an activity. We distinguish between object flow and control flow.

An **object flow** can only transport object tokens, while a **control flow** can only transport control tokens.

Edges are the transport paths for tokens in the activity. In the model we distinguish between object flow and control flow. In the diagram the notation is the same for both types. The difference can be seen only in the context, for example, whether the target of an edge is a pin (object flow) or directly an action (control flow).

The notation is an arrow with solid line. SysML introduces a notation variant, where object flows have a solid line and control flows have a dashed line. Various information that influence the token transport can be added to the edge, including the following.

- A Boolean condition that allows the transport only if it is true. The condition is denoted within square brackets at the edge.
- A weight that specifies how many tokens are transported concurrently over the edge as a minimum. The default (when nothing else is stated) is 1. This weight information is written in the text form *{weight=<n>}*, where *n* is a natural number, or * is used for an unlimited number (Figure 3.45). An arbitrary number means that all tokens that come along will be transported.
- A transformation transforms an object into another value. For example, this can be a single attribute value of the object. The transformation can be denoted in any language. It is written within a comment symbol that is connected with the edge. The keyword *«transformation»* precedes the condition. The transformation in Figure 3.45 describes how to get from the customer object to the PIN check code object. The point indicates that *pinCheckCode* is an attribute of *customer*.

It often happens in activity diagrams that there are very long edges, or edges that run across other elements. The result can be quite messy. To solve the problem, you can conduct such edges through a "tunnel." Both the entry and the exit of the tunnel are denoted with a small circle that has a unique identifier in pairs (Figure 3.47). The UML specification calls this notation variant "connector," not to be confused with the connector used in composite structure diagrams.

3.6.5 Initial and Final Nodes

Definitions

An **initial node** is the starting point for a control flow that is started as the activity is invoked.

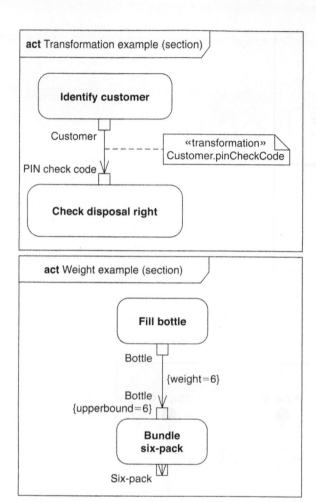

FIGURE 3-45

Example for weight and transformation.

An **activity final node** terminates the entire activity as soon as a single flow arrives at the node.

A **flow final node** terminates the flow in an activity that arrives at this node.

A control token is placed on each initial node, thus starting a flow, as soon as an activity is invoked. An activity can have from none to any number of initial nodes. If there are more than one initial nodes, then there are concurrent flows right at the start of the activity (Figure 3.46). An initial node is denoted as a black filled circle (Figure 3.46).

An activity final node terminates the entire activity as soon as a token hits the node, regardless of how many other tokens (i.e., flows) are still underway in that activity (Figure 3.47). The notation for an activity final node is a black filled circle with an open outer circle. It probably reminds you of a bull's eye from the game

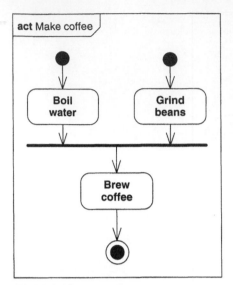

FIGURE 3-46

Example with two initial nodes.

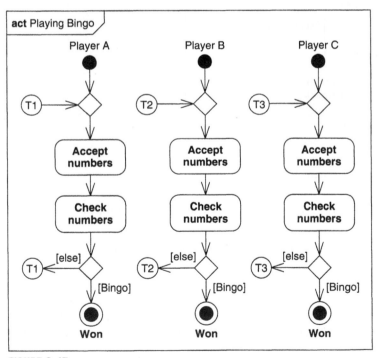

FIGURE 3-47

Example for activity final nodes.

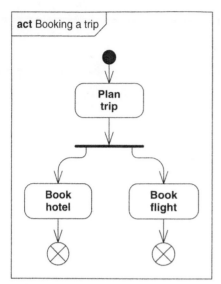

FIGURE 3-48

Example for flow final nodes.

of darts.[12] It's the target you want to hit. In Figure 3.47, you can see an activity that contains three tokens after it had been invoked. The entire activity is terminated as soon as an activity final node is reached.

In contrast to activity final nodes, a flow final node swallows the token that hits it, while all other tokens in the activity continue rolling. This means that only this one flow is terminated. If it is the only or final flow in the activity, then the entire activity is terminated by the motto "the last one turns the light off."

The notation for a flow final node is a circle with a cross, similar to the lamp symbol used in electrical engineering (Figure 3.48). Note that there is no causal connection.

3.6.6 Decision and Merge Nodes

Definitions

A **decision node** is a node in an activity at which the flow branches into several optional flows. There is exactly one incoming edge and an arbitrary number of outgoing edges, which each have a condition.

A **merge node** is a node in an activity at which several flows are merged into one single flow. There is an arbitrary number of incoming edges and exactly one outgoing edge.

A flow within an activity is generally controlled by conditions. If *XY* is true, then do *A*, otherwise do *B*. What we need for this is a decision node. The notation is a

---

[12] In the game of darts you normally try to hit exactly the center of the dart board—the bull's eye.

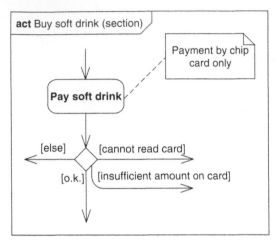

FIGURE 3-49

Example for decision nodes.

rhombus with one incoming edge and an arbitrary number of outgoing edges, at which there is a condition each within brackets (Figure 3.49).

A condition is a Boolean expression in any language.[13] Never more than one condition may be true. Also, exactly one condition must always be met. We can use the *[else]* condition to ensure this. This way is always chosen when all other conditions are false (Figure 3.49).

The notation for merge nodes is the same as that for decision nodes. A merge node is the counterpart that merges several optional flows into one single flow. As flows are merged, no conditions are tested, and there is no waiting for special events (Figure 3.50).

3.6.7 Fork and Join Nodes

Definitions

A **fork node** is a node in an activity that splits a flow into several concurrent flows. There is exactly one incoming edge and an arbitrary number of outgoing edges.

A **join node** is a node in an activity that synchronizes several concurrent flows and joins them into one single flow. There is an arbitrary number of incoming edges and exactly one outgoing edge.

In contrast to a decision node that enables several optional flows, a fork node creates several concurrent flows. To make this happen, the token that arrives at the fork node over the incoming edge is copied several times, so that there is one token available for each outgoing edge. A fork node is denoted as a black bar.

---

[13] The runtime environment of the model must be capable of evaluating the expression. The runtime environment can also be a human.

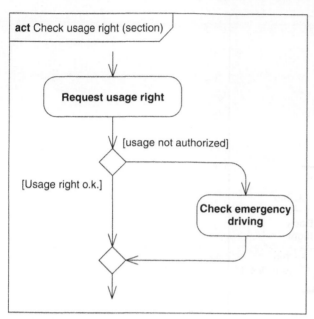

FIGURE 3-50

Example for merge nodes.

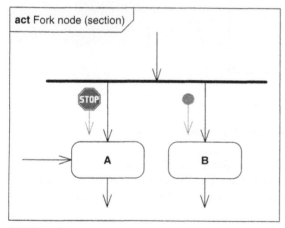

FIGURE 3-51

Example for fork nodes.

A token waits at the fork node bar when the target is not ready to accept it. This can cause a situation, for example, where, at two outgoing edges, one flow already starts while the other flow is still waiting. The waiting token is subject to the FIFO[14] principle if more tokens arrive at the fork node. In Figure 3.51, action A is not ready if no token is present at the edge coming from the far right. The token has to wait at the fork node bar. Action B is ready and can be started. This action's

---

[14] First In, First Out.

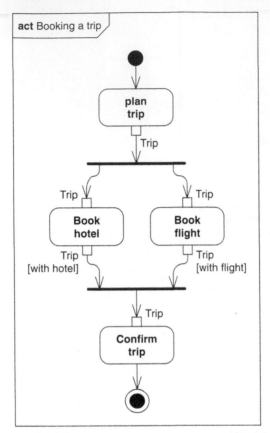

FIGURE 3-52

Example for fork and join nodes.

token doesn't have to wait. The fork node bar is the only control node in the activity model where tokens can wait.

A join node joins concurrent flows to form one single flow. Similarly to fork nodes, join nodes are denoted as black bars. The effect is a synchronization (i.e., the joined flow won't start before all incoming flows have arrived). This is subject to the following rules:

1. If control tokens arrive at all incoming edges, then all tokens except one are deleted. The remaining token is made available at the outgoing edge.
2. All control tokens are deleted if both object tokens and control tokens arrive.
3. If several object tokens arrive, then all of them are made available at the outgoing edge, because a join node does not delete any data from the flow. An exception occurs when several object tokens refer to an identical object. In this case, only one object token is forwarded.

Figure 3.52 shows a simple example. The object token *trip* from the action *plan trip* is duplicated at the fork node. The concurrent actions add a booked

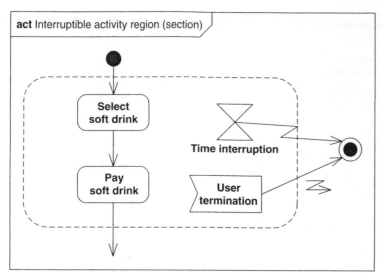

FIGURE 3-53

Example for interruptible activity regions.

hotel and a flight to the trip. Two object tokens *trip* that refer to the identical object arrive at the join node. Only one object token is forwarded according to the synchronization rule. Finally the trip is confirmed. Note that, in this example, two different flows access the same resource concurrently, which can potentially lead to conflicts. However, this is not considered in the activity.

3.6.8 Interruptible Activity Region

Definition

An **interruptible activity region** characterizes a region within an activity, which can be terminated by a token flow at special interruption edges.

Many system flows can be terminated. Either a user pushes a stop button, or a time interruption occurs when a defined time window is exceeded, or another condition occurs. An interruptible activity region supports exactly this flow behavior.

Interruptible actions are denoted as dashed rectangles with rounded corners. Special interruption edges that lead out of this region are denoted by a lightning symbol. An alternative notation is a normal edge to which a small lightning arrow is attached (Figure 3.53).

The interruption edges interrupt every flow within the marked region as soon as a token rolls over them. An interruptible activity region is often used in connection with events that trigger the interruption.

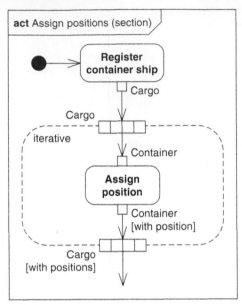

FIGURE 3-54

Example for an extension region.

3.6.9 Expansion Region

Definition

An **expansion region** is a node in an activity that accepts a set of objects, then processes each object individually and finally returns the set with the processed objects.

UML offers the expansion region node to allow us to individually process the single objects of a set. An expansion region is denoted as a dashed rectangle with rounded corners. There are four small squares one next to each other on the rectangle's border for input and output sets. The number "four" has no particular significance. It merely symbolizes that a set is accepted and returned at these points (Figure 3.54).

Inside the rectangle there are actions that form a flow for processing of set objects. Starting from the incoming group of four pins runs an object flow edge to one of the inner actions with an input pin, which can take an object from the set. Vice-versa, the last action of the flow has an output pin, which carries the processed object over an object flow edge to place it in the outgoing group of four pins.

The object *Cargo* in Figure 3.54 is a set of containers that are assigned to a position as the set is being processed. The type of set processing is described in the upper left corner of the dashed rectangle. There are three options:

1. *Iterative*—The objects of the set are processed one after the other in consecutive steps. An object gets into the flow when the previous object has been fully completed.

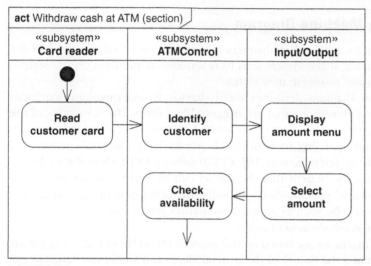

FIGURE 3-55

Example for an activity partition.

2. *Parallel*—The objects of the set are all processed in parallel. This means that there is no defined sequence. They don't necessarily have to be processed concurrently.

3. *Streaming*—The objects of a set are all fed to the processing as one flow. Similar to an assembly line, no object has to wait for processing of the previous object to be complete to place a new object on the assembly line.

3.6.10 Activity Partition

Definition

An **activity partition** divides the nodes and edges of an activity into partitions based on defined common features.

It is common to assign the actions of an activity directly to structures of the system that realize these actions. This can be expressed by an activity partition in the activity diagram. Each partition stands for a structure (e.g., a class) and contains the corresponding actions. Moreover, a control node, such as a decision node or a fork node, as well as edges can be assigned to a partition. However, the focus is clearly on actions. Grouping criteria other than structures are possible as well.

Still common is the UML 1 name for this model element: *swimlane*.

One single partition is denoted by drawing a frame around the activity region (Figure 3.55). The name of the partition goes in a separate area. It describes the grouping criterion. If the grouping criterion is a model element, then the type of element can be denoted within Guillemets[15] above the name.

---

[15] French quotation marks, also called "angle quotes."

3.7 The State Machine Diagram

A system is always in a state that abstracts a combination of values given in the system. Events arriving at the system lead to reactions—depending on the state—that change values and results in new states.

A state machine diagram describes this behavior. It contains state machines with states and state transitions that are triggered by events. The semantics of the state model is defined in such great detail in the UML specification that it can also be executed. Several modeling tools offer this possibility. These tools include, for example, *Rhapsody* by Telelogic and *ARTiSAN Studio* by ARTiSAN Software Tools.

Executability has the benefit that the model can be verified in an early stage (catchword: executable specification). In software development, an executable state machine can also be seen as an implementation, and it can be transferred to the software by source-code generation.

The UML state machines are based on the work of David Harel [22] who, among other things, combined the theory of the general Mealy and Moore machines to create a model that lets you describe complex system behavior.

3.7.1 State Machine

Definition

A **state machine** describes the states and state transitions of a structure.

A state machine describes behavior of a structure that is generally a class. With regard to the concrete execution, we often speak of a context object.

A state machine has no notation of its own. It is represented by the entire state machine diagram. This means that the diagram frame forms the border of the state machine. It is not possible to show a graphical connection between the state machine and the pertaining class in the diagram (Figure 3.56). However, the relationship is explicitly present in the model.

A state machine forms a semantic capsule around states, transitions, and pseudostates. This normally includes the execution rules. A state machine has a queue for events that are consumed by states and transitions in the sequence in which they occur. This means that they lead to state transitions, or to internal actions in a state.

State machines are subject to the so-called *run-to-completion* semantics, which says that the next event will be consumed only provided that all actions of the previous event have been completed. One exception is the state behavior that does not have to be completed before the next event can be processed. An event that cannot be consumed, for example, because there is no matching transition, is discarded.

The state machine in Figure 3.56 can consume the two time events at () and the event *terminate*. The latter event activates the transition that leads to the final state, so that the state machine terminates since no other region is active.

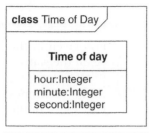

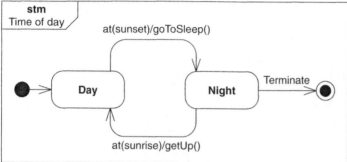

FIGURE 3-56

A state machine, Day of Time, with pertaining structure.

3.7.2 State

Definition

A **state** represents a set of value combinations for the underlying element. It has a name, and may have an internal behavior that is executed based on defined events.

A state represents a set of value combinations, for example, values for the attributes of a class. In Figure 3.56, you can see a class, *Time of Day*, in a class diagram and a corresponding simple state machine diagram. The state *Day* stands for all value combinations of the attributes *hour*, *minute*, and *second*, between the two events, *sunrise* and *sunset*.[16] This example shows clearly that a state is an abstraction of possible value combinations. Not every value combination is a meaningful state, for example, the state "*13:17:31*" (HH:MM:SS), which is not modeled here. What is meaningful and what isn't eventually depends on the domain we model, of course.

States are represented by rounded rectangles (Figure 3.57). The name of the state is within the rectangle. Another compartment shows the internal behavior, which is triggered by events, similar to transitions, but which does not cause the state to be exited.

---

[16] Note that the state machine works meaningfully only provided that the world is created at daytime.

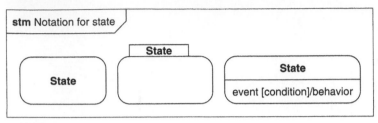

FIGURE 3-57

Notation for state.

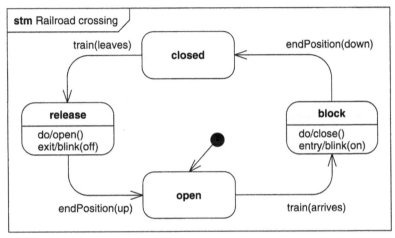

FIGURE 3-58

Example for state behavior.

In addition to the internal behavior, a state can also have three special behaviors that are triggered on the basis of predefined events:

- The *entry behavior* is executed immediately upon entering the state.
- The *exit behavior* is executed immediately before exiting the state.
- The *do behavior* is executed while the state is active.

In Figure 3.58, you can see internal behavior in the state machine of a railroad crossing. This example utilizes the fact that the state behavior is interruptible. For example, the barriers are closed in the state *block*. The state behavior *close()* is interrupted by the event *endPosition(down)*. The entry behavior and the exit behavior are not interruptible.

An important UML extension versus the classic *Finite State Machine (FSM)* is the possibility to decompose states into smaller units. This allows us to first describe states on a general level and then further detailing them.

Figure 3.59 shows the state *Day* after further detailing. It is a so-called composite state, containing a region with states and transitions. We can recognize this by the "spectacles" symbol in the lower right corner of the state in the upper diagram. The detailing itself is not shown here; it is shown in the bottom diagram.

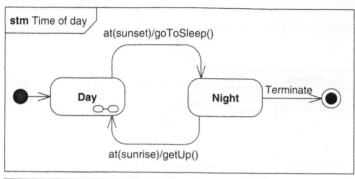

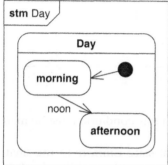

FIGURE 3-59

Example for a state detailing.

A system can also have several states concurrently. When looking out of the window now I find not only that it is afternoon, but also that it is a warm afternoon. To map this on a state machine, we need a so-called orthogonal state. An orthogonal state is divided into an arbitrary number of independent regions, which are each separated from the others by a dashed line. In Figure 3.60, the state *Day* (with the substate *afternoon*) and the state *warm* can now be active at the same time.

3.7.3 Transition

Definition

A **transition** specifies a state transition. It is a directed relationship between two states, and defines a trigger and a condition that both lead to the state transition, as well as a behavior that is executed during the transition.

Together with the states, transitions form the core elements of a state machine. They describe a transition between two states, regardless of one or more triggers and a condition. Triggers and a condition can be stated optionally. A transition without trigger is activated as soon as the source state has completed internal actions, if any, or as soon as the internal final state of a composite state has been

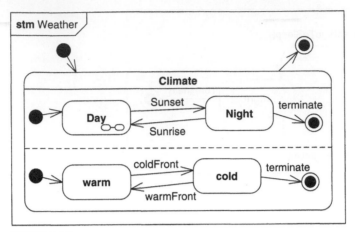

FIGURE 3-60

Example for an orthogonal state.

reached. If a condition is defined at the transition, then this condition must be met in order for the transition to be activated.

In Figure 3.60, the transition from the orthogonal state *Climate* to the final state has no trigger. It is activated automatically as soon as the source state has terminated. In this example, this happens as soon as the final states in both regions of the state *Climate* have been reached.

A transition is denoted as an arrow with solid line and a description in the following syntax:

```
trigger1, trigger2, ... [condition] / behavior
```

Triggers can alternatively be denoted using a special symbol, which corresponds to the symbol for receive signals from activity diagrams (Figure 3.61).

The condition is a Boolean expression that can be stated in any language. For example, you could use a formal language, such as OCL, or a programming language, or a natural language such as English or German. Which one you use depends on the runtime environment that will execute the state machine: man or machine. There is no symbol for conditions. It can be denoted only in text form near the transition.

The flow within a region is often influenced by the state that is active in another region, particularly with orthogonal states. States can be polled by the OCL expression `oclInState(<state>)`, which can be used as a condition. For example, you could add a state poll, `warmFront [oclInState(Day)]`, to the transition from the state *cold* to the state *warm* in Figure 3.60.

The details of the behavior syntax depend on action language of the model. Rather than in text form, actions can be denoted in rectangles on the transition arrow. One of the frequent actions for sending signals is denoted inside the symbol that is also used for send signal actions in the activity diagram (Figure 3.61).

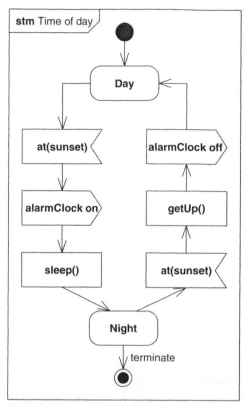

FIGURE 3-61

Example for a transition with behavior.

3.7.4 **Trigger and Event**

> **Definitions**
>
> A **trigger** references exactly one event and establishes a relationship to a behavior.
>
> An **event** specifies some occurrence that can be measured with regard to location and time.

A trigger is the connecting link between event and behavior in the model. Denoted at a transition means that the transition is activated as soon as the event occurs.

UML knows four types of events that can trigger a transition (Figure 3.62):

1. A *call event* occurs when an operation is invoked.
2. A *change event* occurs when a Boolean expression tests to true. This is the case when a value has changed accordingly in the system.
3. A *signal event* occurs when a signal has been received.

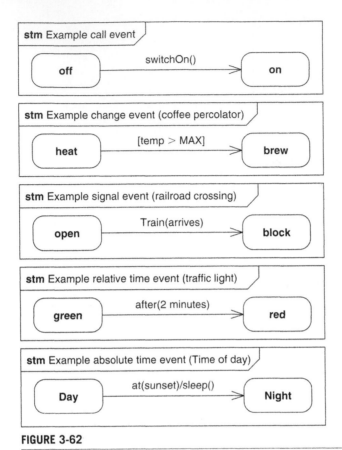

FIGURE 3-62

Examples for the types of events.

4. A *time event* is further distinguished. A *relative* time event occurs when the state from which the corresponding transition originates has been active over a certain period of time (keyword *after(<time>)*). An *absolute* time event occurs when the defined absolute time occurs (keyword *at(<time>)*).

3.7.5 Initial and Final States

Definitions

An **initial state** is a pseudostate with one outgoing transition that points to the initial state.

A **final state** is a state that describes the end of a composite state or a state machine.

A state machine or a composite state has a beginning and generally one or several defined ends. The beginning is shown by the initial state. It is a pseudostate (i.e., its only purpose is to control the state machine) and it does not describe a

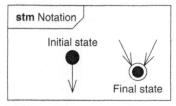

FIGURE 3-63

Notation for initial and final states.

real state of the context object. The transition that originates from the initial state points to the "real" initial state. This transition is mandatory, and there can always be one only. No event or condition is permitted at this transition. However, the transition may define a behavior.

In contrast to the initial state, a final state is a real state (i.e., the context object can be present in this state). There are value combinations that describe the final state. In contrast to the "normal" states, a final state does not have any outgoing transitions of course, and it has no internal behavior and cannot be described in more detail by decomposition. If no other regions of the enclosing state machine are active, then the final state completes the state machine.

An initial state or a final state is denoted similar to an initial or final node of an activity (Figure 3.63).

3.7.6 Pseudostate

Definition

A **pseudostate** is a control element that influences the sequence of events in a state machine. It is not a real state, and a pseudostate does not represent a value combination either.

UML knows 10 different pseudostates. Each of them describes a special property that controls state transitions. For example, the initial state discussed in Section 3.7.5 is a pseudostate. It is responsible for marking the initial state of a state machine.

I'll briefly describe the other nine states below:

- Shallow history
- Deep history
- Join
- Fork
- Junction
- Choice
- Exit point
- Entry point
- Terminate

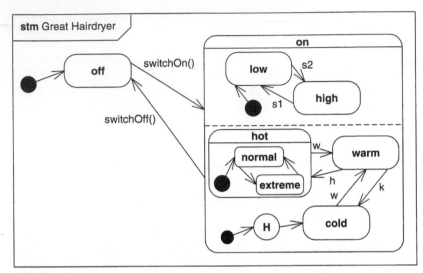

FIGURE 3-64

A state machine, Hairdryer.

There are two types of history state: *shallow history* and *deep history*. To better understand history states, let's first look at the state machine of a hairdryer (Figure 3.64)[17]. Don't pay attention to the circle symbol with the letter "H" for now. As soon as the hairdryer is switched on, it jumps into the initial state configuration, *cold* and *low*. Unless you are particularly concerned about damaging your hair, you will probably switch the hairdryer from *low* to *high* and from *cold* to *hot*. The state *hot* lets you additionally select either *normal* or *extreme*. When you switch it off, the hairdryer changes to *off* state.

The next time you use the hairdryer it will come on in the default state configuration—*low* and *cold*. So again, you have to go through the hassle of resetting it to *high* and *hot*. After the third, fourth, or fifth time you do this, you might come to think that this hairdryer is not fit for everyday use. This situation can be improved, at least in the model, by using history states.

We'll now have a closer look at the circle symbol with the "H." This is the notation for shallow history. Shallow history causes the substate of the pertaining region that was last active to be saved. When you now switch the hairdryer on a second time, when traversing the shallow history, the device will read the state that was last active and activate it directly. This means that the hairdryer will immediately jump into the *low* and *hot/normal* configuration after the second time you use it.

As the name implies, deep history has a "deeper" effect than shallow history. Using shallow history, when you switch it on again, the device sets itself to the state hot, as described above. Within this state, the substate *normal* is activated since the initial state points to it. However, when using deep history, the device

---

[17] Ever noticed the wide range of different, sometimes weird hairdryer systems in hotels?

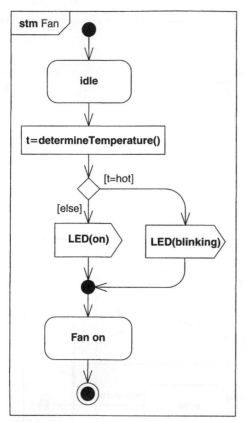

FIGURE 3-65

A state machine with choice and junction.

also restores the substates in the configuration that was active last. More specifically, when you switch it on again, the hairdryer jumps into the state configuration *low* and *hot/extreme*. The notation for deep history is the same as for shallow history, with an additional asterisk (*) behind the "H."

A junction connects transitions and merges them to form a path. It is possible to merge several incoming transitions, or to put several outgoing transitions into a junction. A junction has no additional semantics. Its notation is a black circle (Figure 3.65). In contrast to an initial state, which always has the same notation, a junction has always at least one incoming transition. The merging of transitions is comparable to the merge node in activity diagrams, except that the symbol is different.

A choice has several outgoing transitions that each have a condition. In contrast to junctions, the conditions of a choice can be evaluated on the basis of values that are determined only at the time of the state transition (Figure 3.65). It is therefore also referred to as a *dynamic choice*. A choice is not used for merging of transitions. The notation for choices is identical to the one for a decision in an activity diagram—a rhombus.

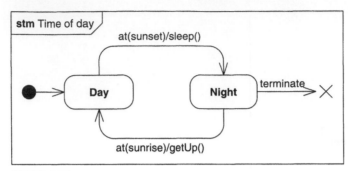

FIGURE 3-66

A state machine with termination.

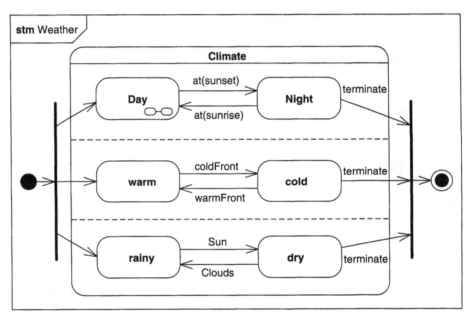

FIGURE 3.67

Example for fork and join.

A terminate state causes the state machine to exit without the context object taking on a new value configuration. Otherwise, it wouldn't be a termination, but a real new state—the final state. A terminate state is denoted as a cross without enclosing circle or rectangle (Figure 3.66).

Fork and join are similar to the elements of the same names from the activity diagram. A fork has one incoming transition and several outgoing transitions that lead to different states, positioned orthogonally to one another. This means that all target states are activated. The outgoing transitions may have neither conditions nor triggers (Figure 3.67).

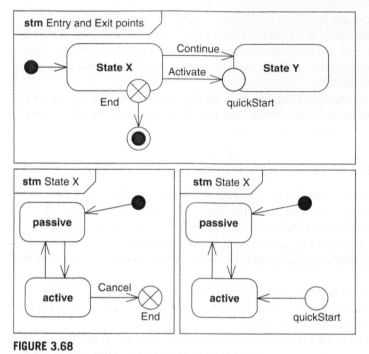

FIGURE 3.68

Entry and exit points.

In contrast, a join has several incoming transitions, which originate from states that are positioned orthogonally to one another, and one outgoing transition (Figure 3.67).

Both elements are denoted as filled bars. They differ in the context of incoming and outgoing transitions.

An entry point describes a special entry into a state machine. A transition leads from the entry point to a state of the state machine, or to one state each of every region in case of an orthogonal state.

An exit point terminates a state machine. If a transition from any region in the state machine reaches an exit point, then the state machine is terminated, and the transition originating from the exit point is activated.

An entry point is denoted as a white circle, and the exit point as a circle with a cross. Viewed from the outside the circle appears on the border of the corresponding state. In the inner view, transitions terminate or start at the circle (Figure 3.68).

3.8 Interaction Diagrams

In UML "interaction diagram" is a generic term for sequence diagram, communication diagram, timing diagram, and interaction overview diagram. Since SysML uses only the sequence diagram the other diagram types will not be discussed in detail in this book.

Sequence diagrams are based on the interaction model that describes the interaction between elements of the system. It answers the question: "When does who call whom and how?" In contrast, the activity model answers the question: "What happens in which sequence?", and the state model: "How does an object respond to events in a specific state?"

The other UML interaction diagrams that are not used by SysML are views on the same interaction model. This means that you don't lose any modeling potential, but only different options of representing the model.

3.8.1 Interaction

An interaction describes a communication between lifelines. This communication is based on the exchange of messages in the form of operation calls or signals.

An interaction describes a behavior of the system, just like an activity or a state machine. The elements of an interaction are essentially lifelines and messages. Lifelines represent communication partners, while messages represent the communication.

Interactions have no notation of their own. They are represented by the entire diagram (Figure 3.69), similar to state machines. In some cases, the diagram frame is included in the modeling (Figure 3.70).

An interaction describes a specific scenario. It represents the participating elements (communication partners) and the sequence showing who sends whom

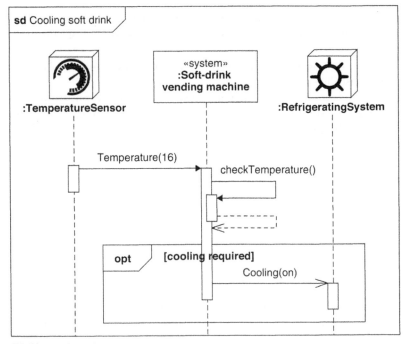

FIGURE 3-69

A sequence diagram, "cooling soft drink."

a message and when. The concrete scenario does not have to be complete. We model only messages that are of interest in the context of the interaction.

Sequence diagrams had not been invented together with UML. They are based on the *Message Sequence Charts* (*MSC*) of the *SDL* (*Specification and Description Language*) modeling language [36, 37]. In addition to UML and SysML, these charts are used in other languages too.

3.8.2 Lifeline

> **Definition**
>
> A **lifeline** represents a communication partner in an interaction. It describes the name, the type, and the lifecycle of the element.

A communication partner represented by a lifeline is a role. The same model element is also used in composite structure diagrams—the internal block diagram in SysML. This diagram shows who the role is connected with (i.e., with whom it can communicate). Here in the sequence diagram we can describe the actual communication.

The header of a lifeline is denoted similarly to the pertaining element from the composition structure diagram. If you are familiar with the sequence diagrams of UML 1 you will probably notice that the name of the lifeline is no longer underlined. The underscore is the notation for objects, and communication partners in UML 1 sequence diagrams are objects. In UML 2—and thus in SysML too—they are roles rather than objects. This is a minor formal difference that shouldn't irritate you in practice.

The body of a lifeline does justice to the name of the model element and is denoted as a dashed line. It shows the lifecycle of the object that assumes the role specified by the lifeline. If the object is destroyed during the interaction, then the line ends, and the destruction event is additionally shown with a cross (Figure 3.70).

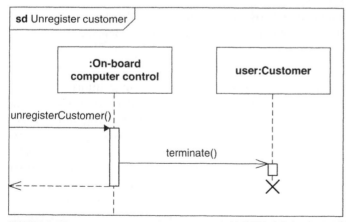

FIGURE 3-70

Destruction of a lifeline.

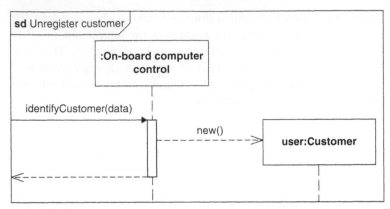

FIGURE 3-71

Creating an object in an interaction.

All lifelines end at the end of the interaction. However, unless there is a destruction event, the objects are not destroyed, but continue living even after the interaction. On the other hand, the header of the lifeline at the beginning of the interaction does not mean that the pertaining objects are only created at this point.

If an object comes into being in the course of an interaction, then the lifeline header is drawn accordingly further below. The message created by that object points directly to the header (Figure 3.71).

Bars can be used on the lifeline to show the positions at which the instance belonging to the lifeline is active (i.e., where it executes behavior) (Figure 3.71). The bar represents a so-called *execution focus*. This notation is optional. Active areas result automatically from incoming and outgoing messages.

3.8.3 Message

> **Definition**
>
> A **message** is a communication between two lifelines. It can be synchronous or asynchronous, and it can invoke an operation, transport a signal, or create an object.

Parts of the system send messages to each other to exchange information and jointly execute a behavior. In the sense of UML and particularly of SysML, this is not to be understood as mere operation calls in the context of a programming language. For example, if you model a pumping system that pumps a liquid from *A* to *B*, then this transmission can be seen as a message between *A* and *B* (send signal).

Both the transmission of a signal and the call of an operation are represented by a message. The notation is an arrow from the sender's lifeline to the receiver's lifeline. Different arrow shapes mark different characteristics of a message.

Figure 3.71 describes a message to create objects. The arrow is dashed. For all other forms of messages the arrow is solid, but with different arrowheads.

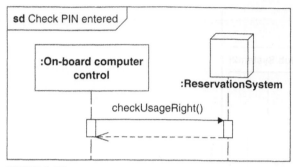

FIGURE 3-72

Example for a synchronous message.

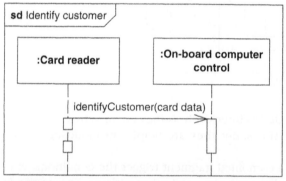

FIGURE 3.73

Example for an asynchronous message.

A synchronous message has a filled arrowhead (Figure 3.72). Synchronous means that the sender waits until the receiver has processed the message. The end (i.e., the return to the sender) is denoted by a dashed arrow.

An asynchronous message has an open arrowhead (Figure 3.73). Asynchronous means that the sender does not wait for the receiver; it can continue its own processing work immediately upon sending the message. This implies that the sender and the receiver are in different execution processes. There is no dashed return arrow here.

3.8.4 Combined Fragment

Definition

A **combined fragment** describes an expression, consisting of an interaction operator and interaction fragments as operands.

A sequence diagram represents a concrete scenario (i.e., an interaction between selected elements in a limited situation). This is the reason why loops and

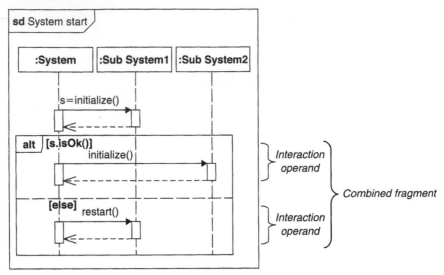

FIGURE 3-74

Example for the interaction operator "alt."

conditional branches are not needed as they are in activity diagrams, which describe sets of possible flows. But they are helpful in modeling simple variants of a flow.

The interaction operators of a combined fragment trigger the conditional execution of an operand, loops, parallel execution, and other variants. The operands are interaction fragments (i.e., a set of messages between lifelines).

A combined fragment is denoted similar to a diagram frame: a rectangle with solid lines and a small pentagon in the upper left corner. Interaction operators appear inside the pentagon. Interaction operands are separated by dashed lines. Depending on the operator, there are interaction conditions as well. They appear at the beginning of the interaction fragment near the first lifeline (Figure 3.74).

In total, there are 12 different interaction operators:

- Branches and loops: *alt*, *opt*, *break*, *loop*.
- Concurrency and order: *seq*, *strict*, *par operator*.
- Filters and constraints: *critical*, *neg*, *assert*, *consider*, *ignore*.

I will explain only a few selected operators in more detail below. You find a full description in [61].

Alternative flows are described with the interaction operator *alt*. There are two operands modeled in Figure 3.74. If subsystem 1 was initialized successfully, then subsystem 2 is also initialized. Otherwise, subsystem 1 is restarted.

The interaction operator *opt* is comparable to the operator *alt*. It is subject to the constraint that only one operand is permitted, which means that this is the operand that describes an optional flow.

The interaction operator *break* is similar to *opt*. They differ in that the enclosing interaction is terminated when the *break* operand has been traversed. In

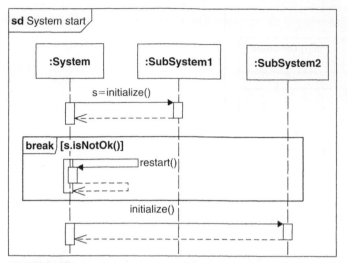

FIGURE 3-75

Example for the interaction operator "break."

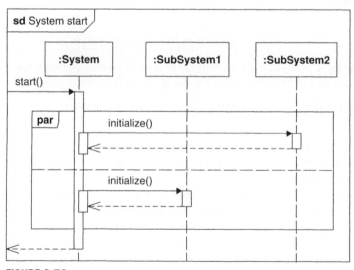

FIGURE 3-76

Example for the interaction operator "par."

Figure 3.75, the subsequent *initialize( )* call is not executed if the condition of the *break* operand is true.

Parallel fragments are marked with the interaction operator *par*. The two messages in Figure 3.76 can occur concurrently or in any sequence.

A loop is specified by the interaction operator *loop*. You can state a minimum and maximum number of loop traversals as well as a termination condition. The

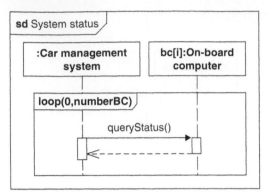

FIGURE 3.77

Example for the interaction operator "loop."

car management system in Figure 3.77 queries the status of all on-board computers (*numberBC*) in a loop.[18]

3.8.5 Interaction Use

Definitions

An **interaction use** is a reference to an interaction. The model is designed such that the reference could be substituted by the referenced interaction.

A **part decomposition** describes the internal interactions of a lifeline.

An interaction use is used to describe parts of interactions from one sequence diagram in a separate sequence diagram. This means that large interaction can be decomposed into manageable units.

Decomposing sequence diagrams into manageable sizes is only one benefit of an interaction use. The fact that it is possible to reference an interaction from within several different sequence diagrams is much more important. This helps avoid redundancies (i.e., several descriptions of the same interaction) and allows you to reuse the interaction.

An interaction use is denoted with the interaction operator *ref*, similar to a combined fragment. The name of the interaction is inside the fragment (Figure 3.78).

There is another decomposition mechanism, in addition to the interaction use. It allows us to decompose a single lifeline. It works like zooming into the lifeline. The reference to the detailed sequence diagram is denoted in the header underneath the name (Figure 3.79).

---

[18] This is a simplified representation; it does not show how each of the on-board computers is determined.

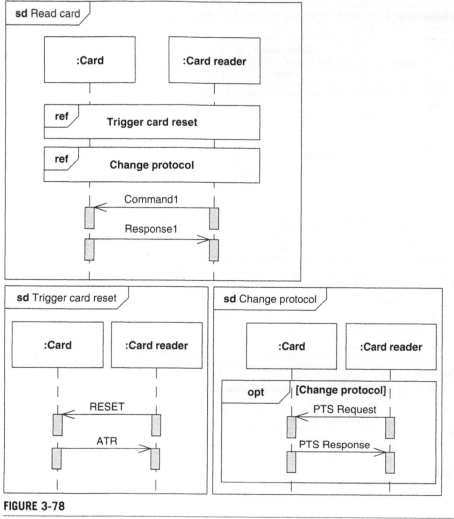

FIGURE 3-78

Example for an interaction use.

3.8.6 State Invariant

Definition

A **state invariant** is a constraint that refers to a lifeline, and which has to be met at system runtime.

A state invariant is a condition that is placed on a lifeline. It specifies that the pertaining instance fulfills the condition upon the next event occurring on that lifeline (e.g., sending or receiving a message).

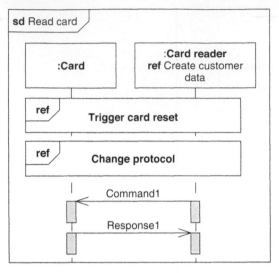

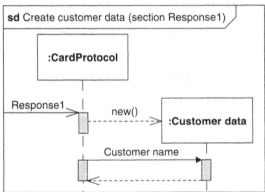

FIGURE 3-79

Example for a lifeline decomposition.

The condition is denoted within curly brackets on a lifeline. The expression can optionally be written within a comment symbol, which is then attached to the lifeline (Figure 3.80).

The third notation option explains the name of the state invariant. If the condition is formulated so that it describes a state from a state machine of the instance that belongs to the lifeline, then you can place the state symbol directly on the lifeline (Figure 3.80).

3.8.7 Time Constraints

UML knows a simple time model. It includes an option to describe and to measure a point in time or a period of time. The measured values can then be used to formulate time constraints.

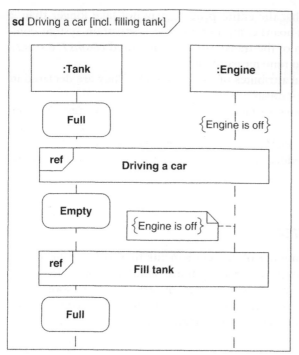

FIGURE 3-80

Example for a state invariant.

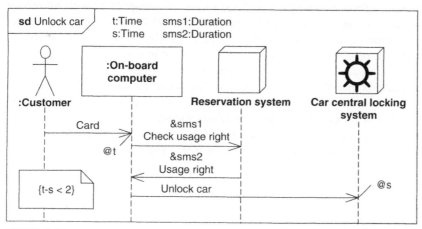

FIGURE 3-81

Example for time constraints.

This time model is not limited to interactions; it can also be used in other model areas. However, its most common use is in interaction diagrams.

In Figure 3.81, the time when the customer card is placed on the card reader (@*t*) and the time when the car doors are unlocked (@*s*) are measured. @ specifies the action at the measurement of time. The measured values are put into the time constraint and describe that the entire process may not take longer than 2 minutes ($\{t - s < 2\}$). The on-board computer and the reservation system communicate via SMS. The duration of the transmission is measured (&*sms1*, &*sms2*). & specifies the action subject to time measurement.

t, *s*, *sms1*, and *sms2* are local attributes of the interaction. They are declared in the upper area of the diagram (<name> : <Type>).

If you need more possibilities to model time aspects, you can use the concepts of the standardized UML Profile for *Modeling and Analysis of Real-Time and Embedded (MARTE)* systems[19] [49]. This profile was created for the development of real-time and embedded systems, but it can also be used in systems engineering.

3.9 The Package Diagram

Most models quickly reach a number of model elements that makes it necessary to somehow structure them, even for small systems. Similar to how directories group files on the hard disk, packages take care of structures in models. The grouping criterion is not explicitly modeled; it is up to the modeler to decide. The package diagram shows the packages and their relationships.

3.9.1 Package

A package groups model elements and forms a namespace.

In addition for forming groups, a package forms a namespace as well. All model elements contained can be identified by unique names. This means that no two elements of the same name can be in one package. The fully qualified name of an element reflects the nesting of namespaces with the double colon, for example, Use Cases::Car usage::Start car usage in Figure 3.82.

SysML demands that elements in diagrams that origin from another namespace than that represented by the diagram be specified with their fully qualified names.

The notation is based on the usual symbols for directories. The name of the package is in the center or on the folder tab, if the content of the package is represented. The contents can also be shown in tree structure using the include[20] relationship (Figure 3.82).

3.10 Other Model Elements

This section discusses UML model elements that do not fit in one of the previous categories such as the class diagram. They offer cross-section functions that can be used in a wide range of different areas. These elements include, for example, the information flow that shows the data flow in various diagrams.

---

[19] OMG is still working on the profile and will probably finalize it in 2007/2008.
[20] Not to be confused with the include relationship between use cases ($\Rightarrow$ page 173 (Section 3.5.3)).

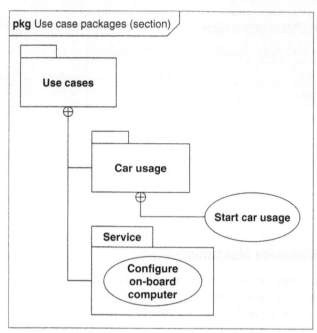

FIGURE 3-82

Example for a package.

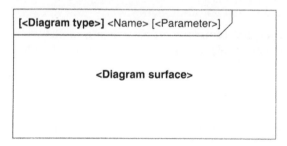

FIGURE 3-83

The notation for diagram frames.

3.10.1 Diagram Frame

All UML diagrams can be drawn with a frame. This is useful especially when you want to integrate your diagrams in a text document.

The frame is a rectangle with a diagram header in the upper left corner, which is separated by the other diagram surface by a pentagon (Figure 3.83).

The information shown in the diagram header includes the diagram type, the diagram name, and parameters, if applicable. All diagram types are specified in UML and described in Table 3.4.

Table 3.4 The UML diagram types.

Diagram Name and Type	Abbreviation
Activity diagram	act
Use case diagram	uc
Class diagram	–
Package diagram	pkg
Interaction diagram	sd
State machine diagram	stm

3.10.2 The Stereotype Extension Mechanism

UML would certainly not be what it is today if there weren't any stereotypes. It is the extension mechanism of stereotypes that allows UML to be generally described (i.e., *unified*) and that it can be used in specific projects. This means that the general UML vocabulary (e.g., use case) can be extended by adding domain-specific, approach-specific, or project-specific vocabulary, such as secondary use case (*«secondary»*).

Definitions

A **stereotype** adds more properties and semantics to an existing model element. A newly defined model element can also have a new notation, in addition to its name.

A **profile** is a set of stereotypes.

An extension extends a UML model element by additional properties that are defined by stereotypes.

Of course, the UML model elements are very general. For example, there is a *class*, but there is no *system*, or *subsystem*, or *hardware unit*, or *software unit*, and so on. The wide range of class categories can be extended by stereotypes. This allows us to extend the UML vocabulary.

In the simplest case a stereotype defines a name and some additional semantics. In Figure 3.84, you can see the definition of the stereotype *EnvironmentalEffect*. The stereotype itself is denoted similar to a class, but with the keyword *«stereotype»*.

The basis of a stereotype—the UML model element—is also denoted like a class, with the keyword *«metaclass»*. The relationship between the two elements is a so-called *extension*. Its notation is an arrow with a solid line and filled arrowhead. Other properties that the stereotype can define are listed as attributes in the stereotype symbol. They are also commonly called *tagged values*. In Figure 3.85, you can see the stereotype definition *Requirement* from SysML.

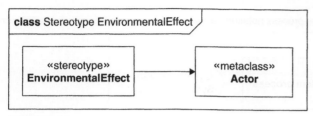

FIGURE 3-84

Example for defining a stereotype, EnvironmentalEffect.

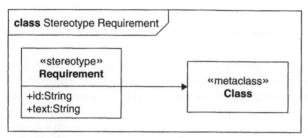

FIGURE 3-85

Example for a stereotype with properties.

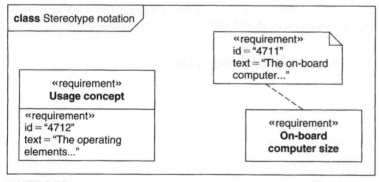

FIGURE 3-86

Example for stereotype notation.

When using the new vocabulary, the name of the stereotype appears within Guillemets[21] near the name of the stereotyped model element (Figure 3.86).

The stereotype properties are listed in a comment symbol for reasons of space (Figure 3.86). The name of the stereotype is shown at the beginning to distinguish the symbol from a regular comment, followed by the values of the stereotype properties.

Since UML 2.1.1, stereotype properties can alternatively be denoted in a separate compartment within the stereotyped model element, provided that the model element supports compartments. This is the case with the class in Figure 3.86, for

---

[21] French quotation marks, also called "angle quotes."

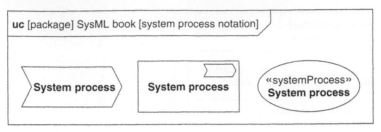

FIGURE 3-87

Example for a stereotype symbol.

example. Of course, this is not possible with relationship elements, such as association or dependency.

If a new symbol is defined for a stereotype, then it can be used instead of the UML notation. A third notation option lets you mix the two symbols. Figure 3.87 uses the system process element, which is a stereotype of the use case, to demonstrate the notation variants.

A profile is a special package that groups stereotypes. Using a profile is the only way to assign a stereotype to a model and use it there (Figure 3.88). There are standardized profiles, such as the *UML Testing Profile* [53], or the UML Profile for *MARTE* systems [49]. This profile includes stereotypes that define test vocabulary (e.g., *test case* or *test context*) to describe a test model. Chapter 5 describes the SYSMOD profile that introduces the SYSMOD approach in this book.

3.10.3 Information Item and Information Flow

Definitions

An **information item** is an abstract UML concept used to model the existence and transmission of information on a rough level.

An **information flow** is a directed relationship between actors, use cases, classes, ports, roles, interfaces, or packages. The relationship expresses that information can be exchanged between these elements.

The information flow concept is the data flow modeling of UML. This concept had been introduced in UML 2. UML 1 lets you model the flowing of data only implicitly, for example, as messages in sequence diagrams, or as object flows in activity diagrams. However, these levels are rather concrete, requiring a view onto the system that are rich in details. Seen on a more abstract level, the exchange of messages between objects could be an exchange of information between actor and use case. From this perspective, the information flow is to be understood as a kind of comment that reflects a concrete detailed exchange of data on a coarser level.

An information item is denoted with a rectangle, like a class. In addition, there is a black triangle in the upper right corner (Figure 3.89). No additional information can be stated, such as attributes and operations with classes.

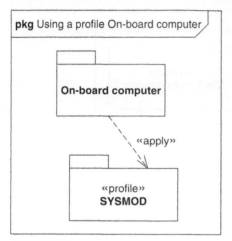

FIGURE 3-88

Example for using a profile.

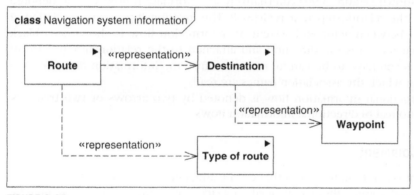

FIGURE 3-89

Example for information structures.

Information structures are modeled using representation relationships. The notation is a dashed arrow with the keyword *«representation»*. Figure 3.89 shows that the route represents a destination and the type of route (fast, short, country road, and so on). Multiplicities are not permitted for this relationship.

In addition to information structures, you can also use the representation relationship to connect an abstract information element with a concrete design element from the model. For example, the design class *Waypoint* in Figure 3.89 is represented by the information item *destination* on an abstract level.

Information items flow through the system in the sense that they get from one element to another element. For example, status information flows from the system class *on-board computer* to the actor *car management system* (Figure 3.90). How the information is transported does not yet play a role in information flow modeling.

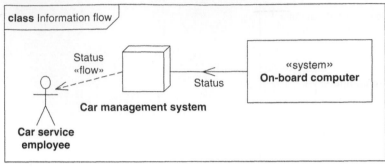

FIGURE 3-90

Notations for information flows.

An information flow is denoted as a dashed arrow with the keyword *«flow»*. At the arrow appear information items, separated by commas, which flow in the direction shown (Figure 3.90). Alternatively, an information flow can be denoted directly at the relationship that realizes it. This relationship is an association, if the flow is between actor and system. An information flow is shown as a black triangle that indicates the direction and attached to the relationship. In case of associations you have to be careful not to confuse the information flow with the direction in which the association names are read.

A bi-directional information flow is denoted by two arrows or two triangles. There are no real bi-directional information flows.

3.10.4 Comment

A comment is a note in text form that can be attached to any element.

In all model areas there is a need to place comments. A comment may be required either to point open issues, or to explain a complicated situation, or to provide general information for the reader.

A comment is denoted as a rectangle with a dog ear on the upper right corner, and it is attached to the commented element by a dashed line.

The comment symbol is often used in UML to capture free text in a diagram. For example, you can denote a constraint in comment form. In this case, however, it is merely the comment notation but not a real comment. A constraint appears in the model.

3.10.5 Constraint

Definition

A **constraint** is a condition that always has to be met, and which restricts the semantics of model elements.

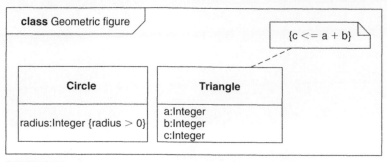

FIGURE 3-91

Example for constraints.

A constraint is a Boolean expression in either a natural language or a machine-readable language. It refers to one or several model elements and restricts their semantics.

A constraint is denoted within curly brackets (Figure 3.91). You can optionally state a name in front of the Boolean expression and separate from it by a colon. A constraint is denoted either directly next to the model element concerned, or in a comment symbol that is attached to the model element (Figure 3.91).

SysML—The Systems Modeling Language

4

"Learn the rules so you know how to break them properly."

(14th Dalai Lama)

The *Unified Modeling Language (UML)* was originally specified as a modeling language for software development. Thanks to its wide proliferation and its integrated extension mechanisms, such as stereotypes, it has been used successfully in other areas as well. Together with the new UML Version 2.0, the bandwidth of its use possibilities has been further extended (see, e.g., [33]). One field of use that has moved closer into focus is systems engineering.

Systems engineering is a discipline that has not had a uniform modeling language. It requires a language that is independent of specific disciplines like software, hardware, or mechanics. UML 2 looks like a good candidate. First, it meets the most important requirements of systems engineering, and second, it is already popular and widely used. In addition, there is a considerable amount of literature, and many seminar programs are offered. The mighty extension mechanisms of this language allow you to adapt it to the needs of systems engineering.

The *International Council of Systems Engineering (INCOSE)*—the worldwide systems engineering organization—set itself the objective in 2001 to establish UML as a standard language for systems engineering. The language has been expanded by several elements, such as a possibility to explicitly model requirements and continuous systems. The adapted UML is called *Systems Modeling Language*, or *SysML* for short.

Now, UML is pretty extensive. This is one of the points the language is criticized on. Nevertheless, more elements have been added. To ensure that SysML will not get too big, even elements explicit to UML but not required in systems engineering are excluded (Figure 4.1). This includes, for example, components that are too much on the software side for systems engineering, and several rather exotic elements for class modeling, such as *power types* and *package merge*. The core of object orientation—classes, objects, inheritance—are moved into the background. An electrical or mechanical engineer won't first have to study object orientation to be able to use SysML. Accordingly, the UML chapter (Chapter 3) describes only those elements of UML that directly or indirectly belong to SysML.

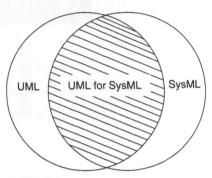

FIGURE 4-1

SysML = UML++−−.

The most important extensions or changes to UML are:

- Classes are called *blocks*. In SysML, the UML class diagram is called *block definition diagram*.
- The UML composite structure diagram is called *internal block diagram* in SysML.
- Item flows between elements in the internal block diagram can be modeled.
- Continuous functions are supported by action and object nodes in activity diagrams, and *Enhanced Functional Flow Block Diagrams (EFFBD)* are also supported.
- New diagram types were added: the requirement diagram and the parametric diagram.
- The ISO AP-233 data format was added to support the exchange of data between different tools.

4.1 History

SysML is a very young language, and its history is accordingly short. Nevertheless it is rewarding to have a look at how it was born to better understand its objectives and structures.

UML has been used in many systems engineering projects, mainly those heavily inclined to the software side, but it lacked a standardized extension. Such an extension was required to satisfy special needs, including, for example, ways to model different forms of requirements, support for continuous functions, and decomposition structures. In September 2001, the *Object Management Group (OMG)*, together with *INCOSE*, founded the *Systems Engineering Domain Special Interest Group (SE DSIG)* [20] to develop a standardized extension of UML to be used as a modeling language for the specification, the design, and the verification of complex Systems. According to the standardization process of OMG [34], a *Request for Information (RFI)* [40] was published in February 2002 to obtain information about requirements to the UML extension. In March 2003, based on the responses to the RFI, a *Request for Proposal (RFP)* entitled "UML for Systems Engineering" [47] was formulated to describe a rough framework and invite submissions of specific proposals.

A work group by the name of *SysML Partners* was formed in May 2003. They called their proposal for the requested extension *Systems Modeling Language (SysML)*. This work group was composed of various representatives from the industry (e.g., Lockheed Martin Corporation, Deere & Company, oose Innovative Informatik GmbH), governmental authorities (e.g., NASA/JPL, NIST), modeling tool manufacturers (e.g., IBM, Telelogic, ARTiSAN Software Tools, EmbeddedPlus Engineering), and other cooperatives (e.g., INCOSE, ISO AP-233).

A first draft of the language was submitted to OMG in October 2003. In Summer 2005, the SysML Partners work group split-up into two (*SysML Partners* and *SysML Submission Team*) due to disputes. In November 2005, the two groups submitted competing SysML specifications to OMG. This caused some confusion in the public perception of this work, the more so as the two specifications had two different version numbers.

At the beginning of 2006, the two separate work groups found together again (*SysML Merge Team*). Eventually, there was a common specification in the end of the entire process, avoiding a crucial vote. At first sight, the separation of the work group appeared to have been destructive. A closer look in arrears reveals, however, that it was rather healthy, encouraging a creative process, and it had a positive effect on the quality of the SysML specification.

At the end of April 2006, at the occasion of the OMG Meeting in St. Louis, SysML was accepted as a standard. At that time, the specification was "frozen" and ready to be used in practice without fearing that there might be more changes. The final standardization process took almost a year and fine-tuned the specification. OMG published SysML™ Version 1.0 as an official standard in September 2007.

Naturally this doesn't mean that the development of SysML is over. SysML Version 1.0 certainly contains errors, and some language elements are still missing. Just as UML evolved from Version 0.9 to 1.5 and finally to 2.1.1, there will be successor versions of SysML, reflecting the experiences gained from practical use. You can report errors or suggest improvements directly to OMG. You can find the online form on the OMG Internet pages at *http://www.omg.org/technology/issuesform.htm*.

The *SysML Revision Task Force* is currently working on Version 1.1, which is scheduled for publication in the first half of 2008. Many companies and individuals from the *SysML Merge Team* are active in this task force, including myself as the representative of oose Innovative Informatik GmbH.

4.2 Structure and Concepts

Since SysML and UML are closely related, their structures and concepts are very similar (see Section 3.2). While SysML is an extension of UML, it omits UML elements (Figure 4.1).

The extensions introduced to SysML are restricted to stereotypes and several new diagrams. The stereotypes can be defined in any UML tool. No special SysML

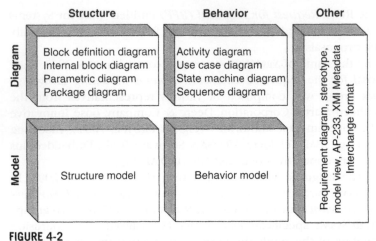

FIGURE 4-2

The structure of SysML.

tool is required. Only the new diagrams require some special support. But this concerns only the diagram level, and not the model. Nevertheless, a SysML modeling tool can naturally support the language better and offer suitable functions.

The fact that several UML elements are missing doesn't play a major role in practice. All SysML tools available so far and planned for the near future are UML tools extended by the SysML language set. The UML elements left out in SysML are still present in the modeling tool and can be used as usual. However, you should be aware of the fact that your model is then neither an UML model nor a SysML model, but a mixed form. This means that you will depend on tools that support such mixed forms. That's no standard.

We can distinguish both between model and diagram and between structure and behavior. The area of the elements to which neither structure nor behavior can be allocated is much larger in SysML than it is in UML, and it includes one of the new diagram forms: the requirement diagram (Figure 4.2).

The extension mechanism of UML (profiles, stereotypes) is also part of SysML. This means that you can define new vocabulary on the basis of existing elements to adapt the language to your needs (see also Chapter 5).

You can see various SysML diagram types in Figure 4.3. The diagrams that are new to SysML, compared to UML, and UML diagrams that were changed in SysML are highlighted. All diagram types not highlighted in the figure were added to SysML from UML in unchanged form. The concepts and artifacts described in the UML chapter (Chapter 3) also apply to SysML.

4.3 **The Requirement Diagram**

SysML defines several elements to describe and model requirements, such as response times, size or functions of a system, which means that it closes a gap in UML. While functional requirements can be modeled with use cases, there is no element in UML to explicitly describe non-functional requirements.

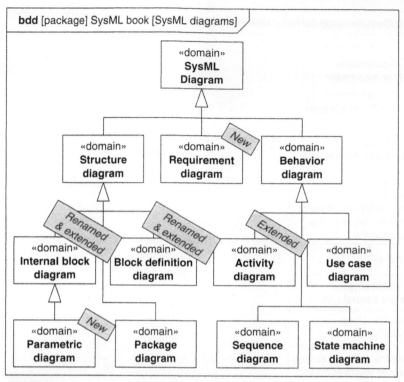

FIGURE 4-3

SysML diagrams.

However, since such elements are needed in practice, a number of different proposals emerged in the course of time to allow you to model requirements using UML. Most of these proposals are based on the definition of special stereotypes. One of these proposals is SysML. It differs from the other proposals particularly in that it is standardized and explicitly supported by tools. To support requirement modeling, SysML has a separate diagram type that shows requirements and their relationships to other model elements (Figure 4.4).

4.3.1 Requirement

Definition

A **requirement** describes one or more properties or behaviors of a system that always have to be met.

It is a stereotype *«requirement»* of the UML element *class*.

Requirements describe a contract between the principal and all those who create the system design and implement the system. A requirement specifies flows or conditions that have to be met by the system.

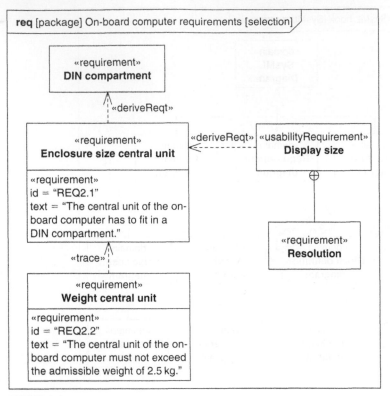

FIGURE 4-4

Example for a requirement diagram.

A requirement is a stereotyped class. This means that a requirement has the semantics of a class, extended by the specific semantics and properties of the stereotype, which will be discussed below.

Two elementary properties of a requirement are a unique identifier (ID) and a descriptive text. They are attributes of the stereotype, which means that they can be described for any modeled requirement.

The ID is a simple string. It is up to the tool or to the modeler to ensure that it is unique. SysML does not dictate a structure for the ID.

The explanatory text is also a simple string. It includes a description of the requirement itself or references an external source, for example, a legal code or a data record in a requirement management tool. In the latter case, the original requirements is stored externally, while the SysML requirement is merely a reference in the model to produce the connection to design and test elements.

Operations are not permitted. Functional requirements are described in more detail in other model elements, such as use cases or interfaces, but not by using operations with the requirement element itself. Attributes are not permitted either.

These two properties of a requirement (ID, text) are not attributes of the requirement itself, but modeled as attributes of the stereotype *«requirement»*. Other properties, such as a priority, can be introduced over an independent

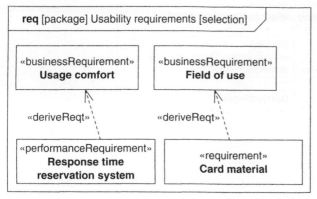

FIGURE 4-5

Example for a derive requirement.

extension of the stereotype. This also includes the introduction of requirement categories (e.g., usability requirements). Section 5.3 describes the extensions for requirements in the SYSMOD profile.

Since requirements are pure specification elements, it wouldn't make sense to create instances of requirements. For this reason, requirements are always abstract.

Requirements must not be generalized. And it wouldn't make much sense, because they have neither operations nor attributes to inherit.

The stereotype *«requirement»* is defined without a notation of its own. This means that the standard notation for stereotypes applies (Figure 4.4).

The term *feature* is often used synonymously for requirement. Unfortunately, there is no uniform definition of this term. It is one of those unfortunate words that are used in almost all projects without having clear definitions of its meaning. This causes many minor misunderstandings that, in total, can lead to serious problems.

4.3.2 The Derive Requirement Relationship

> **Definition**
>
> A **derive requirement** relationship describes that a requirement was derived from another requirement.
>
> It is a stereotype *«deriveReqt»* of the UML element *abstraction*.

Business requirements can result in technical requirements which, in turn, can lead to other requirements. The *derive requirement* relationship shows these relations explicitly. It is permitted only between requirements.

You may already be familiar with the UML *«derive»* relationship, or with derived attributes or associations. The term *derive* is used a lot in UML. To make sure it is not "overstressed," SysML introduces a separate relationship.

The derive requirement relationship is denoted as a dashed arrow with stereotype *«deriveReqt»*. It is read in direction of the arrowhead, as we read in Figure 4.5,

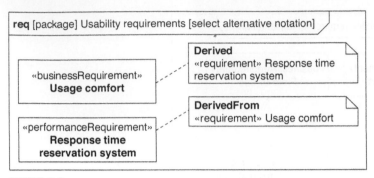

FIGURE 4-6

Alternative notation for the derive requirement relationship.

for example: *The response time of the reservation system is derived from the business requirement usage comfort.*

There are cases when we don't want to represent all elements participating in a derive requirement relationship in the diagram. Figure 4.6 shows the derive requirement relationship from Figure 4.5 in the form of comment symbols—the so-called *callout notation*. This example shows all elements in the diagram for better understanding.

The term *derive* is often used for the generalization relationship as well. You should be careful in discussions and during your modeling work not to confuse the term to avoid misunderstandings.

4.3.3 Namespace Containment

> **Definition**
>
> A **namespace containment** describes that a requirement is contained in another requirement.

Requirements are on different hierarchical levels. Very general requirements that have rather the status of a heading contain more specific, more detailed requirements. A namespace containment shows this relation. It is subject to the rule that the master requirement is satisfied when all of its sub-requirements are satisfied.

Formally the relationship means that a requirement is present in the namespace of the master requirement. The consequence is that a requirement must not contain requirements by the same name, which makes sense. Another consequence is that a requirement must not concurrently be part of more than one requirement.[1] This latter rule contradicts the need to reuse requirements in other contexts. SysML offers the *copy relationship* to this end.

---

[1] You can think of namespaces in SysML as directories on your hard disk. The elements in a namespace correspond to files.

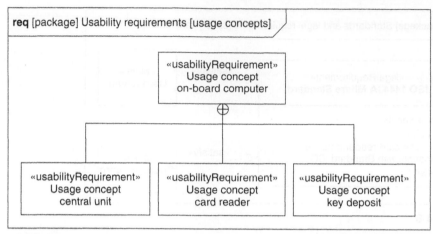

FIGURE 4-7

Example for a namespace containment.

The namespace containment corresponds to the UML notation for the representation of nested classes (think of "inner class"): a circle with a cross, from which starts a line to the contained element (Figure 4.7).

4.3.4 Satisfy Relationship

Definition

A **satisfy relationship** describes that a design element satisfies a requirement.

It is a stereotype *«satisfy»* of the UML relationship *realization*.

Each design element in your model has the direct or indirect purpose of satisfying a requirement to the system. You could also say: The design element realizes that requirement. For this reason, *«satisfy»* is a stereotype for the UML relationship *realization*. If this relation is modeled, then it can be seen what effect changes to the design will have to the requirements. Vice-versa, you can identify the design elements concerned by changes to the requirements.

The startup element for the satisfy relationship can be any arbitrary model element. Naturally, it makes sense to use a comprehensive element of the design (i.e., a package or block). On a level with too fine granularity the cost of modeling would exceed the benefit.

The notation deviates from the standard notation for UML *realization*. SysML uses the notation as a dashed arrow with normal arrowhead and the keyword *«satisfy»* (Figure 4.8).

It is not always meaningful to explicitly draw the relationship in the diagram. Figure 4.9 shows the same scenario from Figure 4.8. We normally don't represent the elements all together in one diagram when we use this notation.[2]

---

[2] In this case, explicitly drawing the relationship would be clearer.

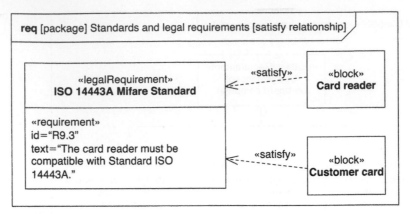

FIGURE 4-8

Example for a satisfy relationship.

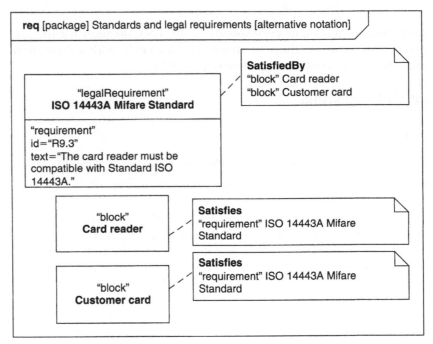

FIGURE 4-9

Alternative notation for the satisfy relationship.

The satisfy relationship does not state whether the requirement is satisfied in full or only in part. You can easily add this information by using a comment or a stereotype. If a requirement is satisfied by several design elements, then you can express this alternatively by using one single relationship. In theory, the satisfy relationship can have several source and target elements. Figure 4.10 shows one single satisfy relationship, which interconnects several elements. In practice, this will most likely fail due to a lack in support by the SysML/UML modeling tool.

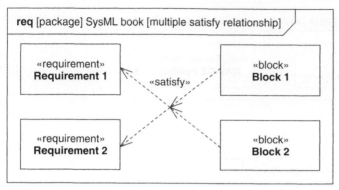

FIGURE 4-10

Relationship with several source and target elements.

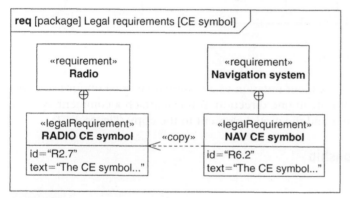

FIGURE 4-11

Example for a copy relationship.

4.3.5 Copy Relationship

> ### Definition
>
> A **copy relationship** describes that a requirement is a copy of another requirement.
>
> It is a stereotype *«copy»* as a specialization of the UML stereotype *«trace»*.

There is often a need in the requirement model to reuse a requirement in another context. This can lead to formal problems in connection with the containment requirement (see discussion in Section 4.3.3). The copy relationship was introduced for this reason, and to enable the use in different contexts.

The copy relationship allows you to create a copy that is maintained consistently with the original. The name and the ID may be different though. The requirement text is write-protected in the copy and always identical with the original.

The copy relationship is denoted as a dashed arrow pointing from the copy to the original and with the stereotype *«copy»* (Figure 4.11).

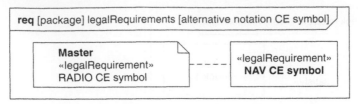

FIGURE 4-12

Alternative notation for copy relationships.

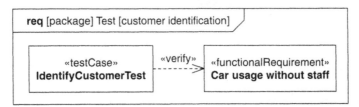

FIGURE 4-13

Example for a verify relationship.

SysML lets you use the callout notation as an alternative notation for the copy relationship as well, but only in one direction. You can attach a comment symbol with the keyword *master* and the model element to the copy (Figure 4.12).

4.3.6 Verify Relationship

Definition

A **verify relationship** connects a test case with the requirement that is verified by that test case.

It is a stereotype *«verify»* as a specialization of the UML stereotype *«trace»*.

The test model normally defines a large number of test cases that test whether or not the requirements are correctly implemented by the system. The verify relationship describes which test case tests which requirement.

It is denoted as a dashed arrow with the stereotype *«verify»*. The arrow points in the direction from the test case to the requirement (Figure 4.13).

The callout notation, which is valid for almost all relationships between requirements, allows you to use an alternative notation to show that an element participates in a verify relationship. Figure 4.14 shows the same scenario from Figure 4.13 in this alternative notation. This notation allows you to represent the verify relationship without the need to use the arrow to all participating elements (i.e., you don't have to show all participating elements in the diagram).

The verify relationship doesn't say anything about the completeness of the test case with regard to the requirement. Similarly to the satisfy relationship, you can use a comment or stereotype to add this information. You could actually use several source and target elements, but this normally fails due to the modeling tool in practice.

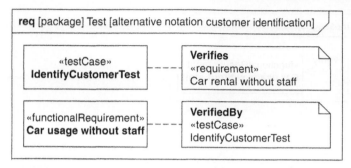

FIGURE 4-14

Alternative notation for verify relationships.

4.3.7 Test Case

Definition

A **test case** is a flow that checks whether or not the system satisfies a requirement.

It is a stereotype *«testCase»* of the UML elements *operation* and *behavior*.

SysML does not offer any model elements to build an extensive test model. Extensive test models can be built with the *UML Testing Profile* [53]. This profile consists of a set of stereotypes you can use to extend your SysML or UML toolbox and test vocabulary.

As far as testing is concerned there is only a test case in SysML. This element is probably sufficient for simple models. However, it was primarily defined to create a kind of basis for a more extensive testing languages, such as the *UML Testing Profile*.

A test case is a stereotype for the model elements *behavior*—that is, activity, interaction, state machine, and free behavior[3]—and *operation*. You can use these elements for a detailed and executable description of a test case (i.e., describing concrete executable testing steps). The notation is a rectangle with the name of the test case and the stereotype *«testCase»* (Figure 4.15).

4.3.8 Refine Relationship

Definition

A **refine relationship** specifies that a model element describes the properties of a requirement in more detail.

It is a standard stereotype *«refine»* of the UML *abstraction* relationship.

---

[3] SysML/UML allows you to define behavior in an arbitrary language (e.g., a programming language) or a natural language, such as English or German. Free behavior is formally called *OpaqueBehavior* [61].

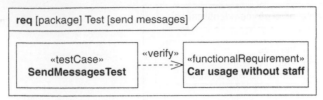

FIGURE 4-15

Test case example.

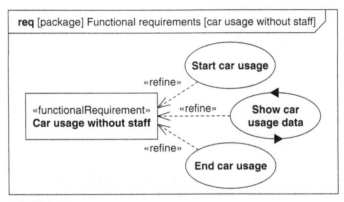

FIGURE 4-16

A refine example.

A requirement is a rather coarse model element. In addition to the name and an ID, you can add some text to describe a requirement. This is not sufficient for a detailed description.

For example, a functional requirement can be refined by one or more use cases (Figure 4.16).

This relationship is used only within the model. It does not serve for refining by external sources, such as a requirement management tool. For this purpose, you'd use the text property of the requirement, which references an external source.

SysML takes this relationship unchanged from UML, but it adds an alternative notation that let's you denote the relationship within a comment symbol (Figure 4.17).

4.3.9 Trace Relationship

Definition

A **trace relationship** is a relationship between a requirement and an arbitrary model element; it describes a general relation for traceability reasons only.

It is a standard stereotype *«trace»* of the UML *abstraction* relationship.

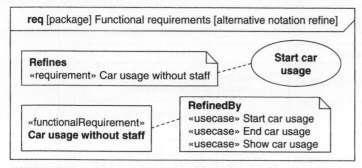

FIGURE 4-17

Alternative notation for refine.

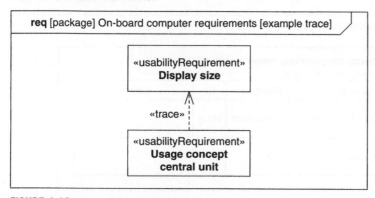

FIGURE 4-18

Example for a trace relationship.

The trace relationship is very general, and its semantics is accordingly weak. It expresses that the model elements have a relationship without specifying this relationship in more detail. The sole purpose of a trace relationship is to create traceability between elements. It does not state why there is a relation.

SysML takes this relationship unchanged from UML, but it adds an alternative notation, similarly to using a comment symbol (Figure 4.17) for the refine relationship. In this case, it uses the keywords *TracedTo* and *TracedFrom*. This alternative notation is useful especially when the participating model elements should not or cannot appear in a diagram.

You can see an example for trace in Figure 4.18. In this example, the usability concept is related to the display size.

4.3.10 Table Notation

Many people like to represent requirements in pure text form—most frequently in tables—rather than in graphical form. This is meaningful mainly when you want to display total overviews of several hundred or thousand requirements (requirements list). SysML offers a table notation. The table is a diagram extension

table [package] On-board computer requirements		
ID	**Name**	**Text**
R1	Car rental without staff	The cars must be picked up and returned by customers without assistance.
R2.1	Enclosure size	The on-board computer has to fit in a DIN compartment.
R2.2	On-board computer weight	The on-board computer must not exceed the admissible weight of 2.5 kg.

FIGURE 4-19

Table notation for requirements.

table [package] On-board computer requirements [with relationships]				
ID	**Name**	**Relation**	**ID**	**Name**
R1	Car rental without staff	deriveReqt	R7.8	...
R2.1	Enclosure size	trace	...	

FIGURE 4-20

Table notation for requirements with relationships.

that cannot be defined by stereotypes. It has to be explicitly supported by the modeling tool.

The columns of a requirements table represent the properties of the ID and the requirement text (Figure 4.19) as well as the relationships of that requirement to other requirements (Figure 4.20).

4.4 Allocation

An allocation is a general mechanism from the field of systems engineering to interconnect elements from different model areas. For example, binding an item flow in the internal block diagram, which occurs in a different form, as an object flow, in an activity diagram (Figure 4.21). Such a binding is normally present in a complete model through a wealth of details and deeply hidden paths, and not visible at a glance. A systems engineer cannot penetrate these detail depths. Nevertheless, they want to model the connections, even in an early project phase.

There are different types of allocations. SysML proposes three general types and let's the developer introduce additional project-specific variants. The predefined types are behavior allocation, structure allocation, and object flow allocation.

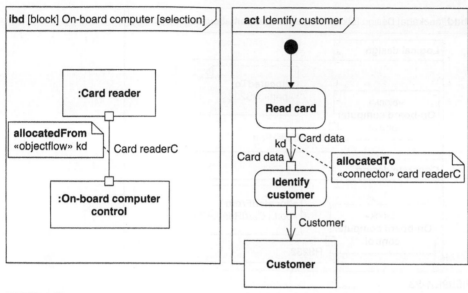

FIGURE 4-21

Example for an object flow allocation.

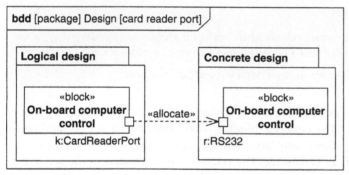

FIGURE 4-22

The notation for allocations.

The object flow allocation is used to connect an item flow in a structure diagram with an object flow edge in an activity diagram (Figure 4.21).

The structure allocation allows you to separate logical structures from physical structures. In a first approach, the systems engineer can build the system logically, while building the concrete hardware structure of the system in a second step. The structure allocation binds elements of both levels. You can see examples in Figure 2.81 and Figure 4.22.

The behavior allocation is used to allocate a behavior (e.g., an activity, or a single action) to a block that realizes this behavior.

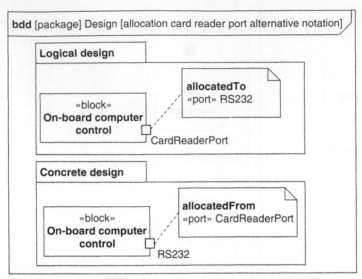

FIGURE 4-23

Alternative notation for allocations.

4.4.1 Allocation

Definition

An **allocation** is an abstract relationship between elements of different type, or on different levels. It allocates a target element to one or more source elements.

It is a stereotype *«allocate»* of the UML element *abstraction*.

Common aspects such as structure and behavior are initially considered separately in the modeling work.[4] The concrete binding—say, behavior *XY* is executed on or by a structure *ABC*—follows only later. The allocation relationship allows you to express this relation in an early stage. The relationship is abstract in the sense that it describes, for example, how a behavior is allocated to a structure, but doesn't say anything about how exactly this allocation looks like.

An allocation is denoted as a dashed arrow with the keyword *«allocate»*. Figure 4.22 shows a structure allocation in this notation.

Similarly to the notation variants for requirement relationships, you can alternatively denote an allocation in a comment symbol at the target and source elements, instead of using a dashed line (callout notation). This is necessary because elements are often in different diagram types (e.g., in an activity diagram and in an internal block diagram) (Figure 4.21), never appearing jointly in one single diagram. Accordingly, we cannot use the arrow notation. You can see the alternative notation for the scenario in Figure 4.22 and Figure 4.23.

---

[4] The strict separation of structure and behavior is not object-oriented. A particular characteristic of an object (block) is the unification of structure and behavior in the form of attributes and operations. This corresponds to objects in the real world.

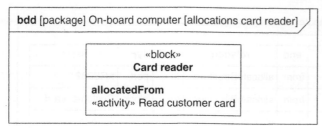

FIGURE 4-24

Other alternative notation for allocations.

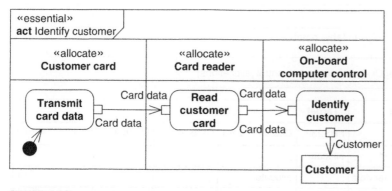

FIGURE 4-25

Example for an allocate activity partition.

When representing allocations we have several options. You already saw two notation forms. There is a third notation for elements that supports compartments, such as blocks (Figure 4.24). The domains are denoted with the keywords *allocatedFrom* and *allocatedTo*.

4.4.2 Allocate Activity Partition

Definition

An **allocate activity partition** is a special activity partition that allocates each action within that partition to the structure that represents this partition.

It is a stereotype *«allocateActivityPartition»* of the UML element *activity partition*.

An activity partition puts actions into groups based on common features. The allocate activity partition restricts the grouping criteria. The common features of actions within an allocate activity partition form a block to which these actions are allocated. This means that an action is the target element (the *from* end) of an allocation relationship, while the structure is the source element (the *to* end). The allocate activity partition is a behavior allocation (Figure 4.25).

table [package] On-board computer control [allocations]

type	name	end	relation	end	type	name
port	k:Card readerPort	from	allocateStructure	to	port	r:RS232
action	Transmit card data	from	allocateBehavior	to	block	Customer card
action	Read customer card	from	allocateBehavior	to	block	Card reader
action	Identify customer	from	allocateBehavior	to	block	On-board computer control

FIGURE 4-26

Allocation relationships in table notation.

matrix [package] On-board computer control [allocations]

Source	Target			
	r:RS232	Customer card	Card reader	On-board computer control
k:Card readerPort	allocate			
Transmit customer data		allocate		
Read customer card			allocate	
Identify customer				allocate

FIGURE 4-27

Allocation relationships in matrix notation.

4.4.3 Table Notation

In addition to the requirement diagrams, SysML extends also the area of allocations by a way to represent allocation relationships in table notation (Figure 4.26).

An additional matrix representation is defined as well (Figure 4.27). This representation is of general interest for all types of relationships, but presently SysML describes it only for allocations.

4.5 Block Diagrams

The central elements in object orientation are classes and objects. Closely related to classes are components in UML as well. Since the two terms are historically at home in the software development discipline, SysML doesn't use them in this form. All static concepts and objects are blocks in SysML.

Blocks describe the structure of a system. They possess information about the block itself (attribute), or they reference other blocks they are bound with

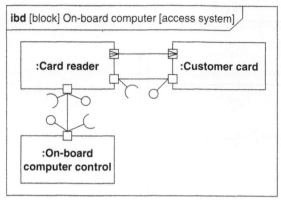

FIGURE 4-28

Card reader in the on-board computer.

(association). In addition to the purely static structure, blocks also describe operations (i.e., behavior they can execute).

Formally blocks are stereotyped classes. Apart from some notation differences, the same as described in the UML chapter applies to them: SysML uses the term *block definition diagram* instead of *class diagram* (as in UML; Section 3.3) and the term *internal block diagram* instead of *composite structure diagram* (as in UML; Section 3.4).

Blocks describe a system as a collection of parts that each play a certain role in a defined context. Look at this specific example: The construction plan of the *card reader* block is described in the block definition diagram (Figure 4.29) and its role is described in the context of the *on-board computer* in an internal block diagram of the on-board computer (Figure 4.28).

4.5.1 Block

Definition

A block describes parts of the structure of a related system.

It is a stereotype *«block»* of the UML element *class*.

Together with the block, SysML defines an element to be used for describing the static structure of systems. A block can be both a logical and a physical unit (software, hardware, functional blocks, and so on).

The notation deviates slightly from the standard representation of stereotyped classes. The stereotype name *«block»* can also be omitted in the notation. Note that I always show it in this book to emphasize the difference to an UML class.

The single compartments of the block rectangle are denoted with a heading each (Figure 4.29). The heading for values of the block is *values*. Values are attributes with either an UML data type or a SysML value type. For example, the value *operatingTemperature* in Figure 4.29 has an interval as its distribution definition.

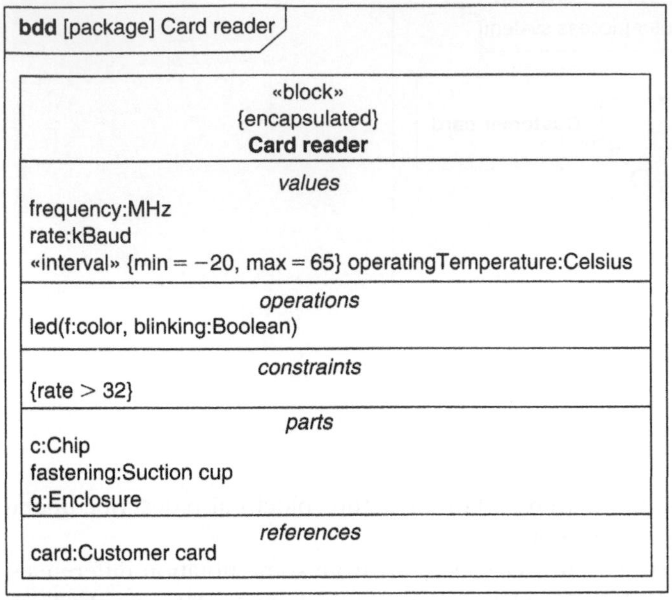

```
bdd [package] Card reader

                        «block»
                     {encapsulated}
                       Card reader
                          values
  frequency:MHz
  rate:kBaud
  «interval» {min = −20, max = 65} operatingTemperature:Celsius
                        operations
  led(f:color, blinking:Boolean)
                        constraints
  {rate > 32}
                           parts
  c:Chip
  fastening:Suction cup
  g:Enclosure
                        references
  card:Customer card
```

FIGURE 4-29

The notation for blocks.

The heading for parts of a block that are bound by means of a composition is *parts*. Properties that are of type *block* but not bound via composition are listed with the heading *references* in a compartment. These are properties, for example, which are modeled by aggregation or association, such as *card* of type *customer card* in Figure 4.29 and Figure 4.30, respectively.

If differentiating compartments in the representation is not desired, then properties of any type can be listed with the heading *properties* in a compartment.

The compartment of operations is denoted with the heading *operations*, while constraints are listed with the heading constraints in the compartment. Altogether you obtain a tabular representation of the properties of a block. You can arbitrarily show or hide single compartments in a diagram, and you can add other user-specific compartments. The SysML/UML tool is responsible for providing you with suitable mechanisms.

In SysML all properties of a block have the visibility *public*. This means that it is not necessary to explicitly represent the visibility.

In addition to the text notation, SysML let's you also represent compartments in graphical form. The structure *compartment* contains an internal block diagram that describes how the block is structured (Figure 4.30). Parts of a block appear as rectangles in the diagram, while references are shown as rectangles with dashed lines, and values are not permitted here.

The internal block diagram can also be used as an independent diagram. You use an internal block diagram to show how the properties of a block are interconnected. This means that it describes the internal structure of a block. The diagram corresponds to the UML composite structure diagram described in Section 3.4.

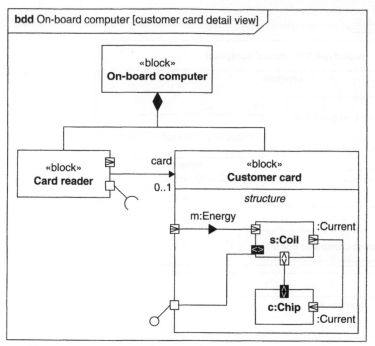

FIGURE 4-30

A block with a "compartment" structure.

You can see in Figure 4.31 that the types *card reader* and *customer card* of two roles, *protoreader7* and *protocard1*, are enclosed by square brackets. They have been extended specifically—for this context only—by initial values for properties. SysML let's you define such context-specific types to avoid having to define an entire new block when all you need is a variant of an existing block in a certain context.

As you can see, the card reader uses the UML version to define initial values. SysML offers yet another possibility. You can state the initial values in a separate compartment with the heading *defaultValues*. This description is more compact since it is separate from the definition that includes both type and multiplicity.

You also have a possibility to pull deeply nested blocks "to the surface" in the internal block diagram. You can see in Figure 4.32 that the left and right representations are equivalent. The notations of arbitrary nesting depths is another extension introduced by SysML. In contrast, UML doesn't allow you to show the internal structures of roles in a composite structure.

As a logical consequence, you can use connectors in an internal block diagram to directly connect the elements across several nesting borders (Figure 4.33). Though this violates the object-oriented encapsulation principle, this form can be often observed in real-world systems. In Figure 4.33, the GPS sender does not communicate with the wrapper of the capsule (i.e., the truck, but directly with a part—the navigation system).

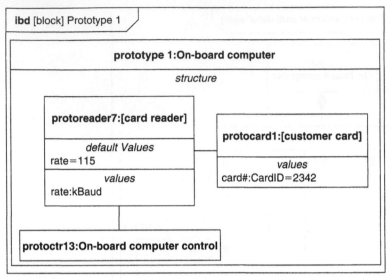

FIGURE 4-31

Specific type of a block attribute.

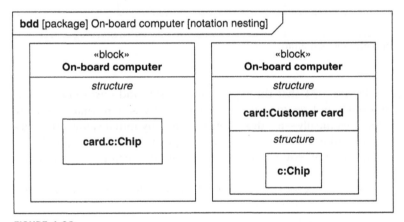

FIGURE 4-32

Nested blocks.

A block can be explicitly modeled as a black box. In addition to the name of a black-box block, we denote the keyword *{encapsulated}* (Abb. 4.29). In this case, a connector must not be connected directly from the outside to a role in the inside. The property is denoted by the verb *{encapsulated}* above the block's name (Figure 4.29).

Since interfaces are rather a software domain in the sense of UML, while blocks are defined in more general terms, and considering that they can also represent hardware elements, they are generally not used in combination with blocks.

However, interfaces are part of SysML. They are used to describe standard ports.

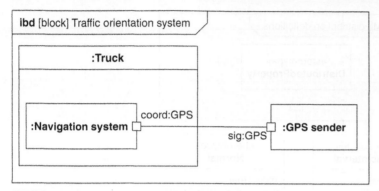

FIGURE 4-33

Nested connectors.

4.5.2 Distribution Definition

Definition

A **distribution definition** describes how values are distributed over a defined value range.

It is a stereotype *«distributedProperty»* of the UML element *property.*

A distribution definition describes how values could possibly be distributed. Specific distribution definitions have to be defined as specialized stereotypes. SysML defines the interval distribution and the normal distribution as basic examples (Figure 4.34).

The notation corresponds to the notation for standard stereotypes. You can see an example for the interval distribution for the value *operatingTemperature* in Figure 4.29.

4.5.3 Value Type

Definition

A **value type** defines values that have no identity, and cannot be referenced by a block, but can have a unit or dimension.

It is a stereotype *«valueType»* of the UML element *data type.*

UML data types describe values that have no identity, for example, integers. This means that two data types with the same value cannot be distinguished. This is different with instances of blocks or UML classes. They can be distinguished, even if they have the same attribute values.

A value type is a data type with the added property that it can have a unit and dimension. This means that you can define a unit as a type (Figure 4.35).

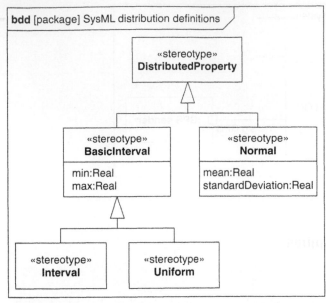

FIGURE 4-34

SysML distribution definitions.

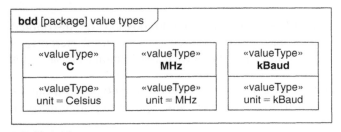

FIGURE 4-35

Value types.

The notation is identical to that for the UML data type, except that we write the stereotype *«valueType»* above the name. The stereotype name also serves as heading of the compartment for which the unit or dimension is described (Figure 4.35).

4.5.4 Unit and Dimension

Definition

A **unit** describes the structure of a physical unit.

It is a stereotype *«unit»* of the UML element *instance specification*.

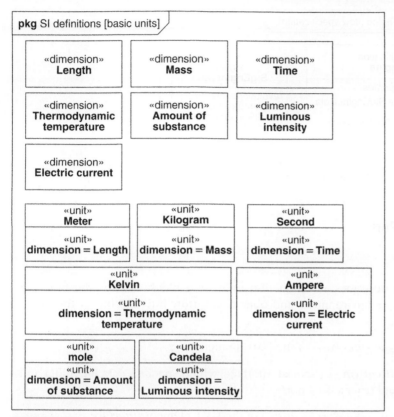

FIGURE 4-36

SI units.

> ## Definition
>
> A **dimension** describes the quantity of a unit.
>
> It is a stereotype *«dimension»* of the UML element *instance specification*.

Many values are normally bound to units in systems engineering models to prevent system errors due to a faulty interpretation of values without units. A tragic real-world example for such errors was the failed Mars mission *Mars Climate Orbiter*. The probe was lost on Mars due to a unit error in the navigation system. While NASA computed using SI units[5] (Newton), a part of the system used the imperial unit system (pound) [14].

A unit describes a specific physical unit. Units are not types. To use a unit as a type in a block property, you have to pack it into a value type (Figure 4.35).

SysML includes a model library that defines SI basic units (Figure 4.36). It let's you easily add more units to the library.

---

[5] The international unit system SI (acronym of the French name *Le Système International d'unités*) is the most commonly used unit system for physical units. It defines many basic units, including meter, kilogram, second, ampere, Kelvin, mole and candela.

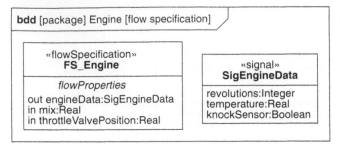

FIGURE 4-37

Example for a flow specification.

4.5.5 Flow Port

Definitions

A **flow port** describes an interaction point of a block used by the block to interact with its environment, and objects can flow into and out of the block over this port.

It is a stereotype *«flowPort»* of the UML element *port*.

A **flow specification** is a special interface, which specifies data incoming and outgoing to and from a flow port.

It is a stereotype *«flowSpecification»* of the UML element *interface*.

Not all interactions of a block with its environment are based on services in the sense of interface descriptions. For example, a block can have an interaction point over which it is supplied with electric power. An UML standard port would not be suitable. You'd have to describe the flow of electric power in an operation of an interface (*givePower( ):Power*).

However, a flow port doesn't let pass just any objects one can think of. The flow specification is a special interface that describes incoming and outgoing data. It has no operations.

You can see a flow specification in Figure 4.37. The data descriptions have the heading *flow properties*. Incoming data is prefixed with the keyword *in*, and outgoing data is prefixed with the keyword *out*. Data that is transported in both directions have the keyword *inout*. The flow port of the block *engine* is denoted with small arrowheads, like an UML port. The flow specification is the type of the port (Figure 4.38).

The opposite flow port requires the same flow specification, except that the incoming data and the outgoing data are swapped. For the sake of simplicity,

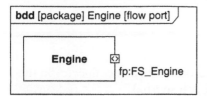

FIGURE 4-38

A flow port in the block definition diagram.

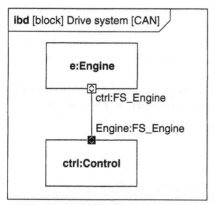

FIGURE 4-39

Example for conjugated flow ports.

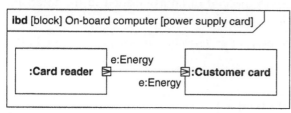

FIGURE 4-40

Example for atomic flow ports.

SysML offers a conjugated flow port that is denoted inversely to the normal flow port (Figure 4.39).

Another variant is the atomic flow port. It allows only one data type to pass it in one direction. In this case, no flow specification is required. The data type that can be transported is directly the type of the port. The direction is denoted by an arrow in the port rectangle (Figure 4.40).

4.5.6 Item Flow

Definition

An **item flow** is a special information flow that describes at a connector in the internal block diagram that specific objects are transported.

It is a stereotype *«itemFlow»* of the UML element *information flow*.

An UML information flow describes only abstract types—information that flows between two elements. SysML extends the information flow by a way to use connectors in the internal block diagram to describe the flow of specific objects. The flowing object is a property defined in the context of the block. While the flow port describes the objects that can flow there, the item flow describes what really flows.

You can see in Figure 4.41 that the object *water* of type H_2O flows from the atomic flow port of a container, *a*, to the atomic flow port of a pump. The flow ports specify more generally that liquids can flow through them.

4.5.7 Association Block

Definitions

An **association block** describes the structural properties of an association.

It is the SysML name for the UML element *association class*.

A **participant property** describes the end of an association in the internal structure of an association block.

It is a stereotype *«participantProperty»* (or *«participant»* for short) of the UML element property.

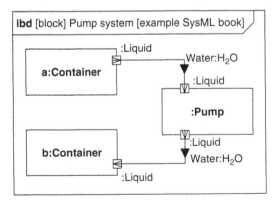

FIGURE 4-41

Example for an item flow.

An association block is the association class of SysML. SysML extends the concept by ways to describe the structure of an association block in an internal block diagram.

The participant property is a property of the association block. It contains a reference to a property that is specified by a participant. This means that you can also list participants in the internal block diagram of an association block, in addition to the usual structures.

As a reference, a participant property is shown with dashes in the internal block diagram. The referenced participant property is denoted as stereotype attribute *end* within curled brackets (Figure 4.42).

4.5.8 Data Types

UML defines four primitive data types: *Boolean*, *Integer*, *String*, and *Unlimited Natural*. SysML adds the data types *Real* for real numbers and *Complex* for complex numbers (Figure 4.43), which are commonly used in systems engineering.

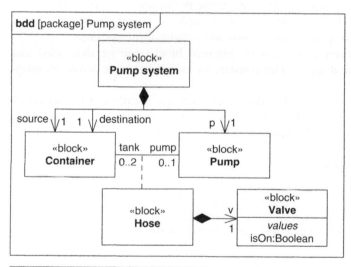

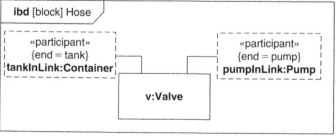

FIGURE 4-42

Example for association blocks.

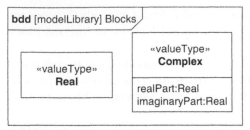

FIGURE 4-43

The "complex" and "real" data types.

4.6 The Parametric Diagram

SysML allows you to define parametric relationships between properties of blocks. For example, Newton's physical law says that force equals mass times acceleration ($f = m * a$). The mass results from the sum of the masses of the single blocks. Acceleration is calculated from the properties of the drive of a system (e.g., a flying object). Now force can also be computed with Newton's law.

We can model such relationships to integrate performance or reliability models in the system model. This allows us, for example, to check alternative design studies with regard to response times, costs, and weight of the system.

The relations between properties of different blocks can be described and defined in a parametric diagram. The constraints form a network across all properties of the blocks.

Figure 4.44 shows a system that describes (strongly simplified) the world of Sir Isaac Newton. We will use this not entirely serious model below to model the legendary fall of an apple on Newton's head.

4.6.1 Constraint Block

Definition

A **constraint block** describes constraints on system structures and the parameters required.

It is a stereotype *«constraintBlock»* (or «constraint» for short) as a specialization of the SysML stereotype *«block»*.

A constraint block is defined free from any context, so that it can easily be reused. This allows you to define a constraint library so that you'll be able to pick constraints for various projects.

Formulated constraints are regular UML constraints. You can formulate constraints in any language. Ideally the language you use can be evaluated automatically, so that you can use a tool to check your constraints.

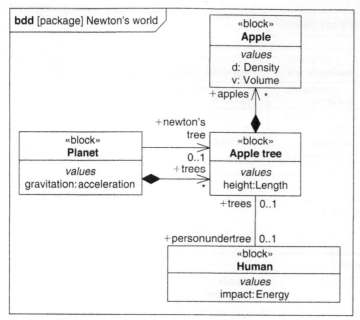

FIGURE 4-44

Newton's world.

A constraint block describes the parameters of its constraints as well. They are defined like attributes.

The notation is similar to that for blocks, except that the stereotype «constraint» instead of «*block*» is written above the name.[6] There are exactly two other compartments. One contains the constraints—denoted as UML constraint in curled brackets—and the other contains the definition of parameters for constraints. Both compartments have their respective heading (i.e., constraints and *parameters*) (Figure 4.45).

You apply a constraint block to the model in a parametric diagram—a special internal block diagram (Figure 4.46). The parameters are denoted in the form of small squares attached from the inside to the rectangle of the applied constraint. In this case, the rectangle has rounded corners. However, you can alternatively denote it as a usual role. Above the name will then additionally appear the stereotype name «constraint». The parameters are bound with parameters of other constraint blocks or with system properties via connectors. Values of blocks can be addressed directly by the dot notation without the pertaining block. This allows you to pull deeply nested values to the surface.

---

[6] It should more exactly read «*constraintBlock*», since that's the correct name of the stereotype for constraint blocks. SysML deviates from the standard notation for stereotypes, using a short form.

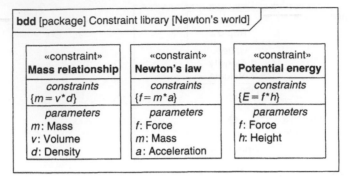

FIGURE 4-45

Example for a constraint library.

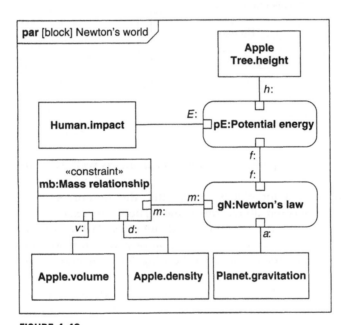

FIGURE 4-46

Using constraint blocks.

4.7 The Use Case Diagram

UML use cases are independent of their realization by a system. They do not contain any information as to whether the serves they describe are implemented in software or hardware, or by an individual. The applications for use cases are accordingly numerous, including systems engineering.

The use case model is integrated in SysML in unchanged and complete form from UML (Figure 4.47).

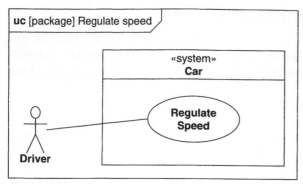

FIGURE 4-47

Example for use cases.

4.8 The Activity Diagram

The activity model specifies flows as well as input and output data, which are required or created during a flow. Flows can run in parallel, or they can be synchronized, or split based on conditions.

More simply, the model shows what will be done in which sequence, which data all of this requires, and which data will be output. The activity model of UML 2 is extended by several properties in SysML:

- Extended control flow with additional information to stop actions or control the flow via so-called control operators.
- Support for modeling of continuous systems.
  - Continuous or discrete object flow.
  - Object nodes can reject data that are no longer current.
- Probabilities of flows.
- Modeling rules for activities in the form of a block definition diagram (function trees).

The activity model of SysML is compatible with the *EFFBD* popularly used in systems engineering.[7] SysML defines an activity stereotype, *«effbd»*, which dictates a few constraints in order to maintain compatibility. For example, such an activity must not have partitions, because they cannot be mapped in EFFBD. You find a complete list of constraints in [44].

SysML introduces an extension of the UML notation, which facilitates distinguishing between different things. The control flow edge can alternatively be shown as a dashed arrow. However, whether or not you can use this notation variant depends on your SysML modeling tool.

---

[7] This diagram is based on the *Functional Flow Block Diagram (FFBD)* developed by TRW in the 1950s; it represents complex flows in a very simple way. EFFBD diagrams add data flow information to a flow.

4.8.1 Activity Composition (Function Tree)

Formally, activities are special classes or, in SysML lingo, blocks. An object of this class is a concrete execution. This means that you can also generalize activities and let them participate in associations. You can use this feature to model a kind of function tree.

You can invoke actions of other actions from within an activity. Actions are denoted with a fork symbol in the lower right-hand corner. If this call is synchronous, then this means for the execution that the called activity is terminated as soon as the call terminates. This corresponds to the semantics of a composition between classes.

You can represent object nodes in an activity as well. This is an association, rather than a composition, from the activity to the element that describes the type of object node (e.g., a block) such as *customer* in Figure 4.48.

You should select a diagram layout that matches a tree structure. The action that invokes the activity is the role name at the composition end in this representation. In practice, activity names and action names are normally identical. In this case you can omit the role name.

Note, however, that this works only with activities. An action is formally not related to the class, so that it cannot become a node or leaf in the function tree. This means, for example, that *confirm usage start* in Figure 4.48 would actually be illegal. We can solve this problem with a modeling trick: We introduce an activity that includes only one single action (Figure 4.49).

Think carefully whether or not you really need function trees since they normally translate in additional modeling work. Your modeling tool may perhaps be capable of doing this work for you, since it requires many steps that can be automated once you have modeled the activity itself.

4.8.2 Control Operator

Definitions

A **control operator** specifies a behavior that can enable and disable actions through control values.

It is a stereotype *«controlOperator»* of the UML elements *behavior* and *operation*.

A **control value** is an enumeration type with values describing the control of a control operator.

The activities of continuous systems normally contain actions that run continually. A control operator allows you to control such actions from the outside (i.e., you can terminate and start them). To this effect, the control operator outputs a

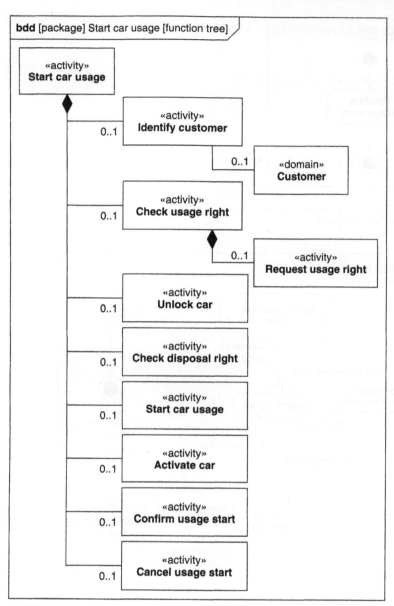

FIGURE 4-48

Function tree for "start car usage."

control value that either starts or terminates the subsequent action, depending on the value.

Figure 4.50 shows an action that invokes a control operator. The stereotype *«controlOperator»* is denoted at this action. The control operator itself is an activity in this example (Figure 4.56). The control operator has an output pin, which is normally not represented. It is shown in Figure 4.50 for better understanding.

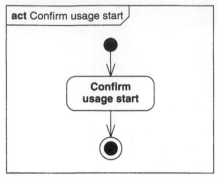

FIGURE 4-49

Modeling trick for function trees.

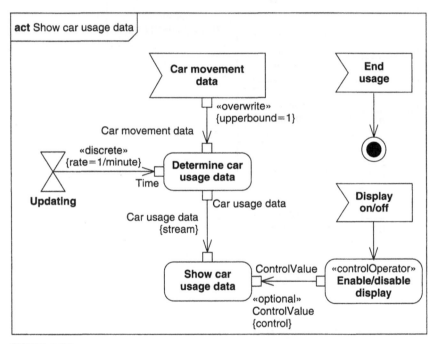

FIGURE 4-50

Example for the control operator «continuous».

In contrast, the subsequent action requires an input pin as well. It is a control pin, which is not normally shown either. This means that it is no longer visible at a glance whether or not it is a control flow or an object flow. The control pin at the action *show car usage data* in Figure 4.50 is an optional parameter.

A control value defined in SysML describes only two values, *enable* and *disable* (Figure 4.51). SysML leaves it up to the modeler to extend the enumeration type, for example, by the values *suspend* and *resume* (Figure 3.22).

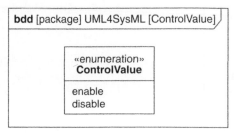

FIGURE 4-51

Example for control values.

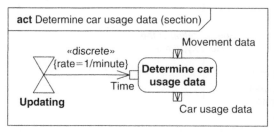

FIGURE 4-52

Example for using a rate.

4.8.3 Rate

Definition

A **rate** describes the frequency in which elements traverse an activity edge, or flow in and out of a parameter.

It is a stereotype *«rate»* of the UML elements *activity edge* and *parameter*.

Elements are transported along an edge between two actions or object nodes. The interval in which they are transported is important for the specification of that flow. The same applies to activity parameters, which can accept or supply data in a certain frequency, provided they have flow property. The rate specifies this frequency (e.g., liters per second).

We distinguish between continuous rate, for example, of a liquid in a pipeline, and discrete rate, such as work pieces on an assembly line. We use the stereotypes *«continuous»* and *«discrete»* (Figure 4.53).

The rate is denoted in curled brackets at the edge. In addition, we can denote either *«continuous»* or *«discrete»* next to it (Figure 4.52).

```
{rate=<constant value>} or {rate=<distribution definition>}.
```

4.8.4 Special Object Node Properties

The stereotype *«nobuffer»* describes object nodes that reject tokens if they cannot be accepted by subsequent edges or actions.

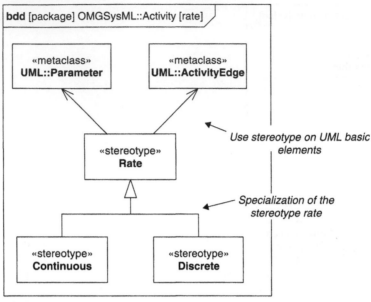

FIGURE 4-53

Stereotypes for rate.

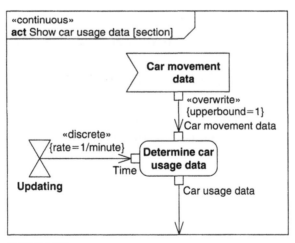

FIGURE 4-54

Example for using «overwrite».

The stereotype *«overwrite»* describes object nodes, the tokens of which are overwritten by newly arriving tokens.

The stereotype *«optional»* describes parameters that do not have to have values in order to execute the pertaining behavior.

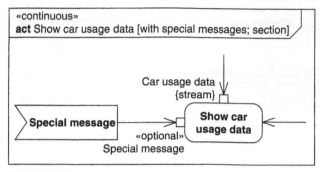

FIGURE 4-55

Example for using «optional».

The standard behavior of an object node is the behavior of a buffer. This means that it can accept an arbitrary number of object tokens, passing them on by the FIFO[8] principle as soon as subsequent edges or actions are ready to accept them. The stereotypes *«nobuffer»* and *«overwrite»* change this standard behavior.

The stereotype *«nobuffer»* suppresses a node's buffer functionality. This is an important property for continuous data streams or data arriving quickly in order to prevent an overflow. It is also important when transient values, such as electric power, are transported, which must not or cannot be buffered. Tokens arriving at an object node with this property are rejected, unless they are immediately forwarded.

The stereotype «overwrite» causes object tokens that arrive at an object node to overwrite existing—buffered—tokens as soon as the object node is full (i.e., when the specified upper limit (*upperbound=n*) is reached) (Figure 4.54). What is overwritten are the oldest tokens in the object node based on a defined order—FIFO (default) or LIFO.[9] An arriving null token removes all existing tokens. The stereotype *«overwrite»* is assigned to a pin that can accept one object token at most. This means that the subsequent action always gets the most current value. This does not disable the buffer functionality, in contrast to the *«nobuffer»* property. The buffer contains the most current element.

Note that both *«nobuffer»* and *«overwrite»* have the same meaning for data that arrive continually (*«continuous»*). It is important to know that these object node properties are independent of the streaming property.

These stereotypes are denoted directly next to the pin, or above the name of an activity parameter.

It is possible to model actions and activities with optional input and output values (i.e., with optional pins or activity parameters).

Figure 4.55 shows the section of an extension from Figure 4.50. With this extension, we can now optionally display special messages.

---

[8] First In, First Out.
[9] Last In, First Out.

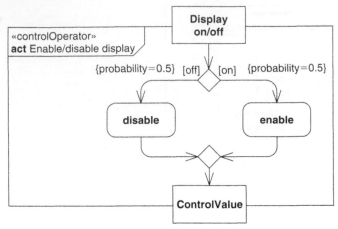

FIGURE 4-56

Example for probabilities.

4.8.5 Probability

> **Definition**
>
> A **probability** describes at an outgoing edge of a choice or an object node how probably it is that this edge will be used by a token.
>
> It is a stereotype *«probability»* of the UML elements *activity edge* and *parameter set*.

Edges outgoing from a choice have conditions and describe OR semantics. This means that a token that arrives at a choice node will continue to flow over one of the outgoing edges only where the condition is true.

A probability is a value between zero and one, which describes at each outgoing edge how probably it is that the token will flow over it. You can state the same at the outgoing edges of an object node, since the OR[10] semantics also applies to them. The sum of probabilities for all edges of the same origin has to result in 1. Probability values can also be attached to parameter sets. Different incoming or outgoing parameter sets have OR semantics.

The probability is denoted at an edge in the following syntax (Figure 4.56):

```
{probability=<value between 0 and 1>}
```

4.9 The State Machine Diagram

The UML state model is used in SysML completely and in unchanged form. The state machines and the corresponding diagram are independent of the respective

---

[10] To be more exact it is the XOR (exclusive or) semantics. However it is more common to speak of OR versus AND semantics.

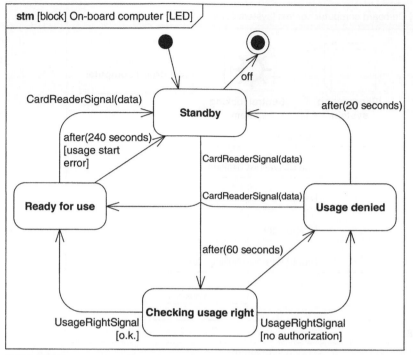

FIGURE 4-57

State machine diagram.

discipline of the system we model, and they do not contain any software-specific elements. Every system, regardless of whether it is a software or hardware system, or a social or biological system has states and state transitions that can be described in a state model (Figure 4.57).

4.10 Interaction Diagrams

In UML, this category includes four specific diagrams: the sequence diagram, the communication diagram, the timing diagram, and the interaction overview diagram. Of these diagrams SysML uses only the sequence diagram (Figure 4.58).

While activity diagrams allow us to describe flows more or less independently of the executing system elements, interaction diagrams show us who calls which system behavior. In interaction, it is normally used to describe a concrete flow (scenario).

4.11 General Modeling Elements

This section introduces model elements of SysML that do not belong entirely to one of the categories discussed above, such as the requirement diagram. They can be used in various diagram categories instead.

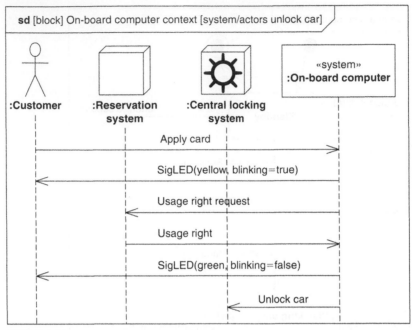

FIGURE 4-58

Example for the "unlock car" sequence diagram.

4.11.1 **Rationale**

Definition

A **rationale** documents the principles or reasons for a modeling choice.

It is a stereotype *«rationale»* of the UML element *comment*.

Your model is full of analysis and design choices. It is normally difficult for a reader of the model to reproduce them. This can lead to difficulty in understanding and misunderstandings. This problem can easily be solved by using a comment that describes the modeling rationale (Figure 4.59).

The stereotype *«rationale»* characterizes this type of comments. It does not add any properties to the UML element *comment*.

4.11.2 **Diagram Frame**

Some of the diagram types that are denoted in the upper left corner of a diagram frame deviate in SysML from the UML identifiers (Table 4.1). Note that I used the UML identifiers for the diagrams in the UML chapter (Chapter 3) (e.g., class for a *class* diagram and not *bdd* for a block definition diagram). In all other chapters, however, I use the SysML convention.

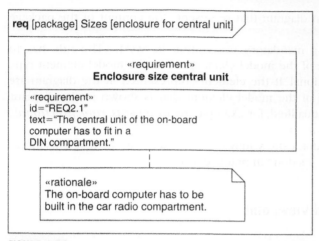

req [package] Sizes [enclosure for central unit]

«requirement»
Enclosure size central unit

«requirement»
id="REQ2.1"
text="The central unit of the on-board
computer has to fit in a
DIN compartment."

«rationale»
The on-board computer has to be
built in the car radio compartment.

FIGURE 4-59

Example for a rationale.

Table 4.1 SysML diagram types.

Diagram Name and Type	Abbreviation
Activity diagram	act
Requirement diagram	req
Use case diagram	uc
Block definition diagram	bdd
Internal block diagram	ibd
Package diagram	pkg
Parametric diagram	par
Sequence diagram	sd
State machine diagram	stm
Matrix	–
Table	–

The matrix and table notations don't belong to the normative part of the SysML specification (i.e., they are recommended) but are not mandatory in order to be SysML-compliant. In SysML the model element and the element type are denoted in addition to the diagram type and the diagram name. The syntax for a full diagram header is as follows:

```
type [model element type] model element [diagram name]
```

For example,

```
bdd [package] system context [with information flow]
```

describes a block definition diagram that represents the content of the package *system context*.

The diagram frame is a mandatory description in SysML. The title has to include the type and name of the model element, while the model element type and diagram name are optional. If the elements represented in the diagram are not within the namespace of the model element that is shown in the diagram, then they have to be fully qualified, for example, *requirements::core::functional:: security* rather than just *security*.

For shortage of space I don't show fully qualified names in the diagrams in this book. This is probably how it's done in practice too.

4.11.3 Model View and Viewpoint

> **Definitions**
>
> A **view** is a representation of the entire system, seen from a defined viewpoint.
>
> It is a stereotype *«view»* of the UML element *package*.
>
> A **viewpoint** specifies the structure of a view based on the goals of a set of stakeholders.
>
> It is a stereotype *«viewpoint»* of the UML element *class*.
>
> A **conform** relationship binds a view with the viewpoint the requirements of which it satisfies.
>
> It is a stereotype *«conform»* of the UML element *dependency*.

A model's target group is very heterogeneous: system engineers, hardware and software developers, analysts, project managers, quality assurance managers, testers, customers, and so on. Depending on the project, this list can get very long.

Each of these groups of individuals has a certain vision of the model and pursues their own interests. For example, a requirement analyst is not much interested in the design, while a hardware developer is not interested in the software, and a project manager doesn't really care about the details hidden deep down in the model.

A view supports all kinds of various interests by providing a view of the entire model especially for a target group. More specifically, a view describes a set of model elements that can be represented in various diagrams. This is a filtered view of the model. It is denoted as an UML package with stereotype *«view»* (Figure 4.60).

Each view realizes exactly one viewpoint. A viewpoint describes the stakeholders and their concerns, the view's purpose, rules as to how the view should be created (methods) as well as languages used to create the view. A viewpoint is denoted as a class with stereotype *«viewpoint»* (Figure 4.60).

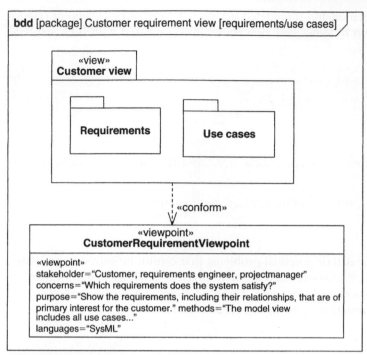

FIGURE 4-60

Example for a view.

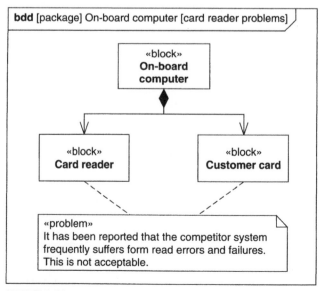

FIGURE 4-61

Example for a problem.

The conform relationship is modeled between a view and a viewpoint (Figure 4.60). The definition of views and viewpoints is coordinated with IEEE standard 1471 [3].

4.11.4 Problem

Definition

A **problem** documents an (potential) error or a flaw in the model or in the modeled system.

It is a stereotype *«problem»* of the UML element *comment*.

We usually discover real or potential problems that cannot be solved in an ad-hoc way during the different system development phases—analysis, design, implementation, test, production, and operation. The model element *problem* allows us to document this information in the model (Figure 4.61).

Systems Engineering Profile—SYSMOD

People who speak too many languages usually don't say much in any of them.
(Peter Ustinov)

Together, the stereotypes discussed in this chapter form the SYSMOD engineering profile required for the SYSMOD approach discussed in this book (Chapter 2). You will most likely introduce additional stereotypes and define an individual profile in your own projects. Depending on the domain, such as aeronautics, for example, and the development process or model simulation used, each project requires its own modeling vocabulary in the form of stereotypes and profiles. The SYSMOD profile is generic, forming a good starting platform for your own project-specific profiles.

The profile extends the SysML language. If you want to use UML only, rather than SysML, you have to additionally use the SysML stereotypes on which this profile depends. For example, the *«domain»* stereotype is a specialization of the SysML stereotype *«block»* which, in turn, is an extension of the UML element *class*.

The UML extension mechanism for stereotypes is discussed in Section 3.10.2. Each good SysML/UML tool supports this form of language extension. Ideally, the profile can be developed independently and used for your respective project model.

Many modeling tools come with various stereotypes. Unfortunately, they are not always explained and often mixed among the pure SysML/UML elements so that it is difficult for developers to see whether they are looking at a pure language element or a stereotype. The situation in the literature is similar. This is why I knowingly paid attention in this book to separate the profile description from the UML and SysML descriptions.

5.1 Actor Categories

Definitions

An **environmental effect** is a factor from the environment that influences the system without communicating with it directly.

It is a stereotype *«environmentalEffect»* of the UML element *actor*.

An *external system* is a system that interacts directly with the system to be modeled. In its role as an interaction partner, the external system is seen merely as a black box.

It is a stereotype *«externalSystem»* of the UML element *actor*.

Definitions

A **user system** is a special external system serving a user as a medium to interact with the system.

It is a stereotype *«userSystem»* as a specialization of the stereotype *«externalSystem»*.

A **boundary system** is a special external system serving another external system as a medium to interact with the system.

It is a stereotype *«boundarySystem»* as a specialization of the stereotype *«externalSystem»*.

An **actuator** is a particular external system that serves the system to influence its environment.

It is a stereotype *«actuator»* as a specialization of the stereotype *«externalSystem»*.

A **sensor** is a special external system that accepts information from the environment and forward it to the system.

It is a stereotype *«sensor»* as a specialization of the stereotype *«externalSystem»*.

A **mechanical system** is a special external system that has only mechanical aspects from the system's view.

It is a stereotype *«mechanical system»* as a specialization of the stereotype *«externalSystem»*.

Actor categories distinguish the different types of an actor, helping us to better understand the system context and the use cases (Figure 5.1). Each category requires a different modeling approach, e.g., when identifying the use cases (Section 2.4.1). The categories defined here are customary and have proven in practice. Nevertheless, there may be a need for additional categories, or a subset of the categories suggested here in a specific project, of course.

Figure 5.2 shows the symbols of actor categories. The figure does not list the user who is a standard UML actor, i.e., users are not part of the profile. The user is denoted as a stick man. In our approach, we introduce the actor categories in Section 2.3.1.

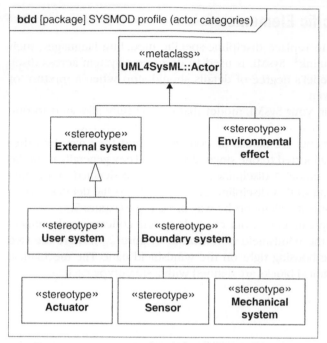

FIGURE 5-1

Stereotypes for actor categories.

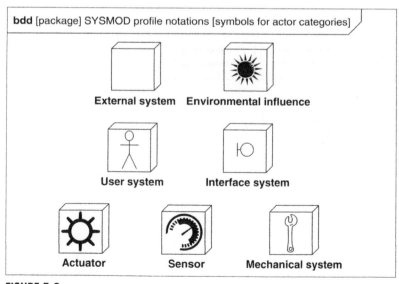

FIGURE 5-2

Symbols for actor categories.

5.2 Discipline-Specific Elements

SysML was not designed to replace discipline-specific modeling languages, such as UML or MATLAB®/Simulink®. SysML is used to describe a system across disciplines. This is why the model's degree of details should stop when a mixture of disciplines is no longer given.

If you have elements in your SysML model that can be fully allocated to one single discipline, then it is meaningful to mark them with a stereotype.

Discipline-specific elements are blocks or connectors, and they may be other elements that can be fully allocated to one single discipline. They generally form the bottom limit of the SysML model. A discipline-specific block is detailed in a model and in a language pertaining to that discipline. The SYSMOD profile defines several stereotypes for discipline-specific elements by way of example (Figure 5.3).

Figure 5.4 shows a simple model for our example system concerning the attachment of a card reader to the windshield of *rentalCar* (Figure 2.3). There are two suction cups that hold the housing tight on the windshield pane. The mechanical connection and the mechanical blocks are defined with a stereotype each.

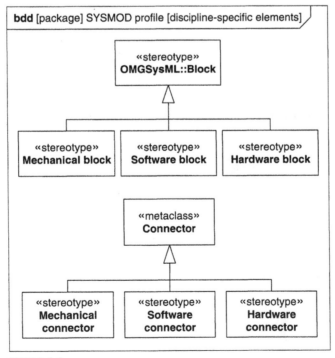

FIGURE 5-3

Discipline-specific elements.

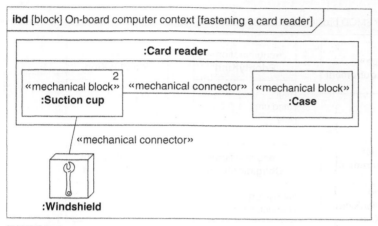

FIGURE 5-4

Modeling mechanical elements.

5.3 **Extended Requirement**

Definition

An **extended requirement** is a requirement that extends the requirement in question by the following properties: *priority, obligation, stability, type,* and *risks.*

It is a stereotype *«extendedRequirement»* as a specialization of the SysML stereotype *«requirement»* (Figure 5.5).

ID and text, the properties defined in SysML for a requirement, are not sufficient in a specific project. The extended requirement shows how we can close this gap. The properties introduced here are common, but not necessarily important or exhaustive in every project. The extended requirement adds the following properties:

- *Priority*: How important is this requirement? This piece of information helps you focus on high-priority requirements.
- *Obligation*: Is the requirement obligatory or just desirable?
- *Stability*: Will the requirement change in the course of the system's development, or will it remain stable?
- *Type*: The *user* type includes requirements specified by the contractor. The *system* type normally includes requirements that emerge from refining contractor requirements and by including a technical solution. Requirement types reflect the difference between user specification and system specification.

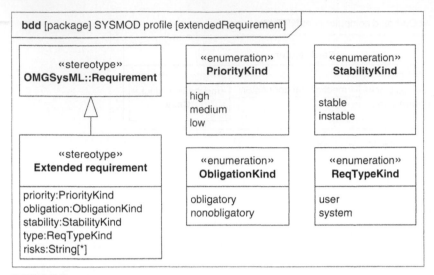

FIGURE 5-5

The *«extendedRequirement»* stereotype.

■ *Risks*: What risks hide behind a requirement? For example, are there doubts whether the technical realization is at all possible, or whether the requirement will encourage political forces that might work against the project?

You can group a large number of possible requirements in categories. The *FURPS* model distinguishes between five categories: **F**unctionality, **U**sability, **R**eliability, **P**erformance, and **S**upportability [19]. It is normally a good idea to define your own stereotypes for these requirement categories. SysML does not provide any specification since the categories are all very project-specific and cannot be defined for general purposes. Figure 5.6 shows the categories of the SYSMOD profile.

5.4 Essential Activity

Definition

An **essential activity** describes the degree of details of an essential use case step.

It is a stereotype *«essential»* of the UML element *activity*.

To ensure that essential steps are directly visible in the diagram and that they can be recognized by document generators, for example, the corresponding activities are defined with the *«essential»* stereotype (Figure 5.7). The stereotype is also visible in actions that invoke such an activity (*CallBehaviorAction*).

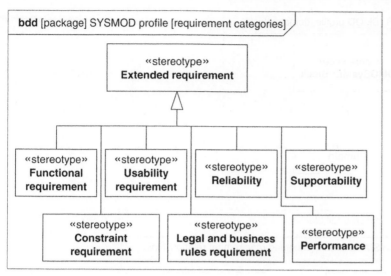

FIGURE 5-6

Requirement categories.

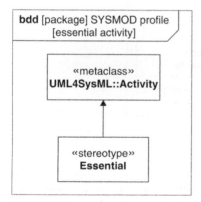

FIGURE 5-7

The *«essential»* stereotype for activities.

You can find an example for essential steps in the flow model in Figure 2.59 in Section 2.4.5.

5.5 Domain Block

Definition

A **domain block** represents an object, a concept, a location, or a person from the real-world domain. A domain block is directly known to the system.

It is a stereotype *«domain»* as a specialization of the SysML stereotype *«block»* (Figure 5.8).

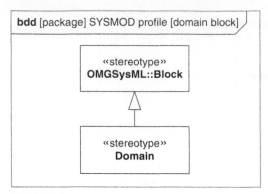

FIGURE 5-8

The «*domain*» stereotype for blocks.

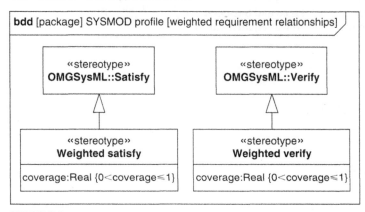

FIGURE 5-9

Weighted requirement relationships.

Domain blocks differ from "normal" blocks in that they do not represent a real object of the system. They are the basic elements of the domain knowledge model, describing domain terms known to the system. The specific flavor in the real-world system is normally specified by other model elements—often from the software discipline.

In our approach, we use domain blocks in the domain knowledge model discussed in Section 2.5.

5.6 Weighted Requirement Relationships

Definition

Weighted satisfy and **weighted verify** add information about the degree of coverage to the SysML *satisfy* and *verify* relationships.

They are the stereotypes «*weightedSatisfy*» and «*weightedVerify*», respectively, as a specialization of the SysML stereotypes «*satisfy*» and «*verify*» (Figure 5.9).

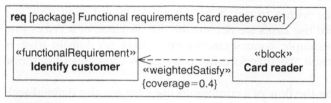

FIGURE 5-10

Example for a weighted satisfy relationship.

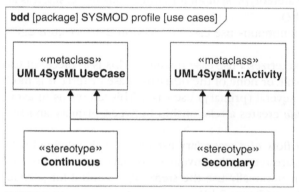

FIGURE 5-11

Stereotypes for use cases.

The SysML *satisfy* relationship merely states that a system element meets a given requirement. It does not say anything as to whether the requirement is fully or partially satisfied. The coverage of the *weighted satisfy* relationship describes the degree of fulfillment. A coverage of 1 means full coverage. Figure 5.10 shows that the card reader meets 40 percent of the functional requirement. The same applies to the *weighted verify* relationship. The coverage describes how muchof the requirement in percent (a number between 0 and 1) is verified by the test case.

5.7 Continuous and Secondary Use Cases

Definitions

A **continuous use case** is a special use case that starts in a defined system state and continually supplies results. No final result is required.

It is a stereotype *«continuous»* of the UML elements *use case* and *activity* (Figure 5.11).

A **secondary use** case is an incomplete use case fragment. It lacks a domain trigger, a result, or an actor

It is a stereotype *«secondary»* of the UML elements *use case* and *activity* (Figure 5.11).

A normal use case begins with a trigger; it has a temporally coherent flow and ends with a result. Normal use cases are not suitable for all kinds of services provided by a system. For example, control circuits often have no domain triggers and hardly ever a final result. We, therefore, use continuous use cases to describe these types of services.

Activities that describe the flow of a continuous use case are also defined with the *«continuous»* stereotype. Actions that invoke continuous use case activities (*CallBehaviorAction*) show stereotypes in their notation.

You can optionally use the stereotype symbol for continuous use cases. It is an ellipse with arrows (Figure 5.12).

In our approach, we use continuous use cases in Section 2.4.1 (Figure 2.37), for example.

A secondary use case characterizes a use case fragment. This is a "piece" of use case that has no trigger, no result, or none of the other use case criteria. It is modeled only if its flow is part of several (primary) use cases. This allows us to avoid redundant descriptions. *Include* creates a relationship between primary and secondary use cases.

Activities that describe the flow of a secondary use case are also defined with the *«secondary»* stereotype, as are actions that invoke secondary use case activities (*CallBehaviorAction*). You can optionally use the stereotype symbol for secondary use cases. It is a dashed ellipse (Figure 5.13).

We have used secondary use cases in Section 2.4.4 (Figure 2.54), for example, in our approach.

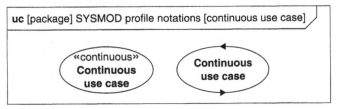

FIGURE 5-12

Notation for continuous use cases.

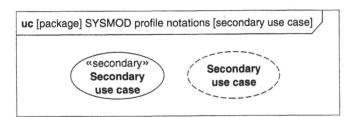

FIGURE 5-13

Notation for secondary use cases.

5.8 Stakeholders

Definition

A **stakeholder** is a person or institution that has an interest in the system, potentially contributing requirements.

It is a stereotype *«stakeholder»* of the UML element *actor* (Figure 5.14).

Section 2.2.1 is fully dedicated to stakeholders. Pragmatically, they are documented in a word processor, for example. You can use the *«stakeholder»* stereotype if you want to explicitly add stakeholders to your model. Though this means that you will initially have more work, compared to documenting them in a word processor, you will then have a possibility to use the *trace* relationship to relate the stakeholders with other model elements, such as requirements (Figure 5.15).

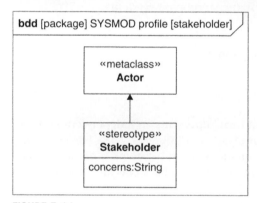

FIGURE 5-14

The stereotype for stakeholders.

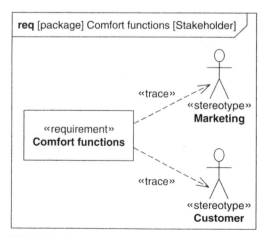

FIGURE 5-15

Example for stakeholders.

5.9 Systems and Subsystems

Definitions

A **system** is an artifact created by humans and consisting of blocks that pursue a common goal that cannot be achieved by the system's individual elements. A block can be software, hardware, a person, or an arbitrary unit [45].

It is a stereotype *«system»* as a specialization of the SysML stereotype *«block»*.

A **subsystem** describes a closed unit within a larger system.

It is a stereotype *«subsystem»* as a specialization of the SysML stereotype *«block»* (Figure 5.16).

A **block** can describe very small elements, but also very large ones. SysML does not dictate anything in this respect. The largest block in a system is the system itself. This special role is emphasized by the stereotype *«system»*.

We introduced the *system* element in Section 2.3.1.

Definition

A **subsystem** is a system block that, in turn, represents an independent system. This is often the case in large system (*System of Systems, SoS*). For example, our on-board computer in Chapter 2 includes the subsystems *radio* and *navigation*. Again, there are no hard criteria as to how subsystems are denoted. It is eventually a project decision.

In our approach, we used subsystems in Section 2.7.3.

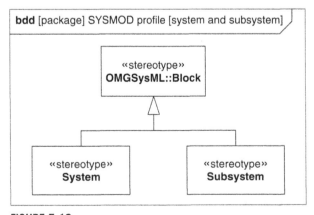

FIGURE 5-16

The stereotype for subsystems.

5.10 System Context Elements

Definition

A **system context element** is a virtual wrapper around the entire system and its actors.

It is a stereotype *«systemContext»* as a specialization of the SysML stereotype *«block»* (Figure 5.17).

SysML itself offers only very few modeling possibilities to describe the environment of a system in more detail. The system context element creates a virtual wrapper, so that the actors are no longer outside the modeling context, but put in relation to the context element within. This supports a more detailed view of the internal block diagram.

Apart from the general stereotype representation, the system context element has no notation of its own. It is normally not represented in a diagram.

We introduced the system context element in Section 2.3.2 in our approach.

5.11 System Processes

Definition

A **system process** describes a flow across use cases. It consists of a set of use cases that have a domain-logical sequence.

It is a stereotype *«systemProcess»* of the UML elements *use case* and *activity* (Figure 5.18).

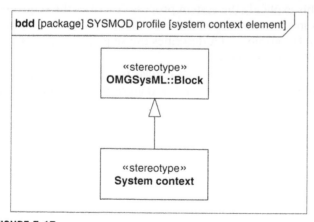

FIGURE 5-17

The stereotype for system context elements.

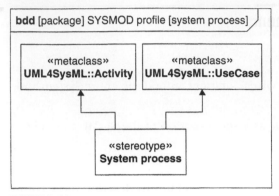

FIGURE 5-18

The stereotype for system processes.

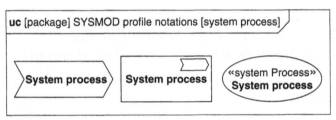

FIGURE 5-19

Notation for system processes.

The use cases of a system can be subject to a domain-logical sequence. This means, e.g., that use case *A* cannot be executed before use case *B* was executed. This is implicitly formulated by defining pre- and postconditions for the use cases. The postcondition of use case *B* is part of the precondition of use case *A*.

If you want to model this explicitly, the system process describes the sequence of selected use cases. It is itself a stereotyped use case that includes the selected use cases via the *include* relationship, and it describes the sequence in an activity that also uses the *«systemProcess»* stereotype.

To distinguish the system process clearly from regular use cases, it has its own notation. It is the most widely used process symbol (Figure 5.19). We have used system processes in Section 2.4.3 in our approach.

Glossary

The important thing is not to stop questioning.

(Albert Einstein)

In addition to SysML- and UML-specific terms, this glossary also includes terms from the SYSMOD approach in particular and systems engineering in general. The origin of each term is marked with either [SysML], [UML], [SYSMOD], or [other]. Of course, the UML terms also belong to the SysML language (Section 4.2).

A

Abstraction [other]: The result of a way of mapping things that emphasizes certain aspects while omitting others.

Abstraction dependency [UML]: The mapping between model elements onto various abstraction levels.

AcceptEventAction [UML]: An elementary ⇒action that receives an ⇒event, or accepts the arrival of a signal.

Action [UML]: An action is an elementary executable step within an activity.

Activity [UML]: An activity describes the coordinated sequencing consisting of elementary actions. The sequencing can be parallel or synchronized, or split and recomposed on the basis of conditions.

Activity diagram [UML]: A diagram that depicts behavior associated with activities using input/output and control flow. It is the visualization of an ⇒activity.

Activity edge [UML]: An activity edge is an abstract class for directed connections between two ⇒activity nodes. We distinguish between ⇒object flow edges and ⇒control flow edges. Synonym: Edge.

Activity final node [UML]: The activity final node terminates the entire ⇒activity as soon as a single flow arrives at the node.

Activity parameter node [UML]: An activity parameter node is an ⇒object node for inputs and outputs to activities.

Activity partition [UML]: An activity partition is a kind of activity group for identifying actions that have some characteristic in common.

Actor [UML]: An actor is a role that interacts with the system. This role can be played by a user or any other system. An actor is external to the system.

Actuator [SYSMOD]: An actuator is a particular ⇒external system that serves another system to influence its environment.

Aggregation [UML]: Describes a ⇒class as an aggregate and specifies a whole-part relationship between the aggregate (whole) and a component part. In contrast to a ⇒composition, the aggregate is not responsible for its parts.

Allocate activity partition [SysML]: A special ⇒activity partition that allocates each ⇒action within the partition to the structure that is represented by the partition.

Allocation [SysML]: An abstract relationship between elements of different types or on different levels. It allocates a target element to one or more source elements.

Association [UML]: An association is a structural relationship between two ⇒classes.

Association block [SysML]: An association block describes the structural properties of an ⇒association.

Association class [UML]: An association class unifies the properties of an ⇒association with those of a ⇒class.

Asynchronous message [UML]: A ⇒message where its sender does not wait for the receiver to complete processing it, but continues with its flow immediately upon sending it.

Atomic flow port [SysML]: An ⇒object flow port that is not typed by an ⇒object flow specification, but which is a ⇒system component or a ⇒data type.

Attribute [UML]: An attribute defines a structural property of a class. This description consists of visibility, name, type, and a multiplicity.

B

Behavior diagram [UML]: A diagram used in ⇒SysML and ⇒UML to describe dynamic aspects.

Block [SysML]: A modular unit that describes the structure of a system or element.

Block definition diagram [SysML]: A diagram that shows the definition of ⇒blocks and their relationships (e.g., a ⇒composition).

Boundary system [SYSMOD]: A special ⇒external system that provides an interface to another external system.

C

Call event [UML]: ⇒Event.

CallBehaviorAction [UML]: An elementary action that invokes a behavior element, such as an activity, directly.

CallOperationAction [UML]: An elementary action that invokes an ⇒operation.

Change event [UML]: ⇒Event.

Choice pseudo state [UML]: The decision is a ⇒pseudo state which, when reached, evaluates conditions to select the next ⇒transition.

Class [UML]: A class describes the structure and behavior of ⇒objects, which have identical characteristics and semantic. The structure is described by ⇒attributes, while the behavior is described by ⇒operations.

Class diagram [UML]: A diagram that shows ⇒classes and their relationships. This diagram is available in UML only. SysML uses a different form called ⇒block definition diagram.

Combined fragment [UML]: A combined fragment describes an expression consisting of an ⇒interaction operator and ⇒interaction fragments as operands.

Comment [UML]: A comment is a textual annotation that can be attached to a set of elements. Synonym: Note.

Communication path [UML]: A communication path is an ⇒association between ⇒actor and ⇒use case, or between actor and system. The name is used synonymously for a relationship in the ⇒deployment diagram.

Complexity [other]: Refers to the number and type of relationships between elements in a system.

Composite state [UML]: A ⇒state that has at least one ⇒region.

Composite structure diagram [UML]: A diagram that describes the internal structure of a ⇒class consisting of ⇒roles and ⇒connectors. The diagram is available in UML only. SysML uses a different form called ⇒internal block diagram.

Composition [UML]: A composition denotes a ⇒class as an aggregate and describes a whole-part hierarchy. The aggregate is existentially responsible for its parts.

Conform [SysML]: A relationship that connects a ⇒model view with a ⇒viewpoint the requirements of which it meets.

Connector [UML]: A connector specifies a relationship between two ⇒roles that allows them to communicate.

Constraint [UML]: A condition that constrains the semantic of model elements, and which must always be met.

Constraint block [SysML]: A block that describes ⇒constraints of system structures and the parameters required for this.

Context object [UML]: A relative term that refers to a behavior and the ⇒object in which that behavior is executed.

Continuous use case [SYSMOD]: A special ⇒use case that starts in a defined system state and continually supplies results. A final result is not required.

Control flow [UML]: An ⇒activity edge that is traversed by ⇒control tokens only.

Control node [UML]: A node in an ⇒activity that controls the flow of ⇒control tokens or ⇒object tokens.

Control operator [SysML]: A control operator specifies a behavior that can enable and disable ⇒actions by use of ⇒control values.

Control pin [UML]: A ⇒pin that accepts ⇒object tokens. It can cause an ⇒action to be executed, but does not forward the ⇒object to the action.

Control token [UML]: ⇒Token.

Control value [SysML]: An ⇒enumerated value that is used to control a ⇒control operator.

Copy [SysML]: A relationship describing that a ⇒requirement is a copy of another requirement.

Core requirement [SYSMOD]: A requirement that refers to the entire system; it is independent of the particularities of system variants.

D

DataType [UML]: A type with ⇒instances that can be identified by their values only.

Decision node [UML]: The decision is a node in an ⇒activity where several optional flows branch. There is exactly one incoming ⇒edge and an arbitrary number of outgoing edges, each having a condition.

Dependency [UML]: A relationship between two elements which describes that one element requires another element for its specification or implementation.

Deployment diagram [UML]: A diagram that shows the hardware structure and the deployment of software. This diagram is not part of ⇒SysML.

Derive requirement [UML]: A ⇒requirement that has been derived from another requirement.

Derived association/attribute [UML]: An association or attribute that can be derived from other model elements. Not to be confused with ⇒generalization.

Destruction event [UML]: An event that specifies the time in an ⇒interaction at which the instance belonging to the ⇒lifeline will be destroyed.

Diagram frame [UML]: A rectangle around a SysML/UML diagram with a diagram heading in the upper left corner, which describes the diagram (type, name, and other information).

Dimension [SysML]: A dimension describes the quantity of a ⇒unit.

Distribution definition [SysML]: A definition that describes in the form of a defined value range how values are distributed.

Do behavior [UML]: An optional behavior that is executed if the ⇒state is active.

Domain block [SYSMOD]: A domain ⇒block represents an object, a concept, a location, or a person from the real-world domain. A domain block is directly known to the system.

Domain experts [other]: A domain consists of domain experts who supply domain-specific ⇒requirements.

Domain model [SYSMOD]: A domain model describes the ⇒domain blocks of a system and their relationships.

E

Edge [UML]: Synonym: ⇒Activity edge.

Enhanced Functional Flow Block Diagram (EFFBD) [other]: A diagram based on the Functional Flow Block Diagram (FFBD), which was developed by TRW in the 1950s, representing complex flows in a simple way. An EFFBD adds data flow information.

Entry behavior [UML]: An optional behavior that is executed immediately upon entering a ⇒state.

Entry point [UML]: A particular point of entry in a ⇒state machine. From the entry point, a transition leads to a state, or to a state in each ⇒region in case of orthogonal regions.

Enumeration [UML]: A special ⇒data type with a value range consisting of a limited set of defined literals.

Environmental effect [SYSMOD]: A factor in the environment that influences the ⇒system without communicating directly with it.

Essential activity [SYSMOD]: An essential activity denotes ⇒activities that describe the details of an essential use case step.

Essential requirement [SYSMOD]: A ⇒requirement describing the pure domain intention, regardless of the technical implementation (solution).

Event [UML]: An occurrence, the time and location of which can be measured, that can trigger behavior in an ⇒object. SysML/UML distinguishes between call, change, signal, and time events.

Execution specification [UML]: Specifies that the ⇒object represented by the ⇒lifeline executes behavior at this point.

Exit behavior [UML]: An optional behavior that is executed immediately prior to exiting a ⇒state.

Exit point [UML]: An exit point stops a ⇒state machine. When a ⇒transition in any ⇒region of the state machine reaches an exit point, then the state machine is terminated, and the transition outgoing from the exit point is activated.

Expansion region [UML]: A node in an ⇒activity that accepts a set of objects, then processes each of these objects individually, and finally returns the set of processed objects.

Extension [UML]: A relationship that extends an UML model element by additional properties that are defined as ⇒stereotype.

External system [SYSMOD]: A system that interacts directly with the system to be modeled. In its role as an interaction partner, an external system is considered merely a black box.

F

Final state [UML]: A ⇒state that describes the end of a ⇒composite state or a ⇒state machine.

Flow allocation [SysML]: Flow allocation connects an ⇒information object flow in a structure diagram with a ⇒flow edge in an ⇒activity diagram.

Flow final node [UML]: A final node that terminates a flow in an ⇒activity.

Flow port [SysML]: Describes an interaction point of a ⇒system block, including its environment, over which objects can flow into the block or out of it.

Flow specification [SysML]: A special interface that specifies data incoming and outgoing over a ⇒flow port.

Fork node [UML]: A node in an ⇒activity, which splits a flow into several concurrent flows. There is exactly one incoming ⇒edge and an arbitrary number of outgoing edges.

Fork pseudo state [UML]: A pseudo state, which splits an incoming ⇒transition into two or more transitions that lead to orthogonal ⇒regions.

Frequency [SysML]: ⇒Rate.

G

Generalization [UML]: A generalization is a taxonomic relationship between a more general ⇒class and a more specific class. Synonym: Specialization, Inheritance.

Glossary [SYSMOD]: The glossary explains all domain-specific terms of a project in a style similar to a lexicon.

H

History pseudo state [UML]: A pseudo state that stores the last state configuration of a ⇒region in which it resides. We distinguish between deep history (with substates) and shallow history (without substates).

I

Include relationship [UML]: A relationship describing that a ⇒use case is included in another use case.

Information flow [UML]: A directed relationship between ⇒actors, ⇒use cases, ⇒classes, ⇒ports, ⇒roles, ⇒interfaces, ⇒packages, or ⇒objects. It shows that ⇒information items are exchanged between these elements.

Information item [UML]: An abstract concept of UML used to model the presence and conveyance of information on a coarse level.

Inheritance [UML]: ⇒Generalization.

Initial node [UML]: An initial node is the starting point for a flow that is started when an ⇒activity is invoked.

Initial state [UML]: An initial state is a ⇒pseudo state with an outgoing ⇒transition that points to the initial ⇒state.

Input pin [UML]: ⇒Pin.

Instance [UML]: Synonym: Item, ⇒Instance specification, Object.

Instance specification [UML]: Describes a specific instance that has been created by the building plan of a type description (e.g., a ⇒class). Synonym: Item, Instance, Object.

Interaction [UML]: Describes a communication between ⇒lifelines. This communication is based on the exchange of messages in the form of ⇒operation calls or ⇒signals.

Interaction diagram [UML]: A diagram that shows the communication between selected interaction partners in a limited situation.

Interaction fragment [UML]: Part of an ⇒interaction.

Interaction operator [UML]: The operator of a ⇒combined fragment. SysML/UML defines these operators: alt, opt, break, loop, seq, strict, par, critical, neg, assert, consider, and ignore.

Interaction use [UML]: A reference to an ⇒interaction. The model is designed such that the reference could be substituted by the referenced interaction.

Interface [UML]: An interface specifies structure and behavior. It does not contain any implementation, and no ⇒object can be created by its building plan.

Internal block diagram [SysML]: A special composite structure diagram that describes the structure of a ⇒block.

Interruptible activity region [UML]: A region within an ⇒activity that can be terminated by a ⇒token flow via special interruptible edges.

Intricacy [other]: Refers to the number of different elements in a system.

Item flow [SysML]: A special ⇒information flow, which describes at a ⇒connector in the internal block diagram that specific ⇒objects are being transported.

J

Join node [UML]: A node in an ⇒activity that synchronizes several concurrent flows, grouping them into one. There is an arbitrary number of incoming edges and exactly one outgoing ⇒edge.

Join pseudo state [UML]: A ⇒pseudo state that groups ⇒transitions from orthogonal ⇒regions.

Junction pseudo state [UML]: A ⇒pseudo state that connects ⇒transitions and composes them into a path.

L

Lifeline [UML]: A lifeline represents a communication partner in an ⇒interaction. It describes the element's name, type, and lifecycle.

Link [UML]: An ⇒instance of an ⇒association (i.e., a specific relationship) between two ⇒objects.

M

Measure of Effectiveness (MOE) [SysML]: MOE, also called Effectiveness Measure, is a metric stating a customer's satisfaction with the technical properties of a system.

Mechanical system [SYSMOD]: A special external system that has only mechanical aspects from the own system's view.

Merge node [UML]: A node in an ⇒activity at which several flows are merged into one flow. There is an arbitrary number of incoming edges and exactly one outgoing ⇒edge.

Message [UML]: A form of communication between two ⇒lifelines. It can be either ⇒synchronous or ⇒asynchronous. It can invoke an ⇒operation, or transport a ⇒signal, or create an ⇒object.

Model [UML]: A model describes a ⇒system for a specific purpose.

Model of Models (MoM) [other]: The ⇒model of a ⇒system of systems. It consists of independent models that, together, describe a system.

Modeling tool [other]: A software application used to create and manage ⇒SysML or ⇒UML models.

Multiplicity [UML]: An interval of positive integers that describes how many objects an ⇒attribute can accept.

N

Namespace [UML]: The namespace contains all elements that can be uniquely identified by their names. Examples for namespaces are ⇒packages and ⇒system blocks.

Namespace containment [UML]: A relationship describing that a ⇒namespace is included in another ⇒namespace.

Navigation [UML]: A property of associations specifying that objects at one ⇒association end can access objects at the other end.

Note [UML]: Synonym: ⇒Comment.

Null token [UML]: A special ⇒object token that contains a value of null.

O

Object [UML]: Synonym: Instance, ⇒Object.

Object [UML]: Synonym: Item, Instance, ⇒Instance specification.

Object Constraint Language [UML]: A text-driven formal language used to formulate ⇒constraints in SysML/UML models. The language supports, among other things, navigation in object models, Boolean Algebra, and set operations.

Object diagram [UML]: A diagram that shows ⇒objects and their relationships. It is a diagram of UML and does not exist in SysML.

Object flow [UML]: An ⇒activity edge that can be traversed by object tokens only.

Object identity [UML]: A property of the ⇒objects of a ⇒class that distinguishes them uniquely from other objects, regardless of the ⇒attribute values.

Object node [UML]: An object node is an abstract ⇒activity node that is part of defining object flow in an activity.

Object token [UML]: ⇒Token.

OpaqueAction [UML]: An elementary executable ⇒action; its implementation is formulated in an arbitrary language (e.g., in a programming language).

Operation [UML]: An operation defines a behavior property of a ⇒class. The description consists of visibility, name, parameters, and return type.

Optional parameter [SysML]: Describes ⇒parameters that do not have to have values for the pertaining behavior to be executed.

Output pin [UML]: ⇒Pin.

P

Package [UML]: A package groups model elements and forms a namespace.

Package diagram [UML]: A diagram that shows how ⇒packages relate, and how model elements are distributed across packages.

Parameter [UML]: A parameter describes values that are forwarded to, or returned from, a behavior element (e.g., an ⇒operation).

Parameter set [UML]: A parameter set is a complete set of input or output parameters of a behavior, which is selected regardless of other parameter sets of that behavior.

Parametric diagram [SysML]: A diagram that shows a network of ⇒constraints for the purpose of modeling performance and reliability models.

Part decomposition [UML]: Describes the internal ⇒interactions of a ⇒lifeline.

Participant property [SysML]: A participant property describes the end of an ⇒association in the internal structure of an ⇒association block.

Partition [UML]: ⇒Activity partition.

Pin [UML]: A pin is a link between the parameters of an ⇒action and the object flow. We distinguish between ⇒input pin and ⇒output pin.

Port [UML]: A port describes an interaction point that is used by a ⇒class (UML) or system block (SysML) of the environment provides or requests services over ⇒interfaces.

Postcondition [UML]: A Boolean expression that is true once a behavior has executed.

Precondition [UML]: A Boolean expression that has to be true before a given behavior can be executed.

Primary use case [SYSMOD]: A ⇒use case that describes a central service of the system.

Primitive type [UML]: A type describing a ⇒data type that has no structures.

Probability [SysML]: Describes at the outgoing edges of a ⇒decision or an ⇒object node the probability that this ⇒edge will be used by a ⇒token.

Problem [SysML]: A problem documents an (potential) error or weakness in the model or in the modeled system.

Profile [UML]: A profile is a set of ⇒stereotypes.

Profile application [UML]: A profile application assigns a ⇒profile to a ⇒package, allowing the use of the ⇒stereotypes contained in the profile at the model elements in the package.

Property [UML]: A property describes a part of the structure of a structural element (e.g., a ⇒class).

Property string [UML]: A string that, in a diagram, shows a certain property of the pertaining model element (e.g., {readonly}).

Pseudo state [UML]: A control element that influences the flow of a ⇒state machine. It is not a real ⇒state, so that the pseudo state does not represent any value combination.

R

Rate [SysML]: The rate describes the frequency in which elements traverse an ⇒activity edge, or in which they flow to or from a parameter. Synonym: ⇒Frequency.

Rationale [SysML]: A rationale documents the principles or reasons for a modeling decision.

Realization [UML]: A relationship that connects an implementation with a specification. The implementation is responsible for realizing that specification.

Refine [UML]: A relationship describing that a model element describes the properties of a ⇒requirement in more detail.

Region [UML]: A region is an orthogonal area in a ⇒state or ⇒state machine.

Representation [UML]: A relationship that describes the model element that is represented by a piece of ⇒information.

Requirement [SysML]: A requirement describes properties or behavior of a ⇒system that always have to be met.

Requirement diagram [SysML]: A diagram that shows ⇒requirements and their relationships.

Risk management [SYSMOD]: Risk management denotes the planned handling of risks. Potential risks are identified and evaluated, and counteractions are formulated for prevention and limitation of damages.

Role [UML]: A role describes a structure in the context of a ⇒class.

S

Satisfy [SysML]: A relationship describing that a design element meets a ⇒requirement.

Scenario [other]: A specific sequence for example, a possible variant of a ⇒use case.

Secondary use case [SYSMOD]: A secondary use case is an incomplete use case fragment. It lacks domain ⇒trigger, result, and ⇒actor.

SendSignalAction [UML]: An elementary ⇒action that sends a ⇒signal.

Sensor [SYSMOD]: A sensor is a special ⇒external system that accepts information from the environment and forwards it to the system.

Sequence diagram [UML]: A diagram that shows an ⇒interaction, focusing on the temporal sequence of messages.

SI – International System of Units [other]: The International System of Units (French: Le Système international d'unités) is the widest used system for physical units. It defines the meter, kilogram, second, ampere, Kelvin, mol, and candela basic units.

Signal [UML]: A signal describes the structure of a communication object.

Signal event [UML]: ⇒Event.

Specialization [UML]: ⇒Generalization.

Stakeholder [SYSMOD]: A stakeholder is an individual or organization that has a direct interest in the ⇒system and that may have requirements.

Stakeholder [SYSMOD]: A stakeholder is a person or institution that has an interest in the ⇒system and may make ⇒requirements.

Standard port [SysML]: Synonym: ⇒Port.

State [UML]: A state represents a set of value combinations for a given element. A state has a name and may have an internal behavior that is executed based on defined events.

State invariant [UML]: A ⇒constraint that refers to a ⇒lifeline, and which must be met at system runtime.

State machine [UML]: A state machine describes the ⇒states and ⇒transitions of a structure.

State machine diagram [UML]: A diagram that depicts a ⇒state machine.

Stereotype [UML]: A stereotype expands an existing model element by additional properties and semantic. The newly defined model element can include a new notation, in addition to the name. Stereotypes are grouped in ⇒profiles.

Streaming [UML]: A property describing that ⇒activities or ⇒actions can accept or supply new values during active operation.

Structural allocation [SysML]: A structural allocation is used to separate logical from physical structures by producing a relationship between the two levels.

Structure diagram [UML]: A generic term for all static diagrams in ⇒SysML and ⇒UML.

Subsystem [SYSMOD]: A subsystem describes a closed unit within a larger ⇒system.

Synchronous message [UML]: The sender of the ⇒message waits until the receiver has processed the message.

SysML [SysML]: The Systems Modeling Language (SysML) is a graphical language for modeling systems in the ⇒systems engineering discipline.

SysML tool [other]: ⇒Modeling tool.

System [SYSMOD]: A system is a collection of system blocks that pursue a common goal, which cannot be achieved by the individual elements. A ⇒block can be software, hardware, a person, or any other unit.

System actor [SYSMOD]: ⇒Actor.

System context diagram [SYSMOD]: A diagram that shows the ⇒system as a black box, including its environment, and information that can be exchanged with the environment.

System context element [SYSMOD]: A virtual wrapper that comprises the entire ⇒system and its ⇒actors.

System of Systems (SoS) [other]: A system composed of ⇒blocks that can, in turn, be independent systems.

System port [SYSMOD]: A port at a ⇒system.

System process [SYSMOD]: The process that describes a flow beyond the use cases. It consists of a set of ⇒use cases that have a domain-specific sequence.

Systems engineering [other]: Systems engineering is a discipline that concentrates on the definition and documentation of system requirements in the early development stage, the elaboration of a system design, and the verification of the system as to compliance with the requirements, taking the entire problem—operation, time, test, creation, cost and planning, training and support, and disposal—into account.

T

Technical requirement [SYSMOD]: A ⇒requirement that describes a requirement based on a solution approach.

Terminate [UML]: A ⇒pseudo state describing that the pertaining ⇒state machine or the pertaining ⇒context object has terminated.

Test case [SysML]: A test case is a sequence that verifies whether or not the ⇒system meets a given ⇒requirement.

Time event [UML]: ⇒Event.

Token [UML]: A virtual element that describes the position of a flow in an ⇒activity. Control tokens mark only the flow, while object tokens additionally show that there is a defined ⇒object at that position.

Token flow [UML]: A flow that uses ⇒control ⇒tokens and ⇒object tokens to describe the flow of an ⇒activity.

Tool [other]: A software application designed to support the development process (e.g., a ⇒modeling tool).

Trace [UML]: A relationship between two model elements, describing a general context.

Transition [UML]: A transition specifies the passing from one ⇒state into another. It is a directed relationship between two states. It defines a trigger and a condition that both cause the state transition and behavior that is executed during that transition.

Trigger [UML]: A trigger connects exactly one ⇒event with a behavior.

Type [UML]: A type defines a value range (e.g., a ⇒primitive data type or a ⇒block).

U

UML [UML]: The Unified Modeling Language (UML) is a graphical modeling language used to describe software and other systems.

UML tool [other]: ⇒Modeling tool.

Unit [SysML]: A unit describes the structure of a physical unit (e.g., kilogram, meter).

Use case [UML]: A use case describes a temporally related and targeted interaction between an ⇒actor and a system. Its beginning is a domain trigger and the outcome is a defined result of domain value.

Use case diagram [UML]: A diagram that shows ⇒actors and ⇒use cases and their relationships.

User [SYSMOD]: A user is a human ⇒actor.

User system [SYSMOD]: A user system is a special ⇒external system that serves the user as a medium to interact with the ⇒system.

V

Value type [SysML]: A type that defines values, which have no identity, and are not referenced by a ⇒block, and which can have a ⇒unit or ⇒dimension.

Variant requirement [SYSMOD]: A requirement that refers exclusively to a variant, and which is valid only for the system design of that variant.

Verify [SysML]: A relationship that connects a ⇒test case with the ⇒requirement that is tested by that test case.

View [SysML]: A representation of an entire ⇒system, seen from a defined ⇒viewpoint.

Viewpoint [SysML]: A viewpoint specified the structure of a ⇒model view based on the targets defined by a number of ⇒stakeholders.

W:

Weighted satisfy [SYSMOD]: A relationship that adds coverage information to a ⇒satisfy relationship.

Weighted verify [SYSMOD]: A relationship that adds coverage information to a ⇒verify relationship.

X

XMI [UML]: The XML Metadata Interchange (XMI) is a data exchange format for models formulated in XML.

References

[1] A.T. Bahill and B. Gissing. Re-evaluating Systems Engineering Concepts Using Systems Thinking. *IEEE Transaction on Systems, Man and Cybernetics, Part C: Application and Reviews*, 1998, 28(4): 516–527.

[2] Kent Beck. *Extreme Programming Explained*. Addison-Wesley Longman, Amsterdam, 2005.

[3] IEEE-SA Standards Board. *IEEE Recommended Practice for Architectural Description of Software-Intensive Systems*. IEEE Std. 1471-2000, September 21, 2000.

[4] Barry Boehm. Some Future Trends and Implications for Systems and Software Engineering Processes. *Systems Engineering*, Spring 2006, 9(1): 1–19.

[5] Grady Booch. *Object-Oriented Analysis and Design with Applications*, 2nd ed., Addison-Wesley Longman, Amsterdam, 2007.

[6] Grady Booch. Software Development Trends. *The Rational Edge*, September 2003, 161–163.

[7] Lewis Carroll. *Alice in Wonderland*. Harper Collins, 2005.

[8] Tom DeMarco. *Structured Analysis and System Specification*. Yourdon Press, New York, 1978.

[9] Tom DeMarco. *The Deadline*. Dorset House, 1997.

[10] DIN 69905—Projektabwicklung, Begriffe, 1997.

[11] Laurent Doldi. *UML 2 Illustrated*. TransMeth Sud-Ouest, 2003.

[12] Bruce P. Douglass. *Real-Time Design Patterns*. Addison-Wesley Professional, 2002.

[13] EAST-EEA. http://www.east-eea.net, January 2006.

[14] Edward A. Euler, Steven D. Jolly, and H.H. Curtis. The Failures of the Mars Climate Orbiter and Mars Polar Lander: A Perspective from the People Involved. *Proceedings of Guidance and Control 2001*, AAS 01-074, 2001.

[15] Martin Fowler. *Analysis Patterns*. Addison-Wesley Professional, 1996.

[16] Martin Fowler. *Refactoring*. Addison-Wesley Professional, 2005.

[17] Martin Fowler. *MF Bliki:IncludeAndExtend*. http://www.martinfowler.com/bliki/IncludeAndExtend.html, January 2006.

[18] Erich Gamma, Richard Helm, Ralph Johnson and John Vlissides. *Design Patterns*. Addison-Wesley Professional, 1996.

[19] Robert Grady. *Practical Software Metrics for Project Management and Process Improvement*. Prentice-Hall, 1992.

[20] Object Management Group. *Systems Engineering Domain Special Interest Group*. http://syseng.omg.org.

[21] Arthur David Hall. *Methodology for Systems Engineering*. Van Nost. Reinhold, 1962.

[22] David Harel. Statecharts: A Visual Formalism for Complex Systems. *Science of Computer Programming*, June 1987, 8(3): 231–274.

[23] DIN ISO 9126—*Software Engineering: Product Quality*, 1991.

[24] ISO/IEC 15288—*Systems Engineering: System Life Cycle Processes*, 2002.

[25] Ivar Jacobson, Magnus Christerson, and Patrik Jonsson. *Object-Oriented Software Engineering*. Addison-Wesley Professional, 1992.

[26] Inc. Jaczone. http://www.jaczone.com, January 2006.

[27] Hermann Kaindl. A Scenario-Based Approach for Requirements Engineering: Experience in a Telecommunication Software Development Project. *Systems Engineering*, 2005, 8(3).

[28] Georg Klaus. *Wörterbuch der Kybernetik (Dictionary of Cybernetics)*, 3rd ed., Dietz, 1969.

[29] Genrich Altshuller. *Innovation Algorithm: TRIZ, Systematic Innovation and Technical Creativity*. Technical Innovation Center, 1st ed., 1999.

295

[30] Philippe Kruchten. Architectural Blueprints—The 4+1 »View« Model of Software Architecture. *IEEE Software*, 1995, 12(6).

[31] Philippe Kruchten. *The Rational Unified Process: An Introduction*. Addison-Wesley Professional, 1998.

[32] Stephen J. Mellor and Marc Balcer. *Executable UML*. Addison-Wesley Professional, 2002.

[33] Bernd Oestereich, Christian Weiss, Claudia Schröder, Tim Weilkiens, and Alexander Lenhard. *Objektorientierte Geschäftsprozessmodellierung mit der UML (Object-Oriented Business Process Modeling with UML)*. dpunkt.verlag, Heidelberg, 2003.

[34] *The OMG Hitchhiker's Guide: A Handbook for the OMG Technology Adoption Process, Version 6.6*. http://www.omg.org/cgi-bin/doc? hh, 2004.

[35] oose Innovative Informatik GmbH. *OEP—oose Engineering Process*. http://www.oose.de/oep.

[36] CCITT Recommendation Z100. *SDL—Specification and Description Language*.

[37] CCITT Recommendation Z120. *MSC—Message Sequence Charts*.

[38] Suzanne Robertson and James Robertson. *Mastering the Requirements Process*. Addison-Wesley Professional, 2000.

[39] James Rumbaugh. Trends in UML and e-Development. *The Rational Edge*, December 2000, 4–10.

[40] James Rumbaugh, Michael Blaha, William Premerlani, Frederick Eddy, and William Lorensen. *Object-Oriented Modeling and Design*. Prentice Hall, 1991.

[41] James Rumbaugh, Ivar Jacobson, and Grady Booch. *The Unified Modeling Language Reference Manual*. 2nd ed., Addison-Wesley Professional, 2004.

[42] Bran Selic, Garth Gullekson, and Paul T. Ward. *Real-Time Object-Oriented Modeling*. John Wiley & Sons, Inc., 1994.

[43] Bran Selic, and James Rumbaugh. Mapping SDL to UML. *A Rational Software White Paper*, 1999.

[44] *OMG SysML Specification. http://www.omgsysml.org/#Specification*, 2006.

[45] Technical Board International Council on Systems Engineering (INCOSE). *Systems Engineering Handbook*, Version 2a, June 2004.

[46] *UML for Systems Engineering: Request for Information. http://www.omg.org/cgi-bin/doc?ad/02-01-17*, 2002.

[47] *UML for Systems Engineering: Request for Proposal. http://www.omg.org/cgi-bin/doc?ad/03-03-41*, 2003.

[48] *UML 2.1.1 Superstructure Specification. http://www.omg.org/cgi-bin/doc? formal/07-02-03*, 2007.

[49] *A UML profile for MARTE. http://www.omg.org/cgi-bin/doc? realtime/07-03-03*, 2007.

[50] *UML 2.0 Diagram Interchange. http://www.omg.org/cgi-bin/doc? ptc/2003-09-01*, 2003.

[51] *UML 2.0 Infrastructure Specification. http://www.omg.org/cgi-bin/doc? ptc/2003-09-15*, 2003.

[52] *UML 2.0 OCL Specification. http://www.omg.org/cgi-bin/doc?ptc/2003-10-14*, 2003.

[53] *UML Testing Profile. http://www.omg.org/cgibin/doc? formal/05-07-07*, 2005.

[54] V-Modell XT 1.2.1: http://v-modell.iabg.de/v-modell-xt-html-english, checked January 2008.

[55] Frederic Vester. *Die Kunst vernetzt zu denken (The Art of Networked Thinking)*, 4th ed., dtv, 2002.

[56] Uwe Vigenschow and Björn Schneider. *Soft Skills für Softwareentwickler (Soft Skills for Software Developers)*. dpunkt.verlag, Heidelberg, 2007.

[57] Uwe Vigenschow and Christian Weiss. Das Essenzschritt-Verfahren: Aufwandschätzungen auf der Basis von Use Cases (The Essential-Step Method: Cost Estimates Based on Use Cases). *ObjektSpektrum*, 2003, 2.

[58] L.v. Bertalanffy. *General System Theory: Foundations, Development, Applications*. George Braziller, 1968.

[59]   Tim Weilkiens. Praxisbericht: Erste Projekterfahrungen mit der UML 2.0 (Initial Project Experiences with UML 2.0). *ObjektSpektrum*, 2004, 3.

[60]   Tim Weilkiens and Bernd Oestereich. *UML 2-Zertifizierung: Intermediate-Stufe (UML-2 Certification: Intermediate)*. dpunkt.verlag, Heidelberg, 2005.

[61]   Tim Weilkiens. *UML 2 Certification Guide: Fundamental & Intermediate Exams (The OMG Press)*. Morgan Kaufmann, 1st ed., 2006.

[62]   *Wikipedia—The Free Encyclopedia*. http://wikipedia.org, 2006.

[63]   Wikiquote. http://de.wikiquote.org, 2006.

[64]   XML Metadata Interchange (XMI) Specification. http://www.omg.org/cgi-bin/ doc? formal/2003-05-02, 2003.

Index

Printed and bound by CPI Group (UK) Ltd, Croydon, CR0 4YY

03/10/2024

01040310-0009